DO GOOD

DO GOOD

Embracing Brand Citizenship to Fuel Both Purpose and Profit

ANNE BAHR THOMPSON

HarperCollins
Leadership

AN IMPRINT OF HarperCollins

Do Good

© 2018 Anne Bahr Thompson

Published by HarperCollins Leadership, an imprint of HarperCollins Focus LLC.

Any internet addresses, phone numbers, or company or product information printed in this book are offered as a resource and are not intended in any way to be or to imply an endorsement by HarperCollins Leadership, nor does HarperCollins Leadership vouch for the existence, content, or services of these sites, phone numbers, companies, or products beyond the life of this book.

Bulk discounts available. For details visit:
www.harpercollinsleadership.com/bulkquotes
Email: customercare@harpercollins.com

ISBN 978-0-8144-3839-8 (HC)
ISBN 978-1-4002-4567-3 (paperback)

ACKNOWLEDGMENTS

Until I began this project, I believed the underlying principles for my model of Brand Citizenship® emerged solely in the CultureQ® trend study my company, Onesixtyfourth, conducted in 2011. As I began developing the proposal with my agent, Jane von Mehren, of Aevitas Creative, I recognized that the concepts that underpin the model are the product of so much more. The five steps of Brand Citizenship represent the values my parents and education instilled in me; what I've learned about business, marketing, and brands over the years; the lessons I've gained through being a volunteer and advocating for fair and equal treatment of women and people in need; my vision for business as an institution that contributes to society; and the energy and passion I've brought to my work from the very start.

Countless people helped to bring this book to life at its various stages. Throughout the process, my husband Ron listened to me deliberate the merits of Brand Citizenship at all hours of the day and night. My son Ronald discussed the tenets of the model with me, benchmarked my take on Millennials, and pushed me to challenge my thinking as I refined the framework. Claire Irving reflected with me more deeply on what the learning from Onesixtyfourth's research meant for brands, as did Chris Lightfoot and Becky Shawl of Whitestone International, Onesixtyfourth's design partner in London. Tricia Heywood worked with me to develop and analyze the CultureQ research. My sister, Rhonda Shannon, added an essential "outsider's" perspective throughout the process, and my executive editor, Ellen Kadin, at AMACOM supported this book even after I walked away from the idea of writing it for several months.

Lance Pauker was instrumental in the early days helping to review and synthesize the results of our quantitative studies, offering an insightful Millennial perspective on what participants were saying. Without David Miles, I would never have set down the pathway of writing the proposal for this book, and many thanks to Dee Dee DeBartlo, whom I met on LinkedIn and who connected me with Gretchen Crary, her business partner at the time. Gretchen ultimately introduced me to my agent, Jane von Mehren, who encouraged me to pursue this project from the first day we met. Janet Goldstein guided me to strengthen the outline for this book, and David Bickerton and Jon Richter offered quotes in support of my work at the proposal phase. Charlene Hoey added encouragement through the highs and lows of writing the first three chapters, which accompanied the proposal. Petra Lewis and Carissa Wright assisted me in researching and completing case studies during my last two months of writing, and my editor, Ann Beaton, provided the essential ingredients for the final polish of the manuscript.

Kim Essency Pillari, an internal communications executive and fellow nonprofit board member, began promoting Brand Citizenship to her colleagues after I shared one of my first articles on the model with her. Her feedback was instrumental as I tested the relevance of the model in real business situations. Daryl Brewster of CECP; Wes Hutchinson, Professor of Marketing and Faculty Director of the Wharton Behavioral Laboratory; Jay Coen Gilbert of B Lab; Simon Fowler of The John Lewis Partnership; Peter Cox, author of *Spedan's Partnership*; and the librarians at the Harvard Business School's Baker Library generously gave their time as I began interviewing experts and doing more formal background research for the book. James Orsini, who was the global CFO of Interbrand during my tenure there, supported Brand Citizenship by introducing me to agency executives and academics. My conversations with these people helped to strengthen the narrative for Brand Citizenship and fine-tune the quantitative assessment tool that measures a company's Brand Citizenship Quotient®, which I highlight in the book.

Further, this book reflects the collaborative spirit of Brad Kahn from the Forest Stewardship Council; Kathleen Dunlop from Unilever; Ben Mand and Ami Hamilton from Plum Organics; Gigi Lee Chang, Founder of Plum Organics, who is now Managing Director of FoodFutureCo; Jenny Lewis, John Federovitch, and Tom Berry from Kimberly-Clark; Janet Tiebout Hanson founder of 85 Broads; Kristy Wallace of Ellevate; and Bob Harlow. All of these people spoke honestly and openly with me about their successes embracing purpose and good citizenship, as well as the lessons they have learned and are still learning. Like the companies they work for, they embody the spirit of good Brand Citizenship and demonstrate how doing good can sit comfortably alongside doing well. Similarly, Anne Waters Westpheling, a Plum Organics fan who posted about the brand on Facebook, readily discussed her perceptions of Plum and real-life experiences with its products over the years. John Ekelin, cofounder of LynxEye a consultancy headquartered in Sweden, shared his company's research with me, as well as explored the role of brands and Brand Citizenship in the context of his experiences with clients. And Archie B. Carroll, Professor Emeritus, Terry College, University of Georgia, readily offered information on his model of corporate social responsibility.

Numerous other executives in corporations and agencies took the time to speak with me about the role of Brand Citizenship in brand development, reputation management, social responsibility, sustainability, enhancing market share, and increasing profits. I'd like to especially thank the large number who trusted me to keep their names anonymous. Your candor helped to clarify outstanding issues and close gaps that my quantitative and qualitative research left open.

And, finally, a big thank-you to my many colleagues and clients over the years. All of our work together helped to shape my perspective on the important role of brands in society and intensify my belief that brands, like the businesses they represent, have a responsibility to create social value as much as financial returns.

CONTENTS

INTRODUCTION

The Call for Brand Citizenship

Over more than twenty years as a Fortune 500 global brand strategist and researcher, I have observed people continuously expecting more from brands. Three years of investigation dedicated to deconstructing the shifting elements of brand leadership, corporate citizenship, and favorite brands through my company's *CultureQ*® research project confirmed that customers unequivocally are demanding more value, more service, better ethics, and a greater focus on sustainability and social good. What people told me in qualitative conversations and quantitative surveys was clear: They want the companies they do business with not only to "do good" and make the world a better place but also to advocate on their behalf and make them feel as though they are part of a larger community or grander mission. Customers are calling for, yearning for—and paying for—a new business ethos that I call Brand Citizenship®.

noun **brand** \ˈbrand\

1. a class of goods identified by name as the product of a single firm or manufacturer : make

2. the factual things someone knows and emotional things they feel about a named product, service, or company

noun cit·i·zen·ship \\'si-tə-zən-ˌship\

1. membership in a community, state, or nation; how together we make society work

2. the qualities that a person is expected to have as an active and responsible member of a community

Brand Citizenship is a way of doing business—from a company's core purpose; to its delivery of goods and services; to its responsibility to its employees, community, the environment, and the world—that people trust, believe in, and rely on. It creates a sense of partnership and belonging, all with the aim of earning profits that are maintainable over the long term.

People who participated in *CultureQ* research beginning in 2011 expressed the belief that companies were better equipped than governments to address and solve problems—from the ordinary needs of daily living to the big issues of our age. Our research also showed that people support companies that demonstrate they have their customers' and employees' best interests at heart. Brands, especially the ones we're most loyal to, represent more than things and services. They signify a lifestyle and an ethos—one that either mirrors our values or ones that we aspire to. As more consumers grow concerned with fairness and sustainability, more of them—in other words, more of us—seek "relationships" with brands that link us to a larger purpose that enriches our modern lives and sustains the planet.

Examples of companies demonstrating small and large elements of Brand Citizenship have been growing every day. They include more than well-known social enterprises like TOMS® shoes, which apply commercial strategies to maximize social impact alongside profits for external shareholders, or conscious capitalist companies like Whole Foods Market, which strive to serve the interests of all major stakeholders—customers, employees, investors, suppliers, communities, and the environment. Consider some of the following examples:

► **CVS Health** becomes the No Cigarette Sales health company. With 97 percent of its nearly $140 billion in sales coming from prescription drugs or pharmacy services, CVS is arguably the largest health provider in the country.[1,2]

▶ **Nike**, inspired by a high school junior with cerebral palsy, lives up to its belief that "If you have a body, you are an athlete" and designs FlyEase, a zip-around shoe specifically for people with disabilities.[3]

▶ **eBay** bans sales of the Confederate flag after the 2015 racially motivated shootings at Emanuel AME Zion, a historically black church in South Carolina.[4]

▶ **H&M** announces in February 2016 that it is providing funding grants to winners of its first Global Change Award, designed to reward solutions that make the fashion industry more environmentally responsible.[5]

Some of the brands participants in *CultureQ* research named as good corporate citizens—and why they chose them—might startle corporate social responsibility and sustainability experts. As far back as the end of 2011, they included:

▶ Apple, for making products that make life more inspired and for making communicating worldwide easier

▶ Walmart, for making prices so low that they make the cost of living and overall quality of life easier

▶ Ford, for making people feel proud by "coming back stronger" and exemplifying the turnaround that all Americans could themselves achieve in the wake of the 2008 recession

As I will explore in this book, customers' perceptions are sometimes counterintuitive and vastly different from what companies expect. Today's consumers are savvy individuals who easily identify efforts that are "bolted on" or straight-up marketing ploys disconnected from what they know or believe is true about a brand. At their best, such initiatives fall flat or fail to grow revenue and fans. At their worst, they significantly erode a loyal customer base. As you'll discover in this book, people don't expect "perfection" from brands: They respect brands that exhibit human traits and thus expect them to be somewhat flawed—provided they're transparent about their imperfections and working to improve themselves.

This dynamic shift can be understood as an Outside-In (customer-first) versus Inside-Out (company-first) view. While the customer-first mentality does exist, at many organizations it's being overtaken by so-called big data, turning each of us into an anonymous consumer to be cross-sold more products and services. Although *engagement* is a word regularly used by marketing communications and customer experience professionals, a truly customer-centric, more human perspective, which is often overshadowed in corporate strategy, planning, and marketing, can no longer be ignored or subverted.

THE IMPERATIVE AND CAPACITY FOR DOING GOOD

Organizations of all sizes are recognizing that having a greater "purpose" than just earning a profit matters more than ever, and studies from major consultancies continue to demonstrate this. A 2014 EY/Harvard Business Review Analytic Services global research study, *The Business Case for Purpose*, found that:

- 87 percent of business executives believe companies perform best over time if their purpose goes beyond profit.

- 89 percent say that purpose-driven organizations encourage greater employee satisfaction, 85 percent better customer advocacy, and 81 percent higher-quality products and services.

- 80 percent of business executives state that business purpose increases customer loyalty.

- Yet, despite nearly 90 percent of executives saying they understand the importance of benefiting local and global society, only 46 percent of them say that their purpose informs operational or strategic decision making.[6]

A 2010 CECP: The CEO Force for Good report, *Shaping the Future: Solving Social Problems Through Business*, based on McKinsey & Company research, also noted that 77 percent of CEOs believe embedding social engagement into the business and organizational structure is the most important action to take to prepare for 2020. Further, according to a Nielsen 2014 report, *Doing Well by Doing Good*, 55 percent of consumers are willing to pay extra for products and services from companies committed to having a positive social and environmental impact.[7]

Although a majority of business leaders have accepted—to varying degrees—that they have a responsibility to help create a better, more sustainable future, they have not necessarily figured out how to do so effectively. For many, the focus has been on *looking* good rather than on actually integrating the elements of *doing* good into the DNA of their organizations. Often, the goal of doing the right thing is seen as a *cost* of doing business, not a *way* of doing business. Although social responsibility has grown in importance as a factor in corporate reputation, a brand purpose centered on doing good is still largely perceived as more specialized and relevant for brands designed around social entrepreneurship or focused on niche target consumers.

As I have listened to people participating in *CultureQ* research, I have heard the call for brands to do good on their behalf growing below the surface of *all* their decisions. The unprecedented level of transparency that social media has generated is placing great power in the hands of customers and employees. And the rise of populism that has continued to surface in different manifestations since the Occupy Wall Street movement is calling for more equity and fairness in business decision making.

With this Outside-In orientation, people are increasingly looking to buy great products and services from companies that have ethical operations, do great things for the world, and advocate for the things they care about. Ultimately, people are demanding greater value for their dollar than ever before, and businesses must holistically align brand development with sustainability and corporate citizenship initiatives. What's most interesting about the shift is the fact that customers and employees—in other words, people themselves—not marketers or advertising agencies are driving the change. Clearly, though, marketers and advertisers have a role to play in making the change happen—and at a faster rate. The concept of Brand Citizenship is reflective of our flattened world, where greater consumer–corporate collaboration can deliver significant benefits to customers, corporations, employees, suppliers, other stakeholders, and society alike. Until now, as long as companies delivered on shareholder value, investment and growth generally continued every quarter. The peak of the economic crisis in 2008, however, accelerated a nascent trend and emphasized a shift from shareholder to stakeholder value. Brand Citizenship champions this notion by embracing profitability and responsibility as harmonious concepts.

Placing a greater purpose at the center of a brand is the starting point, followed by aligning the benefits a brand delivers to individual customers with how it treats employees, suppliers, and the environment, and with the way it helps the world.

THE BRAND CITIZENSHIP MODEL

The qualitative and quantitative studies we conducted over three years as part of *CultureQ* research led me to see something unexpected: People want brands that start with a ME-First orientation to stretch and span themselves across a ME-to-WE continuum. Brands must first deliver value, functionally and emotionally, to individual consumers (ME) and then, depending on the brand's purpose, move outward toward delivering added value to society: the collective WE.

Brand Citizenship isn't about a company sacrificing to better the world. Nor is it boasting about doing good. It's a five-step model that integrates doing good activities—such as fair employee policies, corporate and social responsibility (CSR), sustainability programs, ethical sourcing, and charitable giving—with brand development to strengthen a brand's reputation, foster greater loyalty, and enhance value creation. It's a win-win-win solution that mutually benefits consumers, companies, and society. See Figure I-1.

FIGURE I-1. Brand Citizenship model.

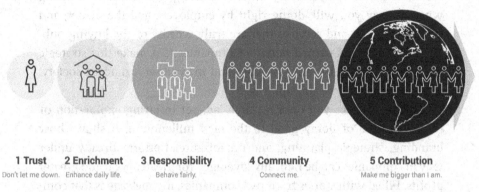

1 Trust	2 Enrichment	3 Responsibility	4 Community	5 Contribution
Don't let me down.	Enhance daily life.	Behave fairly.	Connect me.	Make me bigger than I am.

THE RESISTANCE TO DOING GOOD

For many executives, activities related to corporate social responsibility, environmental sustainability, and doing good may still feel as though they conflict with the classic business school mantra that has dictated corporate behavior for decades: The primary purpose of a corporation is to maximize profits and shareholder value.

Even the phrase *doing good* conjures up images of idealism and altruism—which translates to self-sacrifice and not making a profit. Yet globalized sourcing, production, and sales all insist that long-term success be dependent on meeting the needs of a wide range of stakeholders. In an interconnected world where mashups of all kinds are mainstream concepts—with disparate elements easily coexisting—and where social media enables people to share stories globally of good and bad experiences with products and services, the notions of doing good and earning a profit cease to be at odds with each other.

Doing good and earning a profit are symbiotic and interdependent elements in what I, and others, refer to as a virtuous circle that includes customers, employees, suppliers, communities, society at large, and even the planet. Today, the goal of doing good and becoming a sustainable business is a practical and necessary investment into brand loyalty. This is the new model of Brand Citizenship. A holistic principle that equips businesses to gain lasting credit for sustainability and corporate social responsibility initiatives along a continuum of doing what you say you will, doing right by employees and the planet, and providing goods and services that are truly worthy of the buying public's time and hard-earned dollars. Companies that make this strategic shift are judged to be more relevant and in sync with modern society: empathic, innovative, and uplifting.

This book takes you on a research-led, yet inspiring exploration of the application of doing good in the new millennium. It shows how branding, strategic planning, and organizational efforts already under way in companies can be radically leveraged for greater good and greater profits. Filled with stories from real companies, my message is that companies that stay true to their core purpose, no matter what it is, can garner the benefits of having a stronger value model.

Do Good is organized into three sections. In Part I, I examine the forces leading to the demand that brands address people's growing desire for community and contribution, as well as individual satisfaction, the need to balance social and financial values, and the creation of Brand Citizenship as a model to move from meeting individual needs to nurturing communities to solving global challenges. In Part II, I take a penetrating look at how more than a dozen organizations are taking the necessary steps to meet customer, employee, supplier, and investor requirements to both do good and do well. And in Part III, I discuss specific strategies and techniques that organizations can adopt to align themselves with the goals of Brand Citizenship.

Each chapter of *Do Good* closes with a list of highlights. These can provide a context for your own experiences, as well as point the way for you to navigate the brave new interconnected, transparent, and global world of business.

There is not one type of Brand Citizenship company. Multiple approaches along the ME-to-WE continuum resonate with customers, employees, investors, and other stakeholders of all types, as well as with companies in all industries and of all scales. My intent in writing this book is to provoke more meaningful discussion, accelerate changes already under way, and provide ideas that will catalyze Brand Citizenship methodologies and strategies among start-ups, established teams, brand managers, finance departments, business-line leaders, sustainability and social responsibility experts, and everyone who is inspired to make business more relevant, innovative, enduring, and profitable. Thank you for joining me on this journey.

PART I

IT'S A BRAVE NEW WORLD

A NEW, DEMANDING AND
CHANGING LANDSCAPE

CHAPTER 1

THE NEW DEMAND THAT BRANDS MAKE A DIFFERENCE

In our personal lives, sometimes change comes slowly after we spend weeks, months, or years thinking about how we can be happier, more successful, or more fulfilled. Other times, change is not a choice. It is something that pursues us: We're fired from a job, a natural disaster strikes, our spouse calls it quits, or our child is diagnosed with a potentially terminal disease. Whether by choice or necessity, as we set out to do something differently or adapt to something unexpected, we quickly discover that changing takes time, is full of competing demands, and is far from easy—even when it's a proactive choice.

The process of change is no different for a business, particularly now, because the model that's guided business for the last several decades *must* change. What was an optional path for companies before the millennium has become mandatory. The global economy, technology, climate change, generational shifts, and an evolving cultural landscape are dramatically altering how business is conducted and the ways in which people consume, engage, and even abandon the brands in their lives. Over the past twenty-five years as a researcher studying consumers' and employees' relationships with brands, I've seen the signs of this coming revolution and watched their numbers increase at an exponential rate. If you've been paying attention, you've probably noticed some of these changes, too.

A NEW MILLENNIUM AND A
CHANGING LANDSCAPE

It's hard to remember a time before mobile phones, wireless technology, and the ubiquity of social media. However, it really wasn't all that long ago: The first wireless Palm VII and BlackBerry were released in 1999, Facebook launched in 2004, and Twitter went live in 2006. In 1999 and 2000, as head of the consulting businesses at Interbrand, one of the world's largest brand consultancies with its finger on the consumer pulse in twenty-eight countries, I saw firsthand how technology was transforming our lives and relationships with brands. Through comprehensive discussions with people ranging from CEOs and CIOs to sixteen-year-olds who knew nothing other than living in a digitally connected world, four concepts emerged that captured the ways in which technology was altering our lives: mobility, connectivity, freedom, and humanity.

Today, these concepts may seem like givens, yet the impact they have had and continue to have on us as individuals and as a society is profound. Behavioral psychologists, economists, and marketers alike all look to make sense of how technology is altering our brain patterns and impacting the commercial pact that exists between companies and their customers, employees, and other stakeholders. In other words, between businesses and people.

In 1999, people were seeing the benefits and challenges of this new existence:

▶ We were gaining true *mobility* through the opportunity to plug ourselves in from anywhere to do almost anything—work, shop, make travel plans, and more. . . .

▶ And we were *connected* to the expansive world of the Internet, as well as to our coworkers, families, and friends through email—anytime, anywhere.

▶ Because of mobility and connectivity, we cherished the *freedom* and control to turn our environments on or off with the flip of a switch.

▶ Yet many people reported they were missing the more personal aspects of communications; they were looking for reassurance that they would maintain *human* connections as technology interlaced itself more and more into our daily living.

As our lives became more integrated with machines, the nine-to-five workday was quietly disappearing. As people were expected to be connected anywhere at any time through a growing number of devices, an inherent tension was building: Employers were pressuring workers to be in touch constantly. This existed alongside a growing desire by individuals to use their newly acquired tech tools to stay in frequent contact with colleagues, family, and friends while on the go. Suddenly, we were bringing our communication network with us in our cars, on our travels, and during what used to be our downtime. The ability to turn a device off and escape was an increasingly difficult choice, accompanied by a fear of missing out when doing so. So, did these new mobile communications truly make us free?

At the same time we were becoming *wired*, we craved the intangible and untethered things that made us human. Our intimate ties to technology had changed our social needs and emotions. With a force equal to that of the technological revolution, which was quickly integrating itself into the fabric of our daily lives, an equal energy began to spring up in reaction: a quest for emotional connections and deeper human relationships and experiences.

As Marc Gobé so aptly wrote in his book *Emotional Branding*, "People love brands but brands don't love people back—this results in so many missed opportunities to connect." In response, brand consultants and marketers sought to humanize brands and create more meaningful experiences for connecting companies and their customers, for community building, and for ethical behavior. Sustainability and green consciousness—things more traditionally linked with corporate reputation—started creeping into brand image.

Over the past fifteen years, the research I've conducted on my own and on behalf of my clients has demonstrated that we are developing a deeper connection with the brands we interact with. Brands, especially the ones we're loyal to, represent more than things and services. They signify an ethos, the character of a culture or a group—either one that mirrors our existing values or one that we aspire to. And as more people grow concerned with equality and sustainability, more of us want to feel that our "relationship" with a brand links us to some kind of larger purpose designed to help shape a future that will both sustain the planet and enrich our modern lives.

Since branding became a focus for business in the late 1990s, businesses have looked to nurture consumers who will advocate on behalf of their brands—people who not only buy products or services themselves but who also recommend them to friends, "like" them online, and positively tweet or post about their experiences using them. Today, the tides are turning, and customers and employees alike are looking for the brands they buy and companies they work for to advocate on their behalf, as well as on behalf of those who are disadvantaged and for the planet.

Companies are no longer just companies. We imbue them with the characteristics of friends and family—and even enemies. So it's no surprise that people now demand businesses and their brands to do more than just make a profit. They expect brands to behave like active citizens and partner with customers, employees, and other stakeholders to co-create a better future.

OUR CHANGING ATTITUDE TOWARD BUSINESS

If you're a CEO, marketer, advertiser, entrepreneur, consultant, or other business executive, you're aware of the following movement: Each year, more brands that stand for good principles or causes are surfacing. While they are still in the minority among business enterprises overall, the impact they are having on our collective psyche and expectations for all companies is growing.

Increasingly, politicians, scientists, economists, and the general public are recognizing that our current approach to business needs to change. More and more business leaders are seeking models to guide them through shifting marketplace dynamics. Increasingly, customers and employees are letting companies know that they are no longer willing to accept business as usual, with the attendant human, environmental, and community *costs* of prioritizing earnings above everything else. Ultimately, people want businesses to do more than just earn a profit. They want the brands they buy to go beyond being only bottom line–driven to doing good on their behalf, as their customers.

DOING GOOD REDEFINED

Doing good. For most people this phrase conjures up images of kindness and self-sacrifice: A young Boy Scout helping an old woman to cross the street. A Peace Corps volunteer teaching a Nepalese man to build a smokeless stove. An aid worker in Haiti rescuing a young child from the rubble. Habitat for Humanity, the American Red Cross, Doctors Without Borders, CARE, and other nonprofit organizations come readily to mind. When we hear the phrase *doing good*, few of us think of a business of any kind—whether it's a bank, a fast-food chain, an oil and gas producer, or even a retailer. And if we do, we likely think of "hippy" brands like Tom's of Maine, philanthropic businesses like Newman's Own, social enterprises like TOMS or Warby Parker that apply commercial strategies to maximize social impact alongside profits for external shareholders, or our favorite brand of certified-organic chocolate bars we buy from stores like Whole Foods Market.

Yet today many businesses across industries are doing good and adding social value. According to philanthropic tracking and rating sites, Giving USA and Charity Navigator, U.S. corporations gave $18.45 billion to charities in 2015.[1,2]

By the World Bank's 2015 statistics, that's more than the GDP of Iceland ($16.59 billion), Jamaica ($14.26 billion), the Bahamas ($8.85 billion), and many other countries.[3] It's interesting to note that Giving USA's figures don't include the ways companies are directly contributing to the general good via, for example, initiatives such as employee-volunteer programs, using only ethically sourced materials, recycling waste, and reducing water usage in manufacturing production. If the impact of these and similar efforts were added to charitable donations, the number clearly would be much higher.

So why don't we think of business when we hear the phrase *doing good*? One argument that continues to gain momentum is this: *Even though the number itself is large, corporate giving represents a very small percentage of corporate profits.* Less than 1.2 percent of the Fortune 500's combined $1.5 trillion in profits is donated to causes and communities around the world.[4]

With an average total compensation of U.S. chief executives of the 350 largest publicly traded corporations estimated at $16.32 million per CEO, or approximately a combined $5.7 billion in 2014, when considered alongside executive compensation, the dollar value that 1.2 percent represents seems tiny.[5] However, the issue runs even deeper. Our Western cultural narrative associates doing good with idealism and altruism—two concepts we typically don't associate with corporations.

HOW TECHNOLOGY IS REWRITING OUR CULTURAL NARRATIVE

As technological advances and the digital era are altering our lives overall, and the way we accomplish daily tasks, communicate, produce, and consume media, they are simultaneously changing our cultural narrative. Think about the impact of cutting and pasting, for example. The fact that we can digitally cut two seemingly different images and place them side by side has dramatically changed the way we see things fitting together. The act of mixing disparate elements—how we dress, what we read, what we listen to, what we watch—to create our own individual lifestyles has become practically second nature. This is especially true for Millennials—the generation born between 1980 and 1995—and Gen Z—the generation born between 1996 and 2010—who are far more comfortable with mashups of paradoxical things living side by side than their parents, teachers, and older coworkers have ever been.

We don't need to pick between H&M and Chanel, flip-flops and a suit, Beyoncé and Jimi Hendrix, or even *Brokeback Mountain* and *Back to the Future*. We now have permission to comfortably express the inconsistencies in our personalities daily and even moment by moment. This feature of our wired world has conditioned us to believe we have the right to have it all. We no longer have to decide between seemingly opposite states: competition or collaboration; money or meaning; love or power; sustainability or prosperity.

The digital age has enabled opposites to congruously coexist alongside one another. The transformative result has been to move us beyond a world of *either/or* and into a new universe of *also*. In an interconnected world, where coopetiton (collaborative competition), hybrid cars, mixed racial backgrounds, and gay marriage have moved from the margins into the mainstream, the notions of idealism and realism cease to be at odds with each other as well.

A growing number of CEOs today acknowledge that doing good is as essential a criterion for lasting business success as earning a profit. Organizations such as the CECP: The CEO Force for Good, for example, are growing. Founded by Paul Newman in 1999, CECP is a coalition of CEOs united in the belief that societal improvement is a measure of business performance. Membership now includes more than two hundred of the world's largest companies as diverse as American Express, Coca-Cola, Estée Lauder, Pfizer, Toyota Motor Corporation, United Parcel Service (UPS), and Xerox.[6] Although many of the companies on CECP's roster were once considered part of the proverbial problem, they are now investing in creating social and financial value.

So why shouldn't a business make a profit while simultaneously doing good? Why shouldn't idealism and realism comfortably sit side by side? Just as compelling, why shouldn't doing good or becoming a sustainable business be seen as an investment into brand loyalty rather than simply a necessary cost of doing business?

DOING GOOD IS A MANDATE FOR BUSINESS

For decades, corporate efforts to fund social and environmental programs have been considered, at best, public relations campaigns designed to boost brand reputation and, at worst, a way to right wrongs. They were part of a zero sum game in which companies' positive efforts simply offset their negative behavior.

In the words of *CultureQ* research participants:

Big companies ruin communities in places like Africa or China with their factories. They kill local traditions and use up resources. Then they educate a few kids there and feel they've made up for all the bad things they've done.

I think everyone is equally responsible [for improving society].

No one company can do anything alone. Bigger companies have more pull, though, so they should be the most encouraging.

Consider Nike, for example. Its PR problems began in 1991, when activist Jeff Ballinger published a report documenting low wages and poor working conditions among the company's Indonesian contractors. Then, five years later, Nike's woes escalated when *Life* magazine published pictures of a child in Pakistan assembling Nike soccer balls.[7] The company responded by creating a department to improve the lives of factory workers. More abuses were exposed, and Nike asked diplomat and activist Andrew Young to audit its labor practices abroad. Young's report was positive, and Nike was quick to publish it. Experts, however, criticized the report for being too soft on the company.

In 1997, college students began protesting Nike's practices, and in 1998, faced with lay-offs and significantly weakened demand for its products, CEO Phil Knight conceded in a speech at a press conference at the National Press Club. As *The New York Times* reported, Knight states, "The Nike product has become synonymous with slave wages, forced overtime and arbitrary abuse. . . . I truly believe that the American consumer does not want to buy products made in abusive conditions."[8] He then agreed to allow outsiders from labor and human rights groups to join independent auditors in Asia in their investigations of Nike's manufacturing practices. That day, he did something more powerful than admitting Nike had done something wrong and committing to bettering supplier policies. Through the wording of his statement, he acknowledged his customers' values and aligned the Nike brand alongside them.

Today, Nike sees itself as having been on a "sustainable journey" for nearly twenty years, one that has no ending and for which the bar continuously rises with each accomplishment. As Mark Parker, Nike's current CEO, stated in the company's 2014/2015 *Sustainable Business Report*:

[W]e will never stop trying to achieve our ultimate vision of the future.

A future where we produce closed-loop products—created with renewable energy and recyclable materials.

A future where supply chains are fueled by skilled and valued workers—all of them supported by industry's unified standards.

And a future where NIKE's creative, driven and diverse teams continue to push the boundaries of what's possible—while engaging deeply with local communities.

This represents a new business model, driven by sustainable innovation. I believe it will accelerate change like the world has never seen.[9]

Unlike Nike, McDonald's has been searching for the formula to successfully connect to these new consumer values. Even though it invests heavily in innovation and progressive initiatives tied to shifts in the culture, it is still caught up in the righting-wrongs paradigm.

Remember the documentary *Supersize Me*—in which independent filmmaker Morgan Spurlock chronicled his declining health over a month in which he ate nothing but McDonald's food? Shortly after the release of the film, McDonald's announced that it would phase out its signature menu option for customers to Supersize their orders. As America's obesity rate was sharply increasing, the Supersize menu choice received much criticism. At the time, however, spokesman Walt Riker denied that health concerns were influencing the change: "The driving force here was menu simplification…," he said. "The fact of the matter is not very many Supersize fries are sold."[10]

Although the move was, in fact, officially part of McDonald's "Eat Smart, Be Active" initiative launched in 2003, many believed it was a direct response to Spurlock's film. Despite Riker's claims that phasing out of the Supersize selection had "nothing to do with that [film] whatsoever," the notion that this was a public relations move designed to right a wrong still casts a shadow over all of McDonald's corporate decisions for many activists.

McDonald's 2016 food philosophy, *The Simpler the Better*, affirmed the company's commitment to improve the way it prepares food, to use higher-quality ingredients, and to incorporate sustainable practices at the corporate and retail levels. Although McDonald's isn't 100 percent there yet, the company continues to take steps to become a more progressive brand, and analysts credit investments in food quality and ingredients as factors in the company's improved sales growth in 2015.

Since the Great Recession, Occupy Wall Street, and movements to raise the minimum wage, the zero sum corporate responsibility game has come under even greater scrutiny. People want—and are demanding—that companies do good in both words and deeds. Now more companies than ever have the means to actualize this. A cocktail of consumer desires, technology, and changing culture has made doing good both a practical reality and a new requirement for corporate survival across industries.

AS STORIES GO VIRAL, COMPANIES MUST LISTEN

Every day people across cultures share stories of good and bad experiences with products and services via social media. With so many platforms for far-reaching digital expression, praise is hard-earned, and blame is easily placed when things go wrong. People now require brands to fix problems associated with the things they sell and conduct business sincerely and ethically, addressing the social and environmental issues related to the production and distribution of their products and services.

Few people made the connection between the benefit of fast fashion and its cost on people's livelihoods until the tragedy at Rana Plaza in Bangladesh on April 24, 2013. On that day, a concrete building in the Savar neighborhood of Dhaka collapsed on the 3,500 garment workers inside its factories.[11] It has been labeled both the deadliest garment factory accident in history and the deadliest accidental structural failure in modern human history.

Rana Plaza manufactured apparel for brands such as Benetton Group, Bonmarché, The Children's Place, El Corte Inglés, Joe Fresh, Mango, Primark, and Walmart. According to numerous news reports, 1,129 people died in the aftermath, and 2,515 injured people were rescued from the building. The day before the building collapsed, management ignored warnings about the building's safety and threatened to dock workers one month's pay if they did not return to work.

Images of the disaster were so horrific that many Western consumers considered it a wake-up call, and the Rana Plaza disaster was viewed by many as the start of a "fair trade" movement in ready-to-wear fashion.

H&M was an easy target for activists focused on the poor treatment of garment workers. Even though H&M didn't use Rana Plaza, it was—and continues to be recognized as—the world leader of fast fashion and the biggest buyer of Bangladeshi ready-made garment products, increasing annual purchases to $5 billion in 2016.[12] Through the viral spread of a clever human rights advertisement two weeks after the Rana Plaza disaster, H&M quickly became associated with the unfair treatment of global garment workers. The group behind the advertisement, Avaaz, circulated an online petition that garnered more than 900,000 signatures and demanded that H&M pay to meet fire safety standards and reduce workplace hazards in its Bangladeshi factories.[13]

Initially, H&M did not respond. To increase pressure on the Swedish company, Avaaz then launched a campaign featuring a photo of H&M's CEO, Karl-Johan Persson, juxtaposed above a Bangladeshi woman in tears. Three weeks after the building collapsed, H&M agreed to sign the plan, which was legally binding.

As the fast fashion industry leader in both production and image, H&M's actions to improve the conditions of garment workers in Bangladesh were both lauded and scrutinized closely by consumer and labor groups, as well as by the media. Since Rana Plaza, H&M has further committed itself to green initiatives, such as recycled fashion, reduced waste, and increased use of organic and non-GMO (genetically modified organism) materials.

On April 24, 2014, people across fifty-five countries participated in the first Fashion Revolution Day, sponsored by the industry advocacy group, Fashion Revolution. It marked the first anniversary of the Rana Plaza disaster and galvanized a movement determined not to accept cheap clothing at the expense of the livelihoods—and potentially the lives—of the workers who make the garments. Through a multimedia campaign, celebrities showed their support for garment workers worldwide by both wearing their clothes #InsideOut and asking, "Who Made Your Clothes?" The Fashion Revolution Day event had over 6.6 million hits on Google, trended at number one on Twitter, and reached over 80 million people.[14]

It was one of several social media campaigns designed to pressure retailers such as Walmart, Benneton, Matalan, and Primark to help to better conditions for garment workers and to contribute to the Rana Plaza Donors Trust Fund. The campaign showed positive results: Walmart, along with the Walmart Foundation and Asda, Walmart's British super-market subsidiary, contributed $3 million to BRAC USA ("BRAC" formerly stood for the Bangladesh Rehabilitation Assistance Committee). One-third of that money went to the Rana Plaza trust fund. The Gap Foundation, The Children's Place, and Benetton Group also stepped forward with financial commitments.

In 2016, Fashion Revolution's voice continued to strengthen. Between April 18 and 24 of that year, 70,000 people—a 75 percent increase over 2015—asked brands #whomademyclothes. Even more impressive was the 156 million times the conversation appeared in people's social media feeds.[15] With the goal of greater transparency across the fashion industry, in April 2016, Fashion Revolution and Ethical Consumer also published the first-ever Transparency Index, aimed at giving the public more insight into how and where their clothes are made and motivating companies to publish more about their policies and practices.

It is important to note that the public's interest in fair corporate policies is not limited to workers in the developing world. It's multinational. Just ask AOL. In a February 2014 Town Hall meeting with employees, shortly after the Affordable Care Act (Obamacare) kicked off, AOL CEO Tim Armstrong explained to employees that he was paring down their retirement benefits. He first attributed the reason for the change to rising healthcare costs as a result of the Affordable Care Act. When staff demanded further explanation, he linked the increase to the birth of two distressed babies in 2012 that cost "a million dollars each. . . . And those are the things that add up into our benefits cost. So when we had the final decision about what benefits to cut because of the increased healthcare costs, we made the decision, and I made the decision, to basically change the 401(k) plan."[16]

Employee outrage leaked to the media and created a firestorm. Once TV and online media compared the cost of "million-dollar babies" to Mr. Armstrong's take-home pay of $12 million, the consequences of an internal policy decision became a significant public relations problem. As the general public rallied behind AOL employees' sentiments through social media, Tim Armstrong apologized for his comments and reversed the changes.

As Rana Plaza and AOL each demonstrate, unacceptable corporate policies can easily become news headlines in a flash. Today, unfair labor or environmental practices can have a long-lasting, negative impact on a brand's sales. Consumers care about how a brand brings its products to market and treats employees more than ever before, and they will demonstrate their concerns online through social media, by petitions, with activism, and—perhaps most importantly—with their pocketbooks. Heritage, provenance, quality, transparency of operations, and working conditions all matter.

LEADING FROM THE FRONT, RATHER THAN FROM BEHIND

Just as social media has helped advocates move their causes into the mainstream psyche, it can help brands build movements proactively rather than reactively—and lead from ahead rather than from behind. Chipotle Mexican Grill ("Chipotle"), for example, befittingly used viral marketing to shift the conversation about fast-food production and increase awareness of its brand twenty years after it was founded.

In September of 2013, the company released its video, *The Scarecrow*, which quickly went viral on YouTube. The haunting video opens in a dystopian world with a scarecrow (Scarecrow) heading to his job at the fictional industrial giant Crow Foods Incorporated. Both viewers and Scarecrow grow increasingly sad as chickens are jabbed with hormones to grow faster and cows are trapped in their pens. As Scarecrow heads home from his mechanistic job, he finds a fresh pepper growing in a barren track of land. Inspired to start cooking, he comes to the realization that factory farms are not the future. Scarecrow eventually returns to the city and goes into business for himself, selling wholesome, more natural (Chipotle-style) meals that opens taste buds, minds, and perspectives and is meant to do the same for viewers. The video then signs off with Chipotle's mission: *Cultivate a better world.*[17]

The Scarecrow video was highly effective in emotively bringing the realities of food production into the consciousness and hearts of consumers and in motivating them to connect the dots about healthy food in ways that videos and documentaries like *Food, Inc.* and *Supersize Me* hadn't fully done. By associating its brand with the doing-good side of farming, food processing, and food service, Chipotle created a halo over itself and simultaneously denigrated other brands whose standards were not as high.

In the world of fast food, in particular, food service that uses a better, fairer production process can be a compelling brand differentiator. Whether consciously or subconsciously, *The Scarecrow* video guided people to feel as though they were aligning themselves with a more natural food production process by buying, for example, a Chipotle burrito over a McDonald's hamburger. Walking into Chipotle became a badge that indicated you stood for something more meaningful. Who would have imagined such a thing in fast food twenty years ago?

How seismic was Chipotle's success in shifting public perceptions with *The Scarecrow*? The numbers tell the story: In 2014, a year after rolling out that video, Chipotle's same-store sales grew 16.8 percent, compared with 1 percent for McDonald's global store base, and a 1.7 percent decline in McDonald's same-store sales during that time.[18,19] Chipotle was also off to a strong start in 2015. It opened forty-nine new restaurants and generated revenue of nearly $1.1 billion in the first quarter, an increase of 20 percent on comparable restaurant sales growth of 10.4 percent.[20] However, the aura it created around itself from *The Scarecrow* was not impenetrable. Indeed, having permanently raised the benchmark for fast food, Chipotle's existence was predicated on delivering a consistently higher quality standard, and a series of food-safety scares later in 2015 violated the implicit promise the brand had made to its customers.

LEADING FROM AHEAD DEMANDS AN OUTSIDE-IN PERSPECTIVE IN A SOCIAL WORLD

In August of 2015, after eating at a California Chipotle restaurant, about eighty customers and eighteen employees were sickened by norovirus, a highly contagious food-borne illness.[21] That September, forty-five people became ill from a salmonella outbreak related to tomatoes in seventeen Chipotle restaurants in Minnesota.[22] Then in November 2015, more than forty people fell ill with *E. coli* food poisoning after eating at Chipotle restaurants in six states.[23] By early December, the number of people had increased to fifty-two in nine states.[24]

Few brands, if any, could survive three crises on top of one another without some erosion of trust. But as noted earlier, for Chipotle, a brand "committed to serving food with integrity," the outbreaks were even more ruinous: They destroyed the brand equity *The Scarecrow* had grown. Revenue for fourth quarter 2015 decreased 6.8 percent, compared to the same period in 2014, and by mid-April of 2016, the company's stock plummeted 40 percent, from $758 per share to $456. After proactively redefining and expanding the fast-food debate, Chipotle found itself on the defensive, not unlike McDonald's.[25,26]

On February 1, 2016, the Centers for Disease Control (CDC) declared the *E. coli* outbreak over and the cause of the contamination unknown.[27] Within a few days, Chipotle closed all its restaurants to train employees on the seriousness of foodborne-illness outbreaks as it had promised in a January press release announcing new food procedures.[28] In an effort to be transparent and rebuild trust, the company also placed a timeline detailing its food safety incidents on its website.

Some experts believe the outbreaks may have been a natural by-product of Chipotle's more complex supply chain. The more complicated the supply chain, the higher the risk. Chipotle's promise of ethically sourced, freshly prepared food has additional complexity built into it. For example, onions, lettuce, and cilantro are hand-chopped in restaurants; tortilla chips, rice, and guacamole are handmade; and chicken is also diced and cooked on location.[29] The inherent problems in-house preparation may cause, however, are no comfort to a large number of people looking for a place to buy great tasting, healthy food fast. In July of 2016, eight months after people fell ill from eating at Chipotle chains, the company released its third video, *A Love Story*.[30]

Set in an ideal neighborhood, the film begins with a character named Ivan running a juice stand across the street from Evie's lemonade stand. Ivan clearly pines for Evie, and, aiming to boost sales and earn money to take her out on a date, he starts to advertise his Fresh-Squeezed Orange Juice. Looking to rebuild her lost traffic, Evie responds by marketing her Hand- Squeezed Lemonade. The would-be couple's rivalry begins and grows over the years as each business adds items to its menu and gives way to industrialization and processed ingredients. Disconnected from their businesses and literally thrown out with the trash, Evie and Ivan ultimately rediscover one another and, together, build an authentic brand centered around fresh ingredients and wholesomeness. The video concludes by introducing the company's loyalty program, Chiptopia.

Given the events of 2015, today, *The Scarecrow* appears almost self-righteous or arrogant and *Love Story* a reflection on how, under pressure to grow, Chipotle strayed from fully delivering its purpose. Evie and Ivan's tale of reconnecting with their roots and purpose was charming, but it did not address Chipotle's reputation crisis head-on. While soul-searching is important when a brand loses its way, to lead from ahead and reclaim lost momentum, crisis management requires looking from the outside in, not from the inside out. That said, the impact Chipotle has had on the fast-food industry should not be undermined by the brand's subsequent problems with food-borne illness. *The Scarecrow* everlastingly shifted public perception and expectations of fast food. In Chapter 4, I'll explore further what Chipotle has been doing to regain lost trust and solidly place its mission in the center of its operations and brand experience.

Academics and activists have debated the social responsibility of business for decades, if not centuries. Today, however, social media has moved the debate out of academic hallways, closed-door boardrooms, and print news media into the public square. In the same way that political activists leveraged social media to trigger the Arab Spring, corporate activists, opinion leaders, politicians, and even disgruntled employees are employing it to raise general awareness of harmful, discriminatory, inequitable, and even thoughtless business practices.

From fair trade, to organic, to recycling, to futuristic innovations, people are demanding more from the brands they buy and the companies they work for. They want a product they love from a business that has ethical operations and does great things for the world—or at least one corner of the globe that they care about. Ultimately, people are unequivocally seeking greater value.

HIGHLIGHTS

CHAPTER 1:
The New Demand That Brands
Make a Difference

▶ Profound changes in technology, politics, the global economy, and the rise of social media have reshaped the landscape for business.

▶ The wired, digital world in which brands now operate has had a profound effect on the traditional pact between companies and their customers, employees, and stakeholders.

▶ As people's expectations for their relationships with brands have shifted, businesses are finding that their success is tied to their ability to demonstrate that they are committed to doing good, helping to solve people's bigger social and environmental concerns.

▶ Doing good has come to mean taking responsibility for more than traditional philanthropy or corporate social responsibility initiatives. It now signifies advocating for issues that matter to customers, employees, and stakeholders—whether they be about the local community, people's global concerns, or sustaining the environment.

▶ Technology has reshaped our cultural narrative in significant ways, not the least of which is the expectation that brands should be expected to make a profit while simultaneously doing good.

▶ The power of social media and the impact of stories and images going viral have changed the response time for businesses. Brands must listen and respond in ways that are unprecedented for many of them.

▶ More and more, business success will insist on companies' reflecting and shaping developing trends and exhibiting leadership at the earliest possible opportunity.

CHAPTER 2

BALANCING SOCIAL AND FINANCIAL VALUES

The New Brand and Business Equation

People are frustrated. They want the world to work better, and they have a crazy and exciting idea that companies can help solve many of our problems where governments can't. *Why?* According to my company's research with Millennials, Gen Xers, and Baby Boomers since 2011, it's because *brands unite and inspire us.* They are more in tune with our daily lives and values than branches of government are. And, unlike politicians, brands face no opposing force. Indeed, the Edelman Trust Barometer 2016, an annual global survey in its sixteenth year, strongly confirmed that business was more trusted than government. The study found that:

► 80 percent of the general public agreed that "[a] company can take specific actions that both increase profits and improve the economic and social conditions in the community where it operates."

► 49 percent, up 8 percent from 2015, rated CEOs as extremely or very credible, as compared to 35 percent for government officials or regulators.

➤ 61 percent stated they trust business "to keep up with the changing times," while only 41 percent have faith in government to do so.[1]

To address this shift in trust, companies have been seeking new ways of engaging with people and new ways of doing business. While more and more companies have the will to partner with customers, employees, and other stakeholders to co-create a better future, a large number have not yet figured out how to do so. They struggle to integrate sustainable, environmental, and social initiatives into their corporate mission and align these initiatives with the products and services they offer. Many executives still perceive these activities conflicting with the corporate mantra that until now has defined our economy and our notions of capitalism: *The primary purpose of a corporation is to maximize profits and shareholder value.*

Yet, despite what many in business believe, this guiding principle is not codified in law. It's a notion that was popularized by economists in the 1970s, most notably Milton Friedman. In a September 13, 1970, article in *The New York Times*, Friedman sang the free-enterprise song that we abide by to this day:

> In a free enterprise, private-property system, a corporate executive is an employee of the owners of a business. He has direct responsibility to his employers. That responsibility is to conduct the business in accordance with their desires, which generally will be to make as much money as possible while conforming to the basic rules of the society, both those embodied in law and those embodied in ethical custom.[2]

In the ensuing decades, the pressure for corporate executives to respond to the short-term demands of Wall Street has grown and created a business model that is increasingly disconnected from many stakeholder needs. Between 1926 and 1999, the average length of time shareholders held a stock was four years. By 2012, it had shrunk to 3.2 days![3] However, has shareholder value really ever been only about corporate profits? People today don't think so, and their beliefs and expectations are forcing companies to make a shift that has been more than twenty-five years in the making.

ETHICAL CUSTOMS SHIFTING
WITH THE ZEITGEIST

In 2011, my company launched a new research project called *CultureQ*. Building on research we had been conducting with Millennials formally and informally since 2007, *CultureQ* synthesized our ongoing dialogues with Millennials with exploratory qualitative research, quantitative studies among Xers, Yers, and Boomers, and real-life observations. We wanted to more deeply understand how people's relationships with brands were changing alongside cultural shifts and evolving ideals.

Starting in 2011, over three years of investigation, my company's *CultureQ* project gleaned many fascinating insights about brand leadership, good and bad corporate citizenship, and the things that make some brands favorites. By the third year, it was clear that an increasing and vocal number of participants felt that the long-standing value model taught in business schools was out of step with society. Many indicated that the time had come to stop artificially separating economic and social value. As one of our interview subjects aptly stated it:

> Many companies believe they have a responsibility to "give back" to society and to me. This is wonderful—in the future ... all [businesses will] have to give to get.

Milton Friedman, again in his article in *The New York Times*, noted that business has a responsibility to conform "to the basic rules of the society, both those embodied in law and those embodied in ethical custom." However, what some companies are failing to see is that ethical custom is shifting alongside the Zeitgeist. Relatively new concepts such as "shared-value," "double bottom line," and "triple bottom line," which tabulate a company's value beyond financial returns, demonstrate that more business leaders have recognized that shareholder returns are not creating value when they come at the expense of sustaining the planet, our collective livelihoods, and our quality of life.

Again, it's important to note that, despite what many people believe, the maximization of shareholder wealth is a *standard of conduct*, not a legal rule. The only time a business must forgo long-term benefits for short-term gains is when a company is certain to be sold. This is what has come to be known as the Revlon Moment. In 1985, Ron Perelman, then CEO of Pantry Pride, approached Revlon with a takeover offer, which quickly became hostile. A battle ensued and ultimately ended the following year when Delaware's Court of Chancery found in *Revlon Inc. v. MacAndrews & Forbes Holdings, Inc.* that Revlon's directors had *breached their duty of loyalty* by pursuing their personal interests rather than maximizing the sale price of the company for the benefit of the company's shareholders.[4]

During a period of ongoing, normal operations, a company's directors' *duty of loyalty* does not dictate maximizing the share price for short-term shareholder gains. It's simply about ensuring that each director puts the interests of the company before any personal concerns and avoids potential conflicts of interest (personal and professional). For me, the concept of incorporating society's expanding notions of value creation is something that corresponds with another board duty: the *duty of care*. Assessing the things that matter to all stakeholders is inherently a part of making sound and informed judgments as a board member or part of a firm's C-Suite. Over the long term, creating value beyond the bottom line is a way to promote a company's best interests.

A CALL FOR LONG-TERMISM

Today, there's a growing movement on Wall Street for what's come to be known as long-termism. *Long-termism* aims at improving corporate governance so that it encourages long-term investment strategies. Larry Fink, CEO of BlackRock, the world's largest asset manager with $5.1 trillion in assets under management, is one of its most prominent evangelizers.[5]

Early in 2016, Fink created a lot of buzz when he sent a letter to the CEOs of S&P 500 companies and large European corporations advocating for long-termism. Here's a critical excerpt from his letter, reprinted by *Business Insider*:

> While we've heard strong support from corporate leaders for taking
> such a long-term view, many companies continue to engage in prac-

tices that may undermine their ability to invest for the future. Dividends paid out by S&P 500 companies in 2015 amounted to the highest proportion of their earnings since 2009. As of the end of the third quarter of 2015, buybacks were up 27% over 12 months. We certainly support returning excess cash to shareholders, but not at the expense of value-creating investment. We continue to urge companies to adopt balanced capital plans, appropriate for their respective industries, that support strategies for long-term growth.

We also believe that companies have an obligation to be open and transparent about their growth plans so that shareholders can evaluate them and companies' progress in executing on those plans.[6]

A controversial aspect of Fink's letter was his call for firms to "move away from providing" guidance via quarterly earnings, saying, "Today's culture of quarterly earnings hysteria is totally contrary to the long-term approach we need." However, in an interview on CNBC, Fink later cautioned that he was deemphasizing quarterly earnings—not advocating that companies jettison them.[7]

In his letter, Fink notes, "One reason for investors' short-term horizons is that companies have not sufficiently educated them about the ecosystems they are operating in, what their competitive threats are and how technology and other innovations are impacting their businesses." Instead, he advocates that CEOs "lay out for shareholders each year a strategic framework for long-term value creation." He also calls for new metrics, particularly repurposing CEO shareholder letters so that they're not retrospective but forward thinking and allow both shareholders and stakeholders to understand when and why a company may have to change strategy and pivot.[8]

As highlighted earlier, while many people believe that brands, unlike politicians, face no opposing force, a CEO of a corporation may see things differently. A company's board and shareholders can challenge management as forcibly as an opposing political party does the government. These conflicts may undermine well-intentioned shifts from a shareholder to a stakeholder perspective. If the stakeholder model is about the long term, and shareholder demands for dividends and buybacks are focused on the short term, then even progressive companies with purpose-oriented CEOs and senior management may find themselves stuck in the quagmire of short-termism.

Long-termism promotes a more purposeful corporate orientation in which vision and strategy prevail over short-term goals—and *stakeholders*, not just shareholders, win. Long-termism emphasizes a more holistic approach to value creation.

RETURNING TO THE ORIGINS OF VALUE

When I'm trying to understand new ideas and concepts, I find going back to the origins of the words we use to describe things very helpful. Let's examine the origins of the words *value* and *wealth*: Each word originally suggested an awareness of balance; in other words, they referred to forms of *sustainability*. The word *value* comes from the thirteenth-century Latin word *valere*, meaning "to be strong and well."[9] *Wealth* can also be traced to the thirteenth century, from the word *wele*, Middle English for "well-being."

Wellness. Well-being. When you hear these words, big ideas such as vitality, meaningful activities, supportive relationships, and connections with others may come to mind. When these concepts are placed alongside financial prosperity, it suggests that, in order to maximize shareholder value, a business needs to constructively and effectively manage more than just the bottom line. Globalized sourcing, production, and sales requirements make long-term success dependent on meeting the needs of a wide range of stakeholders: a virtuous—or ethical—interdependent circle that includes customers, employees, suppliers, communities, society at large, and even the planet.

Here's what we already know about how the virtuous circle is formed:

1. A company that provides its employees with a living wage, treats them fairly, and maintains equitable supplier relationships produces higher-quality products and services.

2. When a company prices its products and services at a fair value based on quality, lives up to its product claims, and provides excellent customer service, it is likely to outsell its competitors.

3. When a company incorporates and anticipates consumers' changing needs into its product and service offerings, it further nurtures loyal customers, reduces the cost of sales, and ultimately increases profits.

4. Increased profits enable a corporation to pay out higher returns to investors, provide its workforce with better benefits, foster good community relations, improve its supplier chain, and invest more into R&D. And, as such, the cycle begins again.

The circle becomes truly virtuous. Sustainable shareholder value is created when the purpose of a business embodies goals that include broader societal interests.

THE VIRTUOUS CIRCLE IN ACTION

Conscious capitalism is gaining favor—and not just among Millennial entrepreneurs. Interest in balancing profit with social responsibility is not new. It started long before companies like Whole Foods Market, TOMS, The Container Store, Patagonia, or even Newman's Own were founded. In fact, these more modern socially conscious companies can be seen as swelling tributaries of a *third-wave* movement of companies that are putting good values at the center of profit making.

The concept of conscious capitalism began nearly a century ago. The *first wave* commenced in the modern era of doing business. Wallace B. Donham, Dean of the Harvard Business School, articulated the concept in 1929, when he stated: "Business started long centuries before the dawn of history. . . . But business as we now know it is new—new in its broadening scope, new in its social significance. . . . Business has not learned how to handle these changes, nor does it recognize the magnitude of its responsibilities for the future of civilization."[10]

Two years later, in 1931, Stanford Graduate School of Business Professor Theodore Kreps introduced a course on business and social welfare called Business Activity and Public Welfare, a forerunner of present-day courses in corporate social responsibility.[11] And in 1932, E. Merrick Dodd, a professor at Harvard Law School, wrote, "[T]here is in fact a growing feeling not only that business has responsibilities to the community but that our corporate managers who control business should voluntarily and without waiting for legal compulsion manage it in such a way as to fulfill those responsibilities."[12]

At the time, these ideas did not lead to the consumer-driven behaviors that make up today's Brand Citizenship. Instead, many industrial giants that had put sound, community-facing policies into place became paternalistic, even sleepy, and over time they also became inefficient organizations with outdated corporate structures. John Lewis Partnership, a UK-based company that owns department stores and supermarkets, which I'll explore in greater depth in Chapter 6, is one such company that realized it had fallen behind because of its well-intentioned but antiquated, mode of adding social value. In the early 2000s, after years of sliding profits, the Partnership reviewed its governance structure, which had been in place since the early 1900s, when John Spedan Lewis set up an employee-owned partnership with a vision to establish a *better form of business*. One hundred years later, the Partnership committed itself to updating and modernizing its founder's vision.

To ensure that its founding principles would remain relevant in Britain's intensely competitive modern retail market, the Chairman and Partnership Board took decisive action. They adopted a more decentralized governance model and created a plan to foster operational excellence across their supply chain, become a world-class marketer and e-tailer, and make the in-store shopping experience more engaging. Today, earning a profit, product improvement, and process innovation sit comfortably alongside fairness and social benefit in the organization. As it has done throughout its history, the Partnership still *recruits* and *retains* loyal employees (known as Partners), and attracts long-term customers by nurturing a reputation centered on fundamental characteristics—value, choice, service, honesty, and behaving as a good citizen—and on its ninety-one-year-old motto: *Never Knowingly Undersold*.

John Lewis Partnership was a hundred-year-old company when its management made the changes that would ensure they could become a two-hundred-year-old company. While the notion of adding social value was part of the company's origins, management knew a new model that reflected the current Zeitgeist was necessary for survival. They intuited that they needed to revitalize their purpose, focus, and commitment to their founding values to be a good citizen and a profitable company. They figured out the steps to do so through trial and error and the kind of smarts and patience many of us wish we had as individuals—much more having the moxie to pursue this route as a firm.

Bangladeshi-born Nobel Prize winner and microcredit pioneer Muhammad Yunus, the founder of the Grameen Bank, first officially coined the term that firms like John Lewis Partnership embody: conscious capitalism. More recently, Whole Foods Market co-CEO John Mackey and his cowriter Raj Sisodia, a marketing professor at Bentley University in Waltham, Massachusetts, further popularized the term in their 2013 book, *Conscious Capitalism: Liberating the Heroic Spirit of Business*. Some people believe that Anita Roddick, who founded the Body Shop in 1976, started the conscious capitalist movement long before it was labeled as such.

Today, pragmatists who are looking to sustain capitalism as an economic model by making a profit and doing good business are shaping the current wave of conscious capitalism. They are focused on creating a sustainable future and sustainable value for their companies, customers, employees, trade partners, communities, and the planet.

Over our three years of research at my company, we found that simultaneously creating financial and social value is neither an anomaly nor a choice but a necessity—and, given the growing call for businesses to do good, in the coming years and decades, there will be no other way to succeed. Increasingly, companies are experimenting with new ways to embrace this imperative, to integrate principles that have typically been siloed and isolated in departments—like Corporate Social Responsibility, Corporate Reputation, and Supply Chain Management—and apply them across all of their business operations.

FROM SOCIAL CONSCIENCE TO SOCIAL CONSCIOUSNESS

There's a wealth of academic research on the rise of social consciousness in business. Aiming to establish a process for companies to report their contribution to society in addition to their profits, Stanford's Professor Kreps, who is known as the "the conscience of the business school," coined the term *social audit* in the 1940s. More modern-day Corporate Social Responsibility, commonly known as CSR, was popularized in 1953, with Howard Bowen's book *Social Responsibilities of the Businessman.*[13] In his work, Bowen quoted a 1946 *Fortune* magazine survey in which *Fortune* editors indicated that the "'social consciousness' of managers meant that businessmen were responsible for the consequences of their actions in a sphere wider than that covered by their profit-and-loss statements." [14]

As Baby Boomers came of age in the 1960s, protests and calls for reform altered the Zeitgeist with social movements advocating for civil rights, women's rights, consumer rights, labor rights, and the environment. Our social consciousness and the context in which business operated were shifting. It was in response to this that Milton Friedman published his article about the purpose of a business in *The* New *York Times*, spotlighting the growing tension between a business's financial and social responsibilities.

In 1971, after Friedman's article appeared, the Committee for Economic Development published a model for CSR that included three concentric circles: the inner circle focused on economic development (jobs, products, and economic growth); the middle circle dedicated to societal value (employees and the environment); and the outer circle on social issues.[15]

In 1979, the first widely referenced definition for CSR emerged. Professor Archie Carroll's four-part definition characterized the responsibilities of business as economic, legal, ethical, and discretionary, in respective order of importance. By 1991, he had developed a visual representation of these responsibilities in a pyramid format (Figure 2-1). At the base of the pyramid sat the foundation for all others: a business's economic responsibility to be profitable. Legal responsibility, or playing by the rules of the game based on society's laws, came next, followed by ethical responsibility, which Carroll defined as the obligation to do what's right. Philanthropic—previously discretionary—responsibility sat at the very top of the pyramid and incorporated improving the quality of life through good corporate citizenship.[16]

FIGURE 2-1. Archie Carroll's four-part definition of
corporate social responsibility.

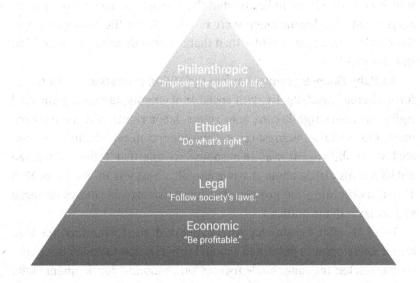

Philanthropic
"Improve the quality of life."

Ethical
"Do what's right."

Legal
"Follow society's laws."

Economic
"Be profitable."

With the prosperity that came with the Reagan years, corporate ethics overshadowed CSR. And as technology spurred globalization in the 1990s and connectivity transformed our knowledge and understanding of business operations and other cultures in the 2000s, CSR and corporate citizenship came to be used as interchangeable terms, which included ethics, corporate citizenship, stakeholder theory, and sustainability.

If you're confused, you're not alone. Based on my company's research into brand leadership, good corporate citizenship, and favorite brands, "real" people define corporate social responsibility and corporate citizenship very differently than academics and experts do. In fact, our research participants told us that the first responsibility of a business is to live up to its promises to its customers and employees, followed by aligning its purpose to behave responsibly, in a way that advances society. This insight links directly to what management guru Peter Drucker, in his 1986 book, *Management: Tasks, Responsibilities, Practices*, identified as the purpose of a business:

> To know what a business is we have to start with its purpose. Its purpose must lie outside of the business itself. In fact, it must be in society since business enterprise is an organ of society. There is only one valid definition of business purpose: to create a customer.... The customer is the foundation of a business and keeps it in existence. He alone gives employment. To supply the wants and needs of a consumer, society entrusts wealth-producing resources to the business enterprise.[17]

According to Drucker, a business is not an end in and of itself; it is an *"organ of society."* *"Society entrusts wealth-producing resources to the business"* to serve—or, to borrow terminology from economics, to supply—the customer. Like the participants in my company's research, Drucker's virtuous circle begins with the customer rather than with the employee as John Lewis Partnership does.

Without customers or access to society's resources, a business isn't sustainable. Therefore, to be successful over the longer term, it's essential that a company understands that it is part of a larger ecosystem. It serves society, not itself, and exists only because of customers.

Social responsibility is a dynamic discipline that has been evolving for decades. Yet even with the microscope focused on ethical issues, fair labor practices, and sustainability, social responsibility remains a specialized department in most companies. While experts are necessary to integrate effective policies and procedures into operations, all employees, beginning with the CEO, should be accountable for social responsibility and good corporate citizenship. Responsible practices of this type should not be segregated to a few departments.

When a CEO pioneers a meaningful brand vision or a purpose for a business, and that mandate emanates from "the tone at the top," doing good is more effectively engrained into a company's DNA. As more people expect companies to respond to an increasingly long list of social and environmental challenges, programs that are aligned with a business's higher purpose will create greater financial and social value over the long term.

CRAFTING BRANDS FOR LIFE

Since becoming CEO of corporate giant Unilever in 2009, Paul Polman has crafted a new vision for the Anglo-Dutch company, whose diverse consumer brand holdings include Vaseline®, Dove, Klondike®, and Knorr. Simply put, Unilever places sustainability and growth at its heart. The company has begun to experiment with new business models that integrate departments historically siloed from one another. The company itemizes fifty timeline-based commitments in its Sustainable Living Plan, which pledges to help more than a billion people improve their health and well-being, halve the environmental footprint of their products, and source 100 percent of agricultural raw materials sustainably by 2020.[18]

Keith Weed, Unilever's chief marketing officer, is focused on making Polman's vision integral to brand marketing through an initiative called Crafting Brands for Life, which was rolled out in 2011 and requires Unilever's consumer-facing brands to define a social purpose and deliver against the timeline they've outlined in the Sustainable Living Plan.[19] In January of 2015, Polman told *Guardian Sustainable Business* that Unilever was considering becoming a B Corp, like its subsidiary Ben & Jerry's.[20] B Corp status is considered by many as the ultimate commitment to benefit society as much as shareholders by pledging to use the power of business to solve social and environmental problems.

THE SIGNIFICANCE OF B CORP STATUS

Like the John Lewis Partnership, Ben and Jerry's, Cabot®, Method, New Belgium Brewing Company, Patagonia, Seventh Generation, and Warby Parker are all committed to balancing earning a profit with doing good and have integrated the elements of the virtuous circle into their corporate charters and cultures. Each of these companies has gone one step further in their commitment to the virtuous circle than the John Lewis Partnership by becoming a Certified B Corporation. To be a Certified B Corp, a company must have a material positive impact on society and the environment and must also meet a rigorous set of standards of accountability and transparency, as set by a U.S.-based nonprofit organization, B

Lab, which was founded in 2006. Certified B Corps embrace the virtuous circle in a notion they call shareholder capitalism, which emphasizes three things: *shared prosperity between the company and society, measuring positive impact, and being the best for the world over being the best in the world*.[21]

Becoming a B Corp is a very involved process for any company. Applying the necessary performance standards and meeting the legal requirement for certification are extremely difficult for a large public multinational company such as Unilever. Ben & Jerry's, which is now a wholly owned subsidiary of Unilever, became a Certified B Corp in September 2012. Therefore, it's not surprising that Ben & Jerry's CEO, Jostein Solhein, had been involved in Unilever's discussions with B Lab.[22]

Certification is not a one-time event. It's an ongoing process of maintenance and change. To ensure that a company stays true to its new charter, B Lab recertifies every company every two years. Although the vast majority of Certified B Corps are small, private companies, more than 40,000 businesses use the B Corps' Impact Assessment as a guideline to improve their outcomes, attract staff, and, ultimately, gain a competitive advantage.[23] These companies know they need to do things differently and aren't certain how. B Corps' assessment tool provides a great structure to get started.

While the difficulties of becoming a B Corp may outweigh the benefits for a large public corporation, these businesses can integrate the spirit of B Corp status across their product portfolio. According to Jay Coen Gilbert, one of the founders of B Lab, there are three ways for large corporations such as Unilever to adopt B Lab's principles: (1) Use the impact assessment to "measure what matters most." (2) Acquire a company that is a certified B Corp. Or (3) become a certified B Corp.[24] Even though it isn't fully formed for large, public multinationals yet, B Lab's certification reflects our changing Zeitgeist and represents an extraordinary movement forward for business. Clearly, a company doesn't necessarily need to be a B Corp to provide social and environmental value alongside financial benefits. The John Lewis Partnership, Whole Foods, TOMS, Newman's Own, and many others are balanced in their approach to business, transparent about their operations, and behaving with a decidedly human face.

HEALING THROUGH PURPOSE

Vaseline®, for example, is one Unilever brand that is effectively aligning its social initiatives with its consumer-facing brand story. In 1859, Robert Chesebrough, a British chemist traveling in Titusville, Pennsylvania, observed oilmen using a naturally occurring by-product of the fuel drilling process to treat cuts and burns. Inspired, he set out to develop a product that would heal dry skin. Eleven years later, Chesebrough opened a factory in Brooklyn, New York, to produce his Wonder Jelly. Confident in the healing power of his salve, Chesebrough traveled around New York demonstrating the product's efficacy on himself—"burning his skin with acid or an open flame and then spreading the clear petroleum jelly on his injury, showing at the same time past injuries that had healed with the aid of his protective petroleum jelly."[25]

Today, Vaseline is more than a household name globally. In most markets it serves, the brand offers products under the Vaseline Jelly, Vaseline Intensive Care Lotion, and Vaseline Lip Therapy sub-brands. In the United States, the brand has a total of thirty-one products under these three lines and the Vaseline Men sub-brand.[26]

With an international portfolio of products and a purpose centered on the essential functional benefit of these products—the power to heal dry skin—Vaseline is aligning its mission with the Unilever Sustainable Living Plan. At the World Congress of Dermatology in Vancouver, Canada, on June 11, 2015, more than 150 years after Chesebrough's original discovery, the brand launched *The Vaseline® Healing Project* in partnership with a nonprofit called Direct Relief. The Project had a measurable goal of helping to heal the skin of five million people living in crisis or conflict by 2020. The initiative is a wonderful example of how seemingly unconnected things come together as our consciousness of the role that brands can play in progressing society expands.

With healing at the center of what Vaseline is about, the brand team intuitively knew its brand purpose should be tied to the physical, not emotional benefits the product delivers to users. While researching ways to do this, the team was serendipitously motivated by an article published in *The Washington Post* about the experiences of two dermatologists on a medical mission to a Syrian refugee camp in Jordan. Vaseline

Petroleum Jelly was an essential item the doctors were missing when treating refugees.

Serendipity Leads to a Solution

Prior to going public with their new project, in December of 2014, the Vaseline division signed an agreement with Direct Relief and worked with the organization to assemble an advisory board for The Project in early 2015. In addition to distributing more than one million units of Vaseline Petroleum Jelly annually, coordinating volunteers, and developing the training curriculum, Direct Relief also measures, tracks, and maps The Project's impact, so that it can sustain and grow its influence over time.[27]

Through its partnership with Direct Relief, the brand provides dermatological care to people across the world. To ensure the sustainability of The Project, the team also trains caregivers and health workers on the ground on how to treat common skin care conditions and identify rare diseases that first appear in the skin. Kathleen Dunlop, a Global Brand Director for Vaseline who heads the team leading the project, recognized from the start that the brand's purpose had to be a long-term ambition that would evolve over time, not a big-marketing or advertising campaign idea.

At its launch to the public at the World Congress of Dermatology, Vaseline shared stories and footage from their first mission trips to refugee camps in Jordan, the Philippines, and Kenya, unveiling their announcement film, which used a split-screen format to show parallel worlds and uses of Vaseline products, with scenes from ordinary life depicted on the left and life in areas of crisis or emergency pictured on the right.[28] The first consumer-facing campaign was later launched in Saudi Arabia, during Ramadan in 2015. They ran the split-screen film and partnered with one of that country's leading retailers to do a "local activation" and create emergency first-aid kits to distribute through a local charity to Saudi Arabians in need. During the promotion, sales of Vaseline products at stores of the retailer they partnered with increased significantly.[29]

In 2016, two cents from every Vaseline product sold in the United States—excepting Vaseline Lip Therapy products—went toward The Project. Globally, the program varied by region. The program expanded to include the Vaseline Lip Therapy collection in the United States in 2017. To increase awareness of The Project with consumers, Vaseline launched a U.S. and a Canadian campaign, featuring actress Viola Davis as the spokesperson in 2016. Through the campaign's videos, Davis makes viewers aware of the brand's aid effort in partnership with Direct Relief, whereby they "provide Vaseline Jelly, dermatological care, and medical supplies to help heal the skin of people affected by poverty and emergencies." As Davis emphasizes, "For people living in areas of crisis, simple skin conditions can turn into serious issues." Encouraging viewers to join Vaseline in its efforts to heal people in need, Davis simply yet powerfully concludes by saying, "That ordinary jar can make an extraordinary difference."[30]

Achieving Success, Integrating Purpose

Eighteen months after the program launched, The Project had proven successful—in terms of both its social impact and Vaseline Jelly's market share. By the end of 2016, Unilever had sponsored nine dermatological missions in Kenya, the Philippines, Jordan, India, South Africa, Nepal, and the United States, with repeat visits to some locations. With a separate NGO in China, the Soong Ching Ling Foundation, they also support a Miao Village near Guizhou. In the United States, the *Healing Project* served up to 500,000 patients per year through donating Vaseline Petroleum Jelly to skin care stations at health and community clinics.

The reach of The Project extends to individuals who would like to contribute to this humanitarian effort. Through Vaseline's brand website, anyone across the globe can "build" a relief kit to help someone in need. Here's how it works: The vaseline.us/kitbuilder site features icon images of medicine kit items to choose from, including a stethoscope, rubbing alcohol, hand sanitizer, and more. As a base, Unilever automatically donates a jar of Vaseline Jelly to each kit. Donors can add items by dragging and dropping the visual icons that represent the other medical essentials they wish to include. As explained on the site, "Each kit item is representative of the types of supplies provided by Direct Relief. By making a donation, you are contributing a dollar value equivalent to the kit item towards Direct Relief's kit programs, directly helping to improve the health of people in need."[31]

To date, Vaseline has donated more than two million units of Vaseline Jelly, as well as Vaseline Lip Therapy and Vaseline Intensive Care Lotion to the kit program. Traditional measures for testing advertising results showed that *The Vaseline Healing Project* increased consumer engagement with the brand and cultivated more meaningful relationships. Sales grew, and after twenty-five periods of declining market share, Vaseline's Lotions and Jelly's business market share increased in the first four weeks post launch.

VASELINE-BRANDED HAND AND BODY PRODUCTS 2016 PERFORMANCE METRICS
(EXCLUSIVE OF LIP PRODUCTS)

OBJECTIVE 1: Program Awareness

Goal: 20 percent awareness in first four months

Results: The campaign exceeded its awareness goal, starting to establish *The Vaseline Healing Project* (TVHP) and making the Vaseline brand more top-of-mind.

► The campaign achieved 700 million impressions by April 2016.

► 22 percent awareness of the project by April 2016.

► Hard-to-budge unaided brand awareness jumped 4 percent by April 2016 vs. December 2015.

OBJECTIVE 2: Brand Reappraisal

Goal: +25 percent increase in brand conviction score

Results: Vaseline saw significant increases in its loyalty numbers.

► According to British multinational market research firm Millward Brown, conviction scores jumped more than 50 percent for consumers who had heard of TVHP vs. those who had not.

► Those exposed scored the brand significantly higher on key attributes. When exposed:

- 70 percent more people said Vaseline "works better than other brands."

- 71 percent more people said Vaseline "appeals more than other brands."

- 61 percent more people said they "would recommend Vaseline to others."

► Ad copy testing showed that 80 percent of viewers were persuaded, with 67 percent now finding the brand appealing. Open-ended responses revealed how substantially we were changing perceptions: "I thought it was a very thought-provoking ad that made me really respect Vaseline and what they are doing."

OBJECTIVE 3: Business Growth

Goal: Reversal of sales volume and market share declines

Results: Vaseline's Lotions and Jelly businesses made a stunning turnaround.

► Market share increased. The campaign's impact was felt after as little as four weeks and continued throughout the media timeframe (and beyond).

► After 25 periods of market share decline, the Vaseline Brand grew share in the first four weeks post launch.

► Sales grew on both Vaseline Jelly and Vaseline Intensive Care Lotions during the campaign period and then continued throughout the year, driven by the heroed Vaseline Jelly product, most especially, and also by Vaseline Intensive Care Lotions.

Penetration Growth:

Penetration of Vaseline Lotions grew 9 percent YOY in Q1 2016.

Penetration of Vaseline Jelly grew 11 percent YOY in Q1 2016.

OBJECTIVE 4: Program Participation

Goal: Raise an additional $1 million in donations

Results:

▶ More than 2 million people helped through TVHP missions in 41 countries.

▶ The $1 million promotional donation goal was secured by year-end.

▶ $23,000 was donated to TVHP through Kit Builder donations via the website.

Source: Kathleen Dunlop, email interview by author, January 9, 2017.

Without a doubt, Vaseline's more mainstream consumer promise, "Truly healthy skin starts with deep healing moisture," is in alignment with the brand's purpose and *The Vaseline Healing Project*. Yet integrating this larger purpose into marketing communications hasn't been straightforward. In fact, discovering the best ways to do this forced the brand team to change the way they think and challenged many of the principles that have guided consumer goods brand management for decades. Even with its early successes, integrating purpose continues to be a work in progress. The brand team and its agencies are on a journey together, gleaning lessons from the first two years in action, seeing what works and what doesn't, and modifying their efforts as they go.

LOOKING "OUTSIDE-IN" AS WELL AS "INSIDE-OUT"

Unilever and John Lewis Partnership are very different organizations, yet equally significant examples of how a new mindset and rationale for business are gaining momentum and importance—even with long-standing legacy brands. The challenge companies face is twofold: (1) aligning strategies that speak to people's real needs and desires with their brand purpose and business operation, and (2) developing criteria that guides managers in making the necessary trade-offs among competing stakeholders.

Adding social value isn't about crafting one-off solutions that managers think are "good" or that look good for executive boards and corporate public relations. It is about integrating greater meaning into the DNA of a company and doing so in ways that are meaningful to customers, employees, investors, and other stakeholders. It requires looking Outside-In as well as Inside-Out in order to truly connect and gain recognition in the marketplace for these efforts.

As our research has shown, and as I'll explore in the next chapter, there are opportunities at each of the five points on the continuum of Brand Citizenship for companies of all types to make a difference and to make a profit. Brand Citizenship focuses on aligning value creation inside and outside a firm, using a brand vision or purpose as the focal point for benchmarking all of the business's activities. It is a collaborative way to optimize value for customers, employees, investors, and other stakeholders, as compared to a top-down dictate to maximize shareholder returns.

HIGHLIGHTS

CHAPTER 2:
Balancing Social and Financial Values

▶ Ethical customs follow changing values and an evolving ethos. To remain relevant, businesses need to follow these changes closely and ensure they adapt to shifting needs and expectations of customers, employees, shareholders, and other stakeholders.

▶ The movement known as long-termism, which emphasizes the need for companies and investors to pursue long- rather than short-term investment strategies, is gaining strength and points the way for businesses to follow.

▶ To maximize shareholder value over the long term, a business must constructively and effectively manage more than the bottom line; success requires balancing the needs of a virtuous circle that includes customers, employees, suppliers, communities, society at large, and even the planet, as well as shareholders.

▶ In action, the virtuous circle embodies the concept of conscious capitalism, which balances making a profit with social responsibility.

▶ Businesses that engrain social responsibility and good corporate citizenship across their operations will create greater financial and social value over the long term.

▶ Unilever's Crafting Brands for Life initiative requires consumer-facing brands to define a social purpose, delivered against a timeline.

▶ B Corporation status certifies that a business has a material positive impact on society and the environment and that it adheres to a rigorous set of standards of accountability and transparency.

▶ *The Vaseline® Healing Project* demonstrates the business case for doing good and shows how a brand that embraces a social mission alongside its consumer promise can consequentially benefit those in need, increase its market share, and improve its financial performance.

CHAPTER 3

BRAND CITIZENSHIP

The Consumer-First Model
for Doing Good and Doing Well

In all kinds of businesses today, the traditional producer–consumer relationship is giving way to an evolving and exciting partnership between people and companies. It's not hard to suppose that, at some time in the not too distant future, either pressure from advocacy groups or innovation from individual companies and whole industries will lead to a new kind of corporate "rating."

Imagine labeling standards that indicate a brand's practices in the realms of sustainability, social responsibility, working conditions, and the like. It might be a little like the Whole Foods Market approach to rating seafood on various measures of health and environment, or Starbucks's information about its coffee sourcing and community involvement, or a cleaning product company that promotes its recycled packaging, eco-friendly ingredients, and charitable activities with kids and families. However, in this new type of corporate rating, all of these metrics and promotional messages would be standardized and aligned. Like today's cereal boxes with ratings for things like fiber, whole grain, and low sugar, imagine familiar icons transparently letting consumers know how each brand fares against the brand practices that I listed at the opening of this paragraph.

As this picture of our future manifests, businesses need to look inward at their production processes, supplier relationships, waste production, and other essential activities, as well as outwardly at what matters most to people, in order to effectively develop their brands. It's already necessary for companies to be much more committed to being "responsible" and identifying the social and environmental issues that matter most to their customers, employees, and other stakeholders. And we already see regular announcements about global firms and fast growing companies that are improving the way that they do business. The most profitable brands win loyal fans by empathizing with their customers and employees, and the most valuable brands marry a clearly defined purpose with deep insight into their customers' hopes and dreams. However, our *CultureQ* research project has shown that this is not enough. This level of connection barely taps buyers' desires and expectations.

So how do people describe responsible companies? Which companies do they think of as good corporate citizens? And what matters most to them? When I first asked these questions, some of the answers caught me off guard.

OUR CHANGING EXPECTATIONS FOR BRANDS

Since 2007, I have formally and informally been speaking with Millennials about their interactions with brands. My team and I annually used the knowledge we gleaned from these conversations to develop proprietary trends based on patterns that emerged. Then in fourth quarter 2011, as part of our *CultureQ* research project, I decided to conduct a more formal quantitative research study to identify high-level social trends that would impact consumers' interactions with brands in 2012.

Many of our clients had been expressing preconceived notions of how Millennials differed in attitudes and behaviors from their Baby Boomer parents; however, a number of their observations were not in line with ours. We fielded this trend study among 763 early technology adopter, news-engaged Millennials and Baby Boomers to uncover how far the generational apple really had fallen from the tree. Using a combination of open-ended and multiple-choice questions, we asked people about their hopes and dreams for the coming year, the things they feared, their outlook for the economy, and the issues that mattered most to them, as well as to name the brands they thought would exhibit leadership in the coming year and the brands they identified as good corporate citizens.

As my team and I read people's responses and compared their answers against one another, the data itself told us a much larger story than the one we had set out to write. It was impossible for us to deny that people's changing attitudes were reshaping their expectations of brands. A large number had a lot to say—a lot more than we expected. It was as if they needed a place to vent because of the insecurity and uncertainty they were feeling about the economy and global events. Rather than listing more typical New Year's resolutions like lose weight or quit smoking as the things they hoped to do in 2012, many referenced more important and fundamental wishes such as:

> I plan on spending very little in 2012; I will only use cash and we'll have no vacations.

> I hope that I'll be able to complete college.

> To stay safe from crime.

For Millennials and Baby Boomers in both the United States and the UK, the goals to "keep my head above water, maintain my lifestyle, keep my job and keep my house" had become an aspiration instead of something taken for granted. Uncertainty about the economy, combined with the perceived absence of inspiring leadership, was increasing people's anxiety levels and making them insecure about their futures.

When we asked about brands they thought would demonstrate leadership in the coming year, they used the same words to describe brand leaders such as Apple, Google, and Virgin as they did effective political leaders: *visionary, inspiring, helping to solve problems*. When discussing the role of the brands they identified as leaders, they further noted:

> Many companies believe they have a responsibility to "give back" to society and to me this is wonderful—in the future. . . . [Businesses will] have to give to get.

> Business is more suited than government to fix things.

I think everyone is equally responsible [for improving society], no one company can do anything alone. Bigger companies have more pull though, so they should be the most encouraging.

Millennials and Baby Boomers alike acknowledged that brands shape our opinions and create new lifestyles for us. And because of this, a notable number wanted what we labeled in the research as *leadership* brands to further break down the boundaries that were dividing what they delivered to shareholders from those they offered to customers and other stakeholders. They believed this was the only way we would be able to sustain our lifestyles and our planet.

While what many market researchers call *opinion elites*—influential consumers who are informed, engaged, and active when it comes to business and social issues—had periodically said things like this before, more mainstream people like many who participated in our survey had rarely done so. Instead they had traditionally spoken about market size, profit, technological advancement, and category leadership when discussing *leadership* brands. Yet the things our participants were saying began to make sense. So much information was available, whether it be via the Web or social media, that a lot more people were doing their "homework" about brands—not just the products and services they represented—before making purchase decisions.

What really didn't make sense to us at first was the brand they named as the number one good corporate citizen: Apple. Although we had expected people to name Apple as the number one *leadership* brand, we hadn't anticipated they would also cite it as a good corporate citizen, especially since the media and corporate social responsibility experts were strongly criticizing Apple for its supply chain integrity at the time of our survey. Yet participants told us that Apple:

Create[s] inventive products to make life easier.

Is very responsible for the way society is shaping [up].

[Offers] technology for today and the future, which makes communicating easier worldwide.

Helps to create and expand knowledge and understanding of just how small and interconnected our world is.

One participant went as far as to note, Apple "giv[es] to society by listening to the consumer."

Even more so than Apple, we were astonished that our U.S. participants chose Walmart as one of the top-five good corporate citizens, although notably fewer cited it than did Apple. While one or two people referred to Walmart's community philanthropy, the majority spoke about convenience and low pricing, telling us:

> In my town it's the only big store we have, and they do well for the town economy.

> [T]hey make their prices low as possible to make life easier.

> [T]hey are good though because of their low prices.

These comments indicated that for consumers of goods and services, the label "Good Corporate Citizen" extended well beyond our traditional notions of corporate responsibility and doing good and also reflected an evolving definition for value creation. People were willing to forgive a lot as long as they perceived a brand offered them fair value or enriched *their* daily lives.

While these insights were unexpected, as I reflected on the findings, I recognized that they fit perfectly with Tom Wolfe's 1976 depiction of Baby Boomers as the "Me Generation" and Jean Twenge's similar view of Millennials forty years later in her book *Generation Me*. In a consumerist society, *Me* inherently comes before *We*, so it makes sense that consumers would rate a brand that benefits "me" as a good corporate citizen.

Simultaneously, however, the other brands that were ranked as the top-five good corporate citizens—Microsoft, Google, and Ford—were chosen for more predictable reasons. Unlike Apple and Walmart that bettered ME, the individual user of products, Microsoft, Google, and Ford were each perceived as focusing on the *greater* good in terms of their corporate citizenship. They were investing in society and bettering life for a larger number of stakeholders, not only consumers of their brands. In other words, they were perceived as servicing the collective WE through their initiatives. For our participants, the halo of the Bill & Melissa Gates Foundation extended onto Microsoft's reputation, and as such they perceived the company as solving meaningful social problems. Participants said:

Gates sets an example with his community and world involvement.

Bill Gates has made an effort to understand social issues and find solutions.

Bill Gates donates his money to very worthy causes with an eye to making them self-sustaining.

Google, according to our participants, adds value to society by:

Working to improve man's existence and the environment.

Tak[ing] care of their employees.

Mak[ing] technology accessible to everyone.

And Ford taps an unexpected emotional core and shows how a "traditional" company is not less relevant or "needed" than a new technology firm or a disruptive, cool Silicon Valley hero by:

Providing support to Detroit, and producing energy-efficient, well-designed cars.

Community service, helping the less fortunate, [and] working to reduce their carbon footprint.

Providing a good sense of who we are as a country.

This last comment about Ford was especially interesting. During a time of economic uncertainty, Ford's story of strong, focused leadership and commitment to its customers inspirationally represented America's pending turnaround.

The research signaled that, despite the resources that companies were investing into corporate social responsibility and sustainability initiatives, good corporate citizenship only seemed to resonate when it was tied in some way to their day-to-day lives or addressed their individual hopes and concerns for themselves or society. Given people's unease with global issues and apprehensions about the economy at the time, we wondered if a new ME-inclusive form of good corporate citizenship had become an essential criterion for brand leadership.

CONSUMERS, BRANDS, AND THEIR NEW RELATIONSHIP

*Leadership brands do what's right, they care about issues
like the environment and advancing social issues and
they go to great efforts to do what's right,
even if it's not the easiest path to take.*

—CultureQ participant

Curious, we used our *CultureQ* research project to investigate further, focusing on pinpointing the criteria consumers were using to identify leadership brands, their definition of good corporate citizenship, and what made people loyal to brands. We fielded five more studies between June 2012 and April 2014, speaking, qualitatively and quantitatively, with more than 5,200 Millennials, Gen Xers (the generation born between 1965 and 1979), and Baby Boomers (the generation born between 1946 and 1964).

We began our research with a highly exploratory two- to three-week journal-based study in order to better understand Millennials' perceptions of brands. A vast number of brand marketers were developing their brands around Millennial's attitudes and behaviors. We instructed participants to track all the brands they interacted with over two weeks and then complete a series of related creative exercises. They told us:

I've yet to find a product that cures my lips like Vaseline can. It's worth it.

Sure deodorant is a leader. It doesn't let me down.

Neutrogena is worth the extra price than cheaper drugstore versions. It may have the same active ingredients, but I feel that the inactive ingredients that make up the scent, texture, moisturizing quality, and exfoliating property are higher quality.

Our participants perceived that leadership brands were convenient, reliable, higher quality, and worth a premium price across categories.

They also felt burdened by the number of choices out there in virtually every product category, so much so that a lot of big brand activity was failing to make it on their radar. Reflecting on the number of brands that were around every day, one participant stated: "Over the week I interacted with so many brands it was shocking. I didn't realize I interact with some brands multiple times a day, and so many I barely noticed [most of them] until I had to write them down."

Our research demonstrated that increased brand promotion and advertising are having an opposite effect than the one brand owners desire: Rather, by increasing the number of brands consumers consider, brand bombardment is leading people to be loyal to a small, trusted circle of a few go-to brands. Out of the twelve or so brands our participants interacted with on average, they labeled one to three of them as favorites. Functionally, favorite brands often traveled with them throughout the day and served more than one purpose. Emotionally, favorite brands mirrored their personal values and said something about them as the purchaser. As several participants shared:

[Using] an Apple product says so much about you as a person. I had a couple of friends go on dates, they'd report back saying, he was OK, but he used a PC!

Ford fits my interests as a young adult: independence, strength, adventure, self-reliance. This is how Ford sells itself, and it resonates with how I think of myself.

I feel like Madewell have pinned my style down to a T.... It is my best friend and stylist rolled into one.

I agree with the philosophy of Philosophy: They say celebrate feeling well and live joyously, I would use the same words as well. I actively tell others about it when I get the chance, and I couldn't imagine finding a better alternative.

As with real-life friendships, the acid test of a satisfying brand relationship is rooted not in grand gestures or even in constant chatter and interactions, but rather in thoughtful, empathic actions and small, meaningful deeds that both improve and enrich our daily lives and help us to feel as though we belong to a group of like-minded people. A majority of participants told us that they felt better about themselves when they bought brands that "did good" and questioned their brand choices when they learned a brand wasn't behaving responsibly. They said:

> Seventh Generation values what I value: My experience with the brand feels like one of solidarity and pride.

> I love ... my Amazon Prime account. But I am concerned with its ethics of warehouse labor after reading an exposé on it, and not sure if I should still use Amazon.

> Google's good corporate citizenship... [makes me] view the brand in a much more positive light. I don't expect them to be malicious. I trust them.

The results of these studies consistently confirmed that, across generations, our research participants desired that brands simultaneously enrich their lives and better society. They felt companies should provide solutions to their personal ME problems, needs, and dreams and to their generalized WE worries about the economy, the problems in the world, and the planet. And this exploratory research gave us amazing insight into how people identified brand leadership, good corporate citizenship, and favorite brands.

Alongside the learning from our first quantitative study, this insight provided us with a wealth of attributes to investigate further. As we continued exploring the issues, each study further confirmed that people were yearning for brands to be more human-like mashups of the traits that shape leadership, good citizenship, and friendship. The characteristics that described the categories of brand leadership, good corporate citizenship, and favorite brands overlapped, and, together, they formed a five-step model of Brand Citizenship that spanned from ME to WE.

BRAND CITIZENSHIP HELPS BRANDS MOVE FROM ME TO WE

Businesses have the potential for effecting societal change in unprecedented ways. Many businesses recognize the magnitude of their responsibilities. However many still don't act on this recognition.

—*CultureQ* participant

Here's what our three years of qualitative and quantitative research told us about how people define businesses's responsibilities to customers, employees, and society, distilled in our five steps that comprise Brand Citizenship:

Step 1. *Trust.* Don't let me down. First and foremost, people want brands that deliver on their promises. Consumers loudly and clearly told us fair value for quality matters more than absolute price. People are faithful to brands that clearly communicate what they offer and follow this up with reliable products and services, sincerity, reciprocity, and listening.

Step 2. *Enrichment.* Enhance daily life. Innovative, hip brands that are ahead of the curve are great, but the notions of new and improved alone are not enough to capture attention. People identify more with—and are less price sensitive toward—brands that understand the things that are important to them individually and that help them to simplify their routines, make mundane tasks less dull, and enrich their daily lives.

Step 3. *Responsibility.* Behave fairly. In a post-recession, flattened, and transparent world, customers expect brands to treat people fairly, behave ethically, and be proactive in their business practices. This doesn't mean a brand has to be perfect. Indeed, people respect and become fans of brands that behave more like people than demigods, provided they are honest about their shortcomings and strive to be better.

Step 4. *Community.* Connect me. The brands we choose are extensions of who we are and act as badges for what we are about to other people. Fans want brands to connect them to other people who share their interests and true passions. Physically, virtually, and emotionally, brands have the power to rally communities, change our behavior for the better, and fix social problems—provided they are not overtly political.

Step 5. *Contribution.* Make me bigger than I am. People insist that brands play an active role in creating a more positive and life-enhancing future. They want to buy from and deal with companies that are making a difference and contributing to our communities and world. As noted earlier in this chapter, participants in our research were clear that the brands they labeled as leaders have the know-how and skills to do this. They yearn for the brands they buy—or aspire to buy—to advocate on their behalf and address the issues that matter most to them. By improving life on the planet, a brand is ultimately enriching its fans' lives.

Brand Citizenship begins with delivering value to the individual person, or ME, through the products and services they buy, functionally and emotionally, and then moves outward to deliver added value to society—or the collective WE. Brand Citizenship is a win-win-win solution that mutually benefits people, companies, and society. It integrates doing good activities, such as fair-employee policies, CSR, sustainability programs, ethical sourcing, and charitable giving with brand development in order to strengthen a brand's reputation, foster greater loyalty, and enhance value creation (Figure 3-1).

Our research demonstrated that, regardless of size and no matter what industry a company is in, it can reap the benefits of Brand Citizenship: more loyal consumers, more engaged employees, more raving fans, more positive reputation, more engaged stakeholders, and more value for shareholders. With so much media attention focused on larger, well-known social enterprises that have "doing good" overtly embedded in

FIGURE 3-1. The five steps of Brand Citizenship.

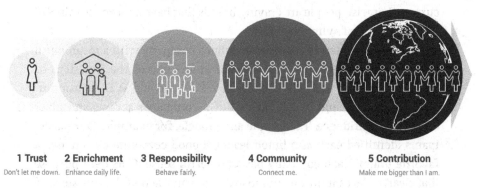

1 Trust	2 Enrichment	3 Responsibility	4 Community	5 Contribution
Don't let me down.	Enhance daily life.	Behave fairly.	Connect me.	Make me bigger than I am.

their vision or brand purpose, Brand Citizenship's five steps equally help the Fords, Vaselines, and Madewells of this world, as well as entrepreneurial start-ups, to connect the dots, so that they, too, can earn a profit and get lasting credit for fair employee policies, CSR, sustainability programs, ethical sourcing, and charitable giving.

THE "WHY" OF BRAND VISION: MORE IMPORTANT THAN EVER

A great vision is a big, audacious statement rooted in a real and timeless unmet human need, truth, or desire. It tells the story of how a company impacts people through the products and services it offers and how that creates societal value. When a company gets this right, the words on a page are more than a collection of empty slogans. They're an embodiment of the company's ethos that is inspiring to executives, employees, customers, investors, partners, and other stakeholders. A brand vision or purpose that is about more than just the products and services a company sells opens a brand up to endless possibilities across the continuum of Brand Citizenship.

While a vast majority of brands have defined their ME product promise to customers, until recently only a smaller number had focused on clarifying a greater WE purpose. With uncertainty about the future economically, politically, and socially being a permanent feature of the current Zeitgeist, people are craving brands that have a more meaningful understanding of why they exist.

Our research clearly corroborated that a company with a meaningful purpose can strategically position itself at any one of the five steps of Brand Citizenship and deliver benefits to both ME and WE. A clear purpose helps guide and benchmark all of a company's actions and gives customers confidence. Take Apple and Google, for example. Our participants identified each as a brand leader, a good corporate citizen, *and* a favorite brand. Each company has a powerful sense of its own purpose that clearly places it on a distinguishable journey across the five steps of Brand Citizenship.

Yet each company goes about articulating and communicating its vision very differently. For our participants, Apple is a ME brand, linked with Step 2—enriching their daily lives and empowering them as individuals—whereas Google is primarily positioned as a Step 5 brand. As such, the latter spans the ME-to-WE spectrum: an innovative tech firm that makes our virtual lives more efficient and richer through breakthroughs that aspire to better us and our physical world.

APPLE: PUT YOUR DING IN THE UNIVERSE

As far as I know, Apple has never published its vision. Yet, among the people I've spoken to over my many years of researching brands, the essence of how they collectively describe Apple's vision is largely the same. This is in part because Apple has used compelling images and words throughout its history to communicate its vision and purpose, more so than a written product promise. Ridley Scott's famous "1984" Apple ad introducing the Macintosh was about the courage to break from the status quo and about people not becoming automatons in the era of personal computing. The essence of Apple's Think Different campaign that followed in 1997 was the same.

More recently, in an interview with *Fast Company* magazine, Apple CEO Tim Cook revealed the company's vision without explicitly labelling it as such. When asked how Steve Jobs's legacy lived on at Apple,

Cook replied, "Steve felt that most people live in a small box. They think they can't influence or change things a lot. I think he would probably call that a limited life...." He continued, "If you embrace that the things that you can do are limitless, you can put your ding in the universe. You can change the world.... He embedded this non-acceptance of the status quo into the company."[1]

Without a doubt, Macs, iPhones, and the iWatch inspire people to believe they are limitless. When you think about Jobs's legacy—about the vision he sowed into Apple's culture—it's no wonder participants in our research named it as the number one Good Corporate Citizen. "Embrace that the things that you can do are limitless." It is this inspiring ethos that makes consumers feel great when they buy an Apple product—and forget that they've just paid a huge premium over competitive products. Apple is a ME brand linked with Step 2 of Brand Citizenship—enriching our lives and empowering us as individuals—so strongly that many people forgive the brand when a product doesn't work. Instead, Apple users willingly make their way to a Genius Bar at the closest Apple Store to have it repaired, sometimes even paying to do so.

Importantly, though, just because Apple is strategically positioned as a ME brand doesn't mean it can't—and shouldn't—run across the five steps of the ME-to-WE continuum of Brand Citizenship. Increasingly, Apple loyalists are calling for the brand to do so. In the post-Jobs era, Cook proactively began the journey to move the company across the continuum and become more responsible. In 2013, Cook hired Lisa Jackson from the U.S. Environmental Protection Agency to minimize Apple's impact on the environment, manage the company's education policy programs (such as ConnectED), oversee its product accessibility work, and direct the company's worldwide government affairs function.[2,3] Enlisting Jackson's assistance didn't mean Cook intended to change the company's vision or primary focus. Indeed, Apple's brand vision is broad enough to readily encompass Jackson's role and embrace the principles in all five steps of Brand Citizenship.

Apple has demonstrated its newer-found focus on responsibility and WE through continual improvement in its supply chain practices and a generous corporate and employee matching gift program. Under Jackson's guidance, through high-profile green initiatives, the company has sought to emphasize that it cares about the planet as much as its customers do. By 2016, three years after she joined Apple, Jackson announced that 93 percent of the company's operations used renewable energy, with offices in twenty-three of the countries it does business in running 100 percent on renewable energy. Apple also committed to switch to all-paper packaging, with 99 percent of the paper used being recycled or sourced from sustainable forests. And it launched a new R&D project, Liam, an automated robot that dissembled iPhones to their basic parts to recycle them.[4] Post-Jobs Apple is working hard to shed its reputation for servicing its own desires and be perceived as more than a ME brand.

With legions of devoted followers and millions of app store users across 155 countries, Apple clearly has a unique opportunity to use its social influence to mobilize support to help solve big issues. And it has started to flex that muscle. For the 2014 holiday season, Apple enabled customers to support World AIDS Day. Over two weeks, it donated a portion of sales from twenty-five apps, including Angry Birds, GarageBand, and FIFA 15, with exclusive new content from (RED), a licensing brand founded in 2006 by U2 frontman Bono and Kennedy descendant Bobby Shriver, which partners with big-name private-sector brands to donate 50 percent of retail sales from campaigns and to raise awareness to help eliminate HIV/AIDS globally.[5]

This was a step in the right direction. However, Apple's focus on AIDS—while laudable—did not necessarily directly or strategically align with the brand's purpose or the specific CSR concerns a large number of its customers had vocalized. In March 2016, Apple set out to put a real ding in the universe and create change by specifically zoning in on issues that a majority of its customers directly told them they cared about. Collaborating with the World Wildlife Fund for Nature, Apple launched apps for Earth Day. For ten days, twenty-seven popular apps, including Angry Birds 2, Jurassic World, and SimCity, offered special paid-for environmental content for Earth Day to support the World Wide Fund for Nature's climate and environmental programs. Through their purchase of this content, customers in turn had an opportunity to amplify and support their concerns in a bigger way than acting alone. In an interview with *The Washington Post* nearly one month after the initiative was launched, Lisa Jackson stated, "Helping the planet is something we hear a lot about from our customers. They love the company [Apple], but they want to be engaged in this mission of leaving the world better than we found it."[6]

As a global brand, Apple's complex business dealings at times have created situations that resulted in controversy for the brand. Apple is one of a handful of global companies—generally headquartered in the United States—targeted for tax evasion by the European Commission. Apple Sales International, which sells the company's products in Europe, India, the Middle East, and Africa, is incorporated in Ireland. All of Apple's sales in Europe, therefore, are recorded in Ireland. In 2014, Apple paid only 0.005 percent in corporate tax for its international activities rather than Ireland's corporate tax rate of 12.5 percent, which is imposed by the EU. At the end of August 2016, the European Commission handed the company a $14.5 billion tax arrears bill.[7] Activists strongly argue that it is irresponsible, bad corporate citizenship for a company with Apple's revenue, scale, and resources to pay virtually nothing, especially when compared to individual tax rates. And the general public in twenty-seven of twenty-eight EU countries agree.[8]

However, Ireland quickly leapt to Apple's defense, stating that they had negotiated Apple's tax status to bolster the country's economy. In an official statement, Irish Finance Minister Michael Noonan "disagree[d] profoundly" with the European Commission's decision, noting he would appeal the ruling.[9] Subsequently, other major U.S. corporations—Amazon, Google, and McDonald's—became the subject of European investigations, fueling speculation that American companies were being targeted unfairly.

In response, members of the Business Roundtable, an association of CEOs whose purpose is to promote sound public policy for U.S. businesses, wrote to heads of the European Union member states. In September of 2016, these business leaders called for the EU to honor the terms of a company's agreement with a sovereign nation. Their defense was that "investments create jobs needed to maintain operations" and that "cross border investments provide for innovation, enhanced standard of living and productive employment opportunities for hundreds of millions of workers across the globe and the EU."[10]

In December 2016, Apple filed an appeal against the European Union ruling, which included a statement that the company was the largest taxpayer in the world. Apple paid a 26 percent tax rate on its worldwide

earnings, mostly in the United States. "Because our products and services are created, designed and engineered in the US, that's where we
pay most of our tax. . . . [T]his case has never been about how much tax
Apple pays, it's about where that tax is paid." In a statement following
Apple's appeal, Ireland's finance ministry noted the European Commission had "misunderstood the relevant facts and Irish law. . . . Ireland did
not give favourable tax treatment to Apple—the full amount of tax was
paid in this case and no state aid was provided. Ireland does not do deals
with taxpayers." Although the case could take years to settle, other companies have responded by moving headquarters to countries where they
have an actual physical business.[11]

Starting at the end of 2011, people we interviewed repeatedly told us
that businesses are better placed than government bureaucrats to improve our lives—whether it be through effective investment in communities, providing jobs, or creating sustainable change. Yet they
simultaneously want their favorite brands—and Apple is their number
one favorite—to empathize with their daily challenges and behave like
responsible citizens. While Apple and other U.S. corporations did not violate tax laws and their investments improve the livelihoods of communities in which they operate, their ability to manipulate the tax code does
not ring fair to some fans. As Apple continues to move along the ME-to-
WE continuum of Brand Citizenship, it may need to adopt more of a
give-to-get strategy to maintain trust and loyalty.

GOOGLE: DON'T BE EVIL

Unlike Apple, Google has actively publicized its vision and brand purpose, beginning with its motto "Don't be evil" and continuing with its
mission to "organize the world's information and make it universally accessible and useful." Google is all about possibilities and materializing
the things we dream will make a better world. As one of our research
participants stated, "Google has created a culture of people in the pursuit
of innovation."

Google—the noun that became a verb—began in the late 1990s as
more than a reliable search engine. Unlike competitors InfoSeek, Alta-
Vista, and even Yahoo!, from the beginning the company's name simul-

taneously indicated a childlike whimsy driving a brand with grand ambitions. Google is a play on the word *googol*—a mathematical term for the number 10100, or the digit 1 followed by 100 zeroes. First seen in 1940, the word comes from the book *Mathematics and the Imagination* by Edward Kasner and James R. Newman and is said to have been coined a year or two before by Kasner's nephew when asked to name an enormous number.[12]

And Google's influence on us as individuals (ME) and society (WE) unequivocally has been enormous and grows every day. Google is a trusted brand that lives up to its main product promise. Every time we "Google" something, we make Google smarter. Through search, Google Maps, and much more, the company learns about what each of us wants individually and adjusts to our needs, making it, as one research participant said, "productive, industrious, easy." Simultaneously, the company's algorithms shape the information we receive and how we perceive the world around us.

Google enhances its users' lives. And it's not only what the company does for us as individuals that fans in our research paid attention to. Equally if not more important were perceptions of the brand's attitude toward its employees. "[Google's treatment of employees] has become infectious. . . . [O]ther industry leaders have adopted these techniques to attract top talent [as well]." As a model for Silicon Valley culture, perceptions of Google's employee policies have helped to set the responsible standard for companies everywhere to treat employees as real human beings, not just as productivity tools. Perceived as bold in its actions, embracing spontaneity, motivating risk taking, and highly valuing employees, Google connects with fans emotionally as well as functionally as a search engine. As one of our research participants said, echoing the sentiment of many others, "[I]f Google ran for President, I'd vote for it."

Whether it's Google Maps, Android, ideas that seed technology-driven initiatives (by connecting users, experts, and engineers around critical issues that people face in times of conflict, instability, or repression), or Sidewalk Labs (dedicated to developing new technologies to improve urban life), Google's highly audacious brand vision has always been about making us—ME and WE—exponentially bigger than we are. And because of this, its corporate foundation, Google.org,

comfortably nestles in alongside other companies in its corporate portfolio—an accomplishment a majority of large corporations cannot
claim.

Giving locally and globally and investing in teams with bold ideas
that create lasting global impact, Google.org donates $100 million in
grants, 200,000 volunteer hours, and $1 billion in products each year.[13]
While participants in our research did not place Google in the same category as TOMS, Whole Foods Market, Newman's Own, or other socially conscious businesses, like these businesses, the company easily
moves across the continuum of Step 1 to Step 5 and back again on the
model of Brand Citizenship.

For some stakeholders, Google's ability to move so facilely was concerning. As Google added complex pet projects, a number were judged
as being too brazen or off the mark. Examples included fuel from seawa-
ter, Internet access beamed from stratospheric balloons, giant blimps
hauling cargo, and jetpacks. Other stakeholders, especially investors,
began to insist on greater transparency (fiscal or otherwise) and accountability across the corporation in order to keep Google's new endeavors
focused and on track.

Responsibility—Step 3 of the model of Brand Citizenship—is the
transitional point of a company moving from being perceived as a ME
brand to being seen as a WE one. To credibly align a WE-based vision
with a ME product and service promise, any brand—particularly a public company such as Google—must behave responsibly and be accountable and create value for all constituents: customers, employees, business
partners, and investors alike.

Founders Larry Page and Sergey Brin heeded the call from investors
by rolling out a new corporate structure aimed at improving oversight
and transparency, while simultaneously facilitating the freedom necessary for the company to take risks and live out its higher brand purpose.
On October 2, 2015, Google became Alphabet Inc., a holding company.
Sundar Pichai became CEO of Google, the largest subsidiary of Alphabet, and companies that were "further afield" from Google's main Internet product were spun off from Google as subsidiaries of Alphabet.[14]

Like the name *Google*, *Alphabet* is also a play on words. Page, Brin, senior management, and their branding team chose Alphabet not only because it represents "a collection of letters that represent language, one of

humanity's most important innovations, and is the core of how" Google indexes searches but also because it represents the reward the company is aiming for in investing in innovative, risky ventures. In other words, when deconstructed, an "alpha bet" (where alpha is the investment return above the market benchmark).[15] As a holding company, Alphabet is not a consumer-facing brand. And although, like Apple, it has not published its vision or mission, its activities, which are broad yet centered on using technology to influence society and improve lives, remain true to Google's brand heritage.

For example, in September of 2016, Verily, Alphabet's life-science company, entered into a joint venture with French pharmaceutical company, Sanofi. The joint venture, named Onduo, is aimed at improving and simplifying the management of diabetes by uniting software, medicine, and professional care.[16] Through businesses like Onduo, Alphabet focuses on delivering products and services that enhance our daily lives (ME), progress society (WE), and are also economically viable. Revenue in second quarter 2016 for the corporation was up by 21 percent year-on-year, despite $859 million in losses from experimental initiatives.[17]

BRAND CITIZENSHIP ENHANCES ALL BRANDS

As the comparison of Apple and Google illustrates, Brand Citizenship is not an all-or-nothing proposition. Nor will the ideal moment to purposefully begin to practice Brand Citizenship emerge simply. The need to balance commercial realities with ideal notions of doing good will also be ongoing. Indeed, three years of *CultureQ* research demonstrated that, as people require more of brands, many companies are practicing one or more of Brand Citizenship's elements by initiating things like corporate matches, ad campaigns about sustainability, or promotional initiatives in partnership with nonprofits. Each of these can set the wheels in motion for a business to align its brand development with responsible policies and initiatives across the five steps, provided they stem from a clear vision or understanding of the business's larger purpose.

In Part II, you'll learn more about Brand Citizenship's five-step path. Through case narratives highlighting different elements of a range of companies—from decades-old large corporations to successful start-ups—you'll see how longstanding and newer businesses alike are positioned on different steps of Brand Citizenship and gaining meaningful recognition through creating lasting social value. Each of the brands profiled in the following chapters has a rich history of Brand Citizenship. To explore the myriad ways these brands embody trust, enrichment, responsibility, community, and connection in their relationships with customers and stakeholders is beyond the scope of this book. Please consider these case studies an invitation to learn more about their compelling stories.

Perhaps most importantly, you'll also see that successful Brand Citizenship is not formulaic. It's an iterative process that includes trial and error in part and a continual journey of adapting to our shifting Zeitgeist.

> *Now that businesses and companies are inextricably*
> *linked to society, their effects on the world, due to their*
> *practices, are directly reciprocal, similar to karma.*
> *Companies need to be sustainable, honest,*
> *concerned for the consumer, and reliable in order to live*
> *as a successful entity. In this way, society can progress*
> *forwards through mutualistic*
> *consumer–corporation relationships.*
>
> —CultureQ participant

HIGHLIGHTS

CHAPTER 3:
Brand Citizenship

▶ Today's consumer demands that the brands they buy meet an ever more expansive and deep range of functional and emotional needs.

▶ Increasingly, people are seeking brands that both enrich their lives and better society.

▶ The five-step model of Brand Citizenship enables a brand to move from satisfying people's individual needs (ME) to addressing their desires to belong to communities that reflect their values and concerns to their interest in contributing something meaningful to the wider world (WE).

▶ Now more than ever, brands need to articulate what drives and informs their business vision, so that people can relate to them in the same way they connect with other people and develop the sense of loyalty that is crucial to ongoing success.

▶ Without a written brand statement, Apple succeeds in conveying its vision, best summed up in Steve Jobs's words, "Put your ding in the universe," through the products it offers.

▶ Beginning with its reputation for treating employees well, Google is perceived by fans as effectively enhancing our individual lives, progressing society, and creating economic value.

▶ Regardless of size or industry, all brands can reap the benefits of Brand Citizenship, progressing on a continuum from ME to WE and encompassing the attributes that build and secure brand loyalty.

PART II

THE PATH OF BRAND CITIZENSHIP

CHAPTER 4

TRUST

Don't Let Me Down

Do what you say.

Although academics have debated the specific definition of brand loyalty since the 1950s, most business leaders would agree that building a strong relationship with a loyal customer base provides competitive and economic benefits. Whether we define brand loyalty as repeat purchases, a predisposition to a brand, a brand that is a favorite and the only one you'll buy, or all three, it's relatively safe to say loyal customers cost less to keep and are more likely to recommend a brand than nonloyal users. Similarly, loyal employees are more productive and cost less to train than new or disgruntled ones. Ultimately, brand loyalty enhances profitability.

Over the three years my team and I spent deconstructing the elements of brand leadership, good corporate citizenship, and brand loyalty, we confirmed that, as in any healthy relationship, trust is the starting point for brand loyalty—not the endgame or the highest accolade a brand can achieve. Indeed, trust is the foundational building block for any positive relationship between a brand and its customers. As distrust of politicians and established institutions has increased, people have grown more media savvy, and multimedia advertising campaigns have aggrandized brands, it has become increasingly difficult for companies to effectively cultivate trust. Today people accept little at face value and are fairly adept at seeing through crafted messaging, political rhetoric, and marketing hype.

With video recorders in living rooms, a camera on every phone, last night's exploits posted on Facebook, and an audit trail on every keycard, we're all watching one another. We count on eventually seeing businesses, politicians, and other people as they really are and thereby are not necessarily surprised when they don't live up to their promises. We're trained by social media to contrive our images, just like the political leaders we revile, celebrities we adore, and companies we work at and invest in do. We stylize our Facebook posts, Instagram pictures, LinkedIn professional profiles, and iPhone playlists to project a personal brand. And as savvy manipulators of identity ourselves, we're prone to be skeptical of a brand's claim of provenance and excellence.

Further, many marketing pundits have argued that brand loyalty—and even the very concept of a brand—is a thing of the past. As Kevin Roberts, former chairman of the advertising agency Saatchi & Saatchi, observed in his 2005 book *Lovemarks: The Future Beyond Brands*, brands have become ubiquitous. Everything has become a brand.[1]

Others believe that brands themselves are no longer needed as markers of trustworthiness or credibility. Taken together, product parity (or the functional differences between products in the same category) being minimal, the ability to learn everything you might ever want to know about a product online, and big data helping products and services find us (as well as the other way around) have all made it hard for brands to maintain the attention and loyalty of existing customers—and to convert prospects to new customers. Indeed, Havas Media Group's 2015 Meaningful Brands® index (which "measures the potential business benefits gained by a brand when it is seen to improve our wellbeing and quality of life") demonstrated that "most people would not care if 74 percent of all brands disappeared for good."[2]

However, over the last twenty-five years, my work researching brands has demonstrated the opposite: It's shown that the roles brands play in culture and society have increased dramatically. And as people have become overwhelmed by the number of brands that try to capture their attention every day, their loyalty to a select few trusted brands is growing. Brands matter today more than ever. Yet it's more difficult than ever for a brand to find a way to break through, to connect in a meaningful way with its target customers, and to be among the select few favorite brands that a given customer trusts. Technology has conditioned us to believe we can have it all, and today's digital social landscape has naturally blurred the lines that historically divided products from service enhancements and communications. With too many choices in virtually every product category, endless claims of "new and improved," countless loyalty programs, and perpetual price discounting, the brands that our friends and families trust have become even stronger filters for acceptable choices. Indeed, in my company's *CultureQ* research, three of the top five attributes people chose to describe leadership brands reflected a yearning for trustworthy icons that deliver the basics, such as producing reliable goods and services, offering value for quality, and excellent customer service.

The role of a brand was never meant to be varnish. It was—and will continue to be—about fostering emotional connections that pull people toward products, services, and even companies by promoting meaningful interactions. No matter what a company's size, scale, or purpose, Brand Citizenship starts at the very beginning: cultivating relationships rooted in trust. Bottom line: *Do what you say, reliably and with excellence—every time.* If a company makes a mistake—something that is bound to happen—it should offer the best service available to fix the problem and be honest when it can't fix it. Brand Citizenship, and indeed cultivating brand loyalty, begins with not letting me—the purchaser of your goods and services or your employee—down.

Although this may seem like Positioning 101, it's not. Like people, it's easy for brands to become too focused on celebrity hype, the latest app, and all the trappings of new and improved technology. Since the Great Recession, anger toward corporate greed has magnified, and the pace at which corporate scandals have been uncovered has accelerated. So it really is not surprising that people trust those brands that deliver on their promises to ME first.

In this chapter, I'll examine the characteristics that embody trust in a brand and see how several organizations across a range of industries—from retail to fast food to finance—work to build trust with customers, employees, and the public.

FIVE CHARACTERISTICS FOR
EARNING FAITHFULNESS

As the model of Brand Citizenship emerged from our research, my team and I spent a lot of time discussing trust. While countless brands include trust as a value or personality attribute in their strategy, no brand can own trust. In the same way a new friend, colleague, or neighbor gains our trust by the way they behave, a brand must earn trust over time through its collective actions. We each have different expectations of the people we trust. You, for example, may trust someone who is there to listen when you're down and not care if they tell a mutual friend about it or share personal stories with you. Your sister, on the other hand, may only trust a friend who keeps her secrets and who also confides theirs. In the same way, trust can mean something different to each customer, employee, or stakeholder of a business.

Different participants in our research used varying words when describing the brands they trust, including reliable, dependable, honest, transparent, having integrity, selfless, respectful, and more. Combing through our qualitative journal exercise with Millennials and all the participants in the quantitative surveys' open-ended responses, we determined that favorite brands cultivated the most trust—or *deep faithfulness*, as my team and I often referred to it—when they embodied five characteristics: Clarity, Reliability, Sincerity, Reciprocity, and Active Listening.

CLARITY: BE CLEAR ABOUT WHO YOU ARE—
WALMART

As with any relationship, starting things off right is the best way for a brand to begin to nurture trust. When a brand clearly communicates what it delivers, it provides customers with a benchmark from which to measure all their interactions with that brand. Taken one step further, when a brand shares why it exists and how it helps to create meaningful societal value, it is more likely to foster an emotional connection with its fans.

Walmart is a ME brand that is clear about why it exists and, for a significant number of participants in our research, creates meaningful societal value through its brand purpose. For these people, as for many others, Walmart is a good corporate citizen: a brand they trust because its pricing policies afford them a better standard of living. As one *CultureQ* participant explained, "[Walmart] offers me access to products I wouldn't otherwise be able to afford."

Through its *everyday low cost* approach, Walmart unequivocally helps people "Save money. Live better." On the other hand, an even greater number of participants in my company's *CultureQ* research between 2011 and 2014 perceived Walmart as an untrustworthy brand not responsibly living up to its purpose. They judged Walmart as a symbol for much of what has been wrong with big-box retailers and other mass employers. Their perceptions in large part were fueled by press about the company's employee, environmental, and supply chain policies. Although Walmart continues to face vocal opposition today, it was voted one of the most trustworthy brands by Americans surveyed in a *Reader's Digest* study in both 2015 and 2016.[3,4]

In October of 2005, Walmart embarked on a long-term journey to be a more socially responsible company and, in doing so, set itself up to shift from being perceived as a ME brand to a WE one. In a speech broadcast worldwide to Walmart's 1.6 million associates (employees) in its 6,000-plus stores worldwide and shared with 60,000-plus suppliers, then president and CEO of Walmart Stores, Inc., Lee Scott, announced a strategic sustainability initiative designed to significantly reduce the company's impact on the environment. He ambitiously stated that Walmart aimed to be "the most competitive and innovative company in the world." Further, he acknowledged, "Being a good steward of the environment and being profitable are not mutually exclusive. They are one and the same." Scott committed Walmart to three sustainability goals:[5]

1. To run 100 percent on renewable energy

2. To create zero waste

3. To sell products that sustain resources and the environment

That same month, responding to years of criticism from activists that its employee health insurance was out of reach for many of its 1.2 million workers in the United States, Walmart introduced a cheaper option for employees called the Value Plan, with premiums as low as $11.[6]

Much, if not all, of the goodwill the company intended to cultivate with
this was thwarted less than one month later when *The New York Times*
published an article referencing an internal memorandum addressed to
the Board and written by M. Susan Chambers, Wal-Mart Stores' then executive vice president for benefits. The memo proposed ways to curb the
cost of benefits, most notably healthcare, while aiming to minimize
damage to the brand's reputation. Chambers acknowledged the world's
largest retailer "had to walk a fine line in restraining benefit costs because critics had attacked it for being stingy on wages and health coverage."[7]

In November of 2005, after *The New York Times* article appeared, director Robert Greenwald released a documentary titled *Walmart: The
High Cost of Low Price*. Through interviews with former employees,
small business owners, and footage of Walmart executives, and with statistics interspersed between interviews, Greenwald reinforced the negative view of Walmart's business practices and its effects on individuals
and communities, despite the company's recent announcements to improve itself.[8,9] Then, in April of 2006, the company outraged many activists when it promoted Susan Chambers—who, in her memo, also had
included ways to discourage unhealthy people from applying for jobs—
to head the company's human resource division.[10] Nearly eighteen
months later, Walmart was working hard to regain lost trust and project
itself as a trustworthy brand adding real value.

A New Tagline and a New Business Orientation

When a company changes its tagline, it's a signal that they've changed
their product and service offering or their value proposition to customers, to other external stakeholders, and to employees. On September 12,
2007, Walmart made a public declaration of a new orientation to business when it launched its new tagline, "Save money. Live better." This
new promise replaced its nineteen-year-old slogan, "Always Low Prices,
Always."[11] Without a doubt, "live better" reflects a big, meaningful
brand ambition—one that pledges something more than selling goods at
lower prices than competitors. It explains what Walmart does (helps
customers save money), as well as why it does it (helps people live
better). "Save money. Live better" extends well beyond the store experi-

ence itself and sets Walmart up to easily glide across all five steps of the ME to WE continuum of Brand Citizenship. With its new tagline, Walmart is communicating that it is a brand that sells products at low prices and cares about people's quality of life—presumably its employees' quality of life as well as its customers'.

In 2008, the brand signaled an even bigger change as the new Walmart when it refreshed its logo, dropping the star that acted like a hyphen and punctuating itself with a bright, optimistic starburst at the end of its name. [12] One month after Mike Duke became CEO in March of 2009, the brand announced it was paying $933.6 million in bonuses to every full- and part-time worker. [13] And, in 2011, going one step further in its journey to help stakeholders "live better," the company introduced a plan to improve, over five years, the nutritional value of its store-brand foods, including eliminating trans fats and lowering the quantities of salt and sugar used. Walmart also promised to negotiate nutritional issues with suppliers, to reduce retail prices for whole foods and vegetables, and to open stores in lower-income areas.[14] As the world's second-largest retailer, changes in Walmart's policies and operations have a meaningful social impact.

Over the past two years under the company's fifth CEO, Doug McMillon, who joined in February of 2014, the brand has taken further steps to cultivate trust with the general public, not only with its fans. By focusing on responsibility—Step 3 of the model of Brand Citizenship—Walmart is setting itself up to be trusted as a WE brand as much as a ME brand. In 2014, it rolled out an initiative to replace lighting in its U.S., UK, Latin American, and Asian stores with LED lights, for increased energy efficiency. [15] And in 2015, Walmart took a big leap, using its influence to positively impact three big social issues in the United States that are focused on bettering lives:

- ► *Religious freedom:* McMillon issued a statement in March urging Arkansas Governor Asa Hutchinson to veto the now dead HB1228 "religious freedom" bill.[16]

- ► *The Confederate flag:* Following the shooting of nine black churchgoers in Charleston, South Carolina, the retailer stopped selling any merchandise depicting the divisive and controversial flag.[17]

▶ *Guns:* McMillon also altered Walmart's gun sales policy. In an interview with *CNNMoney*'s Cristina Alesci on August 26, 2015, he said Walmart's selection of firearms should be geared toward hunters and sports shooters. That same month, the company ceased selling military-style semiautomatic weapons.[18]

A Focus on Responsibility, Trust, and Transparency

In the company's 2015 *Global Responsibility Report,* McMillon asserted "by embracing responsibility and collaboration with others, we can make a significant difference in the world that will serve us well in the long term."[19] Kathleen McLaughlin, who joined the company as Chief Sustainability Officer in 2013, later confirmed in the 2016 *Global Responsibility Report,* "We have learned that lasting change requires collective action to reshape social and environmental systems, and that the most viable programs are those that create shared value—value for business and society."[20]

In November of 2016, at the Net Impact Conference in Philadelphia, McMillon spoke about a future based on *a new era of trust and transparency* for the brand. As he stated when he detailed the company's plans for the environment, employees, and community, "We want to make sure Walmart is a company that our associates and customers are proud of—and that we are always doing right by them and by the communities they live in."

WALMART INITIATES A NEW VISION FOR ITS ROLE IN SOCIETY WITH ITS 2016 COMMITMENTS

Environment:

▶ Power half of its energy from renewable sources designed to achieve scientifically derived targets

▶ Achieve zero waste to landfill in key markets by 2025

▶ Sell more sustainably produced products while maintaining their commitment to low prices

Employees:

► Be the place to go for a first job

► Provide career advancement through training in the United States

► Foster predictability and stability through paid time off and better scheduling in the UK

Community:

► Source $20 billion in products from U.S. women-owned businesses by the end of 2016 and $260 billion in products that support American jobs by 2023

► Support the human dignity of workers in the supply chain

► Donate four billion meals to help fight hunger by 2020 and contribute $25 million to disaster recovery

Source: Walmart. "Walmart Offers New Vision for the Company's Role in Society." November 4, 2016. http://news.walmart.com/2016/11/04/walmart-offers-new-vision-for-the-companys-role-in-society

At the conference, McMillon appealed to other retailers to join Walmart in aiming to be an employer of choice. In a company press release, he's quoted as saying, "Today we are asking other retailers to join us in helping people live better. Let's use our collective power to create good jobs with good training that become good careers for all our associates."[21]

It's exciting to envision the ways in which Walmart can move even further along on the continuum of Brand Citizenship. By better informing people about the money it donates and its sustainability initiatives, Walmart can help its customers feel that they're creating a better world by shopping there. Imagine if Walmart let you know what portion of your purchases helped support its Fighting Hunger Together initiatives, for example. Envision being handed your purchase receipt by the cashier and seeing, "You saved $25 by shopping with us today. Your purchases also support our fight against hunger in America. Through them you helped us donate ten meals to feed hungry Americans." Wouldn't you feel better about buying things at Walmart? Wouldn't you feel that through your purchases you were helping Walmart to combat hunger and contributing to help others more than you could by yourself? And what if Walmart invited shoppers to join its associates in delivering Thanksgiving meals to elderly and housebound people in its local communities? Wouldn't this motivate you to shop at Walmart more often? In connecting its social responsibility initiatives with its low-cost promise, Walmart can demonstrate how saving money will indeed help us *live better* in a more expansive way.

RELIABILITY: DELIVER WHAT YOU PROMISE, TIME AFTER TIME—CHIPOTLE

Once a brand clearly commits to what it is and does, it must follow through. Walmart has been awarded trusted-brand status because it makes good on its promises, not because it makes exciting claims it never intends to deliver. Although we're often easily wooed by shiny new toys and impressed by the large number of "likes" that successful viral campaigns deliver, consistency and dependability are the essential tools for building trust and developing a loyal customer base. It's only logical that we think twice about repurchasing a product or service from a company that claims more than it delivers or that we can't rely on time after time.

A Story of Resilience

Chipotle, whose story began in Chapter 1, lost its fans fast in the third and fourth quarters of 2015 when several health scares significantly reduced sales and the company's share price. Even as *E. coli* and norovirus made people ill, the germs also poisoned customer loyalty. If history provides any lessons, Chipotle will eventually win back the trust it lost, provided it follows through on its purpose.

McDonald's certainly did just that after food scandals in China in July of 2014 and sanitary violations in Russia. Unlike McDonald's or indeed any other fast-food brand, though, Chipotle faces greater challenges in winning people back. After all, its reputation stems from a purpose that is the very thing the contaminated food violated: great-tasting, healthy food delivered through an efficacious food supply chain that "cultivates a better world."

Without a doubt, the company has done many of the right things, although not necessarily in the right order. It quickly acknowledged the food crises, closed stores, and made improvements to its supply chain and food preparation procedures. Steven Ells, the company's founder and co-CEO, even hired a new executive director of food safety, Jim Marsden. Marsden, a former Kansas State University (KSU) meat science professor, has been focused on making Chipotle's food chain the "safest restaurant to eat at."[22]

As I reviewed in Chapter 1, as part of its recovery plan from the health scare, the company created Chiptopia, its summer loyalty program promoted at the end of its *A Love Story* video. The impact on long-term sales is still unclear. According to media reports, more than three million people signed up for the program, and 85,000 achieved "hot" status, meaning they earned up to nine free meals, plus a $240 Catering for 20 bonus. Although these numbers are impressive and indicate success in the short term, YouGov BrandIndex data indicates that customer perceptions of the brand have not improved. On September 20, 2016, when Chipotle was offering free drinks for high school– and college–aged customers and free meals for kids alongside its rewards program, customer perceptions of brand quality was only 6.8 on a scale of −100 to +100. [23]

Seeking to Rebuild Trust in Products and Processes

Later in September, the chain did what it should have done much earlier: It overtly communicated the improvements it made in its food safety procedures to ensure high-quality, good-tasting burritos, every time. In other words, it explained the changes it had made as part of its commitment to being a trustworthy brand focused on cultivating a better world. In a video and a full-page open letter published in several newspapers, Steve Ells described the eight things Chipotle has done to improve food safety since the crises.[24,25]

Shortly after, Chipotle launched a new ad campaign, its first since 2012: *Ingredients Reign*. Although it's more whimsical than Chipotle's *Back to the Start* advertisement in 2012, *The Scarecrow*, and *A Love Story*, *Ingredients Reign* is an animated feature developed to rebuild the trust that the brand lost in 2015. The ad opens in a fairy tale–like manner to tell the story of Chipotle's "obsession" with finding the best ingredients. Tomatoes, cheese, avocados, and jalapeños all get the "royal treatment" as they're lovingly prepared by Chipotle staff. As the ad states, "Tis their world, we just cook in it."[26]

The message of *Ingredients Reign* is much simpler and more straightforward than the brand's previous videos: Chipotle sources only the best ingredients, and it takes great care when handling them. Using words like *marinating*, *hand dicing*, and *hand mashing*, it gives us deeper insight into their food preparation process. Interestingly, some participants in our *CultureQ* research project have said that while *Ingredients Reign* communicates Chipotle's dedication and commitment to food preparation, the emphasis is too strongly on their corporate story. As one participant stated, "The message 'we are so great we only choose the best' is less compelling than if the focus was on ME. I think they should say, 'You're deserving of nothing but the best, so Chipotle gives you ingredients fit for a king.'"

Meeting the Challenges Every Day

There are many aspects to delivering reliability in the food service industry, and Chipotle exemplifies that complexity—and not always in a positive way. The idea that the staff is obsessed by the ingredients is often at odds with the experience of being served and eating there—at least the experiences I've had. When I've been in a Chipotle, I've noticed many customers who feel rushed by the staff, who often have a fast-food server mentality rather than that of a foodie, which the ad implies. While *Ingredients Reign* may increase perceptions of the brand as trustworthy, only the in-store customer experience will or will not deliver this. Closing all Chipotle's restaurants to train employees on the seriousness of food-borne illness outbreaks was a great step, but it may not have been enough.

The brand must also focus on excellent customer service. A starting point might be to educate servers on the quality and excellence of Chipotle's supply chain so that they can truly appreciate the food they're serving and more lovingly, as well as efficiently, craft burritos and salad bowls. To live the brand's promise and thereby fully deliver it to customers, servers should be trained to view themselves as food artisans rather than as expediters, consistently blending ingredients together in perfect proportion.

Since the crisis, I've also wondered why Chipotle has focused on opening new stores over bringing a "better food" dining experience to the seating and eating areas, beginning first with the basics such as cleanliness and neatness—especially during rush hour, when the Chipotles I've visited have been unkempt. The wall space also offers an ideal untapped place to educate customers about food and the company's supply chain through art or visual narratives that tell the story of Chipotle ingredients.

In December of 2016 at the Barclays 2016 Eat, Sleep, Play—It's Not All Discretionary Conference in New York, Steve Ells himself stated:

> I'm particularly not satisfied with the quality of the experience in some of our restaurants. While the majority of our restaurants are running well, some are not delivering a terrific guest experience. When we invite new or lapsed customers into restaurants that are less than perfect, we believe those customers will return less frequently and that we will needlessly slow our recovery by allowing that to happen. Therefore, we are focused relentlessly on creating an excellent dining experience in every one of our restaurants.[27]

Less than one week after the conference, on December 12, 2016, Chipotle announced that it was abandoning its co-CEO structure and that Steve Ells would manage all operations.[28]

At the same time, the company announced a new, "expanded" mission statement: "Ensure that better food, prepared from whole, unprocessed ingredients is accessible to everyone." Without a doubt, the new mission statement is designed, at least in part, to focus the brand more on the product it delivers than on changing the way people think, as did its original mission, "Change the way people think about and eat fast food."

The new mission necessitates a change in how Chipotle speaks with consumers. *Back to the Start*, *The Scarecrow*, and *A Love Story* pull at our heartstrings to change the way we think about factory farms and fast-food restaurants. Focused on the quality of the ingredients, *Ingredients Reign* is more in line with the new mission. The Chipotle Cultivate Foundation also aligns with the new mission, despite the word cultivate in its title. Founded in 2011, it is all about developing better food through funding grants to organizations that promote sustainable agriculture, innovation in farming, food literacy, cooking education, and nutritious eating.[29]

Although Chipotle has shifted the spotlight on which aspects of its customer-service experience it wants to emphasize (ingredients and food safety), the sincerity and passion that helped it to become a fast-food change agent remain at the brand's core. With continued commitment to its core principles and vigorous leadership, it can likely look forward to continued success.

SINCERITY:
ACT SINCERELY FROM THE HEART—TRADER JOE'S

Sincerity always wins our trust, especially over the long term. With corporate reputation being top-of-mind these days, many communications experts equate sincerity with transparency. But our research, as well as that of others, has shown time and again that sincerity builds trust more than transparency. So how does a brand that's sincere behave as compared to one that's transparent?

Like a sincere person, a sincere brand is honest and genuine, and it exhibits deeply human characteristics. It openly shares its point of view on the world and expresses this not only in its communications but also in its actions and the experiences it offers. Being sincere doesn't necessarily mean brands voluntarily tell all or operate with complete transparency. However, it does involve speaking frankly and being truthful when asked a question, whether in a routine customer service call or by an investigative reporter. As savvy consumers of media, participants in our *CultureQ* research acknowledged that information sometimes needs to be filtered. And they simultaneously told us they're not always trusting of brands when they claim they're being transparent. They recognize candor may be forced or even contrived when a brand is responding to a crisis.

Even though most consumers don't expect full disclosure in everyday marketing communications, they judge the omission of facts in watershed moments as something done only by those with something to hide. In times of crisis or during a product recall, people insist that brands put the interests of their customers and other stakeholders first. Although it's had a hard time winning back customer trust, Chipotle understands this. A brand that's *human*, like Chipotle, is self-reflective and recognizes that it will never be flawless. And a brand that's genuine, like Chipotle, balances a deep sense of purpose with the pursuit of market share and/or profits and commits to being better when things go wrong. A brand that's honest also demonstrates its true intent to put customers first by improving its practices and fixing mistakes through its actions, not just its words—as Chipotle did.

A Distinctive Experience with a Focus on Value—and Fun

Trader Joe's, or "TJ's" as its loyal customers call it, is a ME brand, with WE sensibilities, that has cultivated an eclectic, cult-like following, especially with Millennials. Fans love everything about TJ's, from its products to its happy employees to its kitschy store and packaging design. As participants in my company's *CultureQ* research told us:

> Trader Joe's is uncharacteristically self-aware, especially compared to other supermarket chains. I shop at TJ's every week or so . . . and while I supplement my weekly shopping with a few choice items at other stores, I rarely cheat on TJs with my weekly shop.

> Trader Joe's positions itself as your neighborhood grocery store. They are not located in my neighborhood, but that's the impression I get when I go there.

> Trader Joe's stands for humor and casualness. They make silly, energetic announcements over the loudspeaker, and they have bells and flags that signal open registers, and employees wearing tacky Hawaiian shirts.

The experience of a Trader Joe's perfectly fits the way I see and understand the brand.

Product labels, unique package sizes (and thereby product pricing), in-store samples, product flavors, and even its consistently fun, light tone that includes literary and philosophical references in its marketing and branding all add up to a distinctive Trader Joe's experience that no other grocer comes close to matching. Like Chipotle, Trader Joe's positions itself to attract foodies who appreciate quality ingredients yet don't necessarily label themselves as serious gourmands. Value is integral to Trader Joe's brand purpose. And like everything else at the chain, even value has a decidedly TJ's feel to it. As the company states on its website: "It's not complicated. We just focus on what matters—great food + great prices = Value." [30] The choice of the word "great" makes all the difference. It communicates a personality characterized by honesty, genuineness, and humanness. It's the *wow!* factor Trader Joe's delivers time and time again across its brand experience.

Founded originally as Pronto Market Convenience Store by Joe Columbe, the first Trader Joe's opened in Pasadena, California, in 1967. As myth has it, Joe developed the store's Tiki theme while on holiday in the Caribbean. From its inception, Trader Joe's has mashed up warm sunny cultures to create its own, unique persona. Employees first donned their trademark Hawaiian shirts in 1969.[31] And as of February of 2017, the chain had expanded into a small grocery empire of over 461 stores in forty-one states and Washington D.C.[32] The company was purchased in 1979 by Theo Albrecht of Aldi, the global discount supermarket giant headquartered in Germany, and has experienced considerable growth since.[33] Yet Trader Joe's has retained its "neighborhood feel despite being a chain," as one participant in our *CultureQ* research noted. Promoting itself as "Your Neighborhood Grocery Store," Trader Joe's stores are tucked away in intriguing locations that another one of our *CultureQ* research participants labelled "palace[s] of food." Signage in each store is created by local artists, so they feel like they're "of" the neighborhood, not from a cookie-cutter template. The chain's uniquely local and original ambience helps to make the brand highly trustworthy.

Few question whether the food itself is of great value. As it states on the "Insider Pages" of its *Fearless Flyer*, a newsletter, comic book, and catalogue mashup available in print or online eight times per year:

> You won't find genetically modified ingredients, artificial flavors, artificial preservatives, MSG, partially hydrogenated oils, or colors derived from anything other than naturally available products. We could go on, but we'll let our products speak for themselves.[34]

Eighty-percent of the items Trader Joe's stocks are their own brand. A search on the Internet quickly shows that many of TJ's SKUs are suspected of being sourced from well-known manufacturers such as Pacific, Amy's, and Annie's. Yet Trader Joe's loyalists who know this don't seem to mind. The company stocks a mere 4,000 items as compared to big-box grocers like Walmart or even Wegman's, which typically stock over 50,000.[35] The limited selection isn't a drawback because everything they carry is carefully curated, making its customers feel as though the chain truly understands what they desire. As one participant in our research stated, "When you go to Walmart and you're looking for one thing you have fifteen options in front of you. I never know which one to pick. At Trader Joe's I know the one they have is the one I want." Its fanatical customers are known to go to Trader Joe's first to get everything they possibly can on their grocery list and then go elsewhere for the rest. You can't get Two-Buck Chuck (wine), Chili-Lime Cashews, or Chocolate Covered Power Berries at a Wegman's, Costco, Publix, or Raley's.

TJ's humanness and genuineness come in large part from its potentially uncool coolness. Dorky Hawaiian shirts, along with artsy, homemade signage and an obsolete bell-ringing system directing checkout traffic (a low-tech system when compared with Whole Foods's electronic, number- and color-coded queuing process) are all just cheesy enough to make you smile. Eager employees make enthusiastic announcements over the intercom and regularly interact with shoppers. When you consider Millennials' love of humor and nostalgia, Trader Joe's elusive offbeat and alternative appeal makes perfect sense.

Crisis Management: Swift and Sure

Trader Joe's is known for responsibly sourcing food and paying its employees well. However, this doesn't mean that the brand is perfect. Unlike Walmart, which has often been characterized as a soulless business, TJ's friendly and sincere persona has helped it to skirt the potentially negative impact of newsworthy issues such as high levels of arsenic in the wine the store carries and, as the chain has expanded to the East Coast, the poor treatment of its employees. On March 19, 2015, CBS News broke a story about a proposed class-action lawsuit that was about to be filed in California, claiming Trader Joe's and twenty-three other winemakers and sellers were misrepresenting their wine as safe when it had up to four or five times the maximum levels of arsenic that the Environmental Protection Agency allows for water.[36] Although arsenic is naturally present in many foods and the federal government has few requirements for including the ingredients in wine on labels, as compared with water, for example, Trader Joe's was fast to respond. The next day, on March 20, the company posted "A Note to Customers About Arsenic in Wine" on the "Announcements" section of its website that addressed the issue head-on.

TRADER JOE'S
A NOTE TO CUSTOMERS ABOUT ARSENIC IN WINE

With recent media coverage raising concerns about levels of arsenic in wine, we'd like to clarify some important points.

We will not offer any product we feel is unsafe. Ever. We have no reason to believe the wines we offer are unsafe.

Trader Joe's is among 28 companies named in a recently filed legal complaint. 83 wine products are listed in the filing, covering a range of brands, including one varietal of Charles Shaw—White Zinfandel.

The filing alleges that plaintiffs tested certain wines and found them to contain more arsenic than the level considered safe for drinking water. The complaint does not provide any specific test results nor has plaintiffs' counsel provided those test results to us.

CBS News has reported testing results on Charles Shaw White Zinfandel, said to contain 31 parts-per-billion of arsenic. CBS News also stated it had conducted its own testing on four wines listed in the filing and that "the arsenic levels were all considerably lower than BeverageGrades' results," citing a result for Charles Shaw White Zinfandel "at more than twice [the] standard."

Out of context, this sounds alarming. We would like to provide some context for the claims.

There are no US governmental standards for arsenic in wine.

The EPA has set the limit for Total Arsenic in drinking water in the US at 10 parts-per-billion.

In Canada, the limit for Total Arsenic in wine is 100 parts-per-billion.

The International Organization of Vine and Wine (OIV) is a Paris-based, intergovernmental organization comprised of 45 different wine-producing countries dealing with technical and scientific aspects of viticulture and winemaking. One of the activities of OIV is the compilation of global statistics within its field. The OIV limit for Total Arsenic in wine is 200 parts-per-billion.

Again, we will not offer any product we feel is unsafe. We have had no reports of adverse reactions to Charles Shaw wines—or other wines—related to the potential presence of arsenic. We continue to have no reason to believe the wines we offer are unsafe, including Charles Shaw White Zinfandel.

Additional comment from the WINE INSTITUTE:

> [W]e believe this allegation is false ... Arsenic is prevalent in the natural environment in air, soil and water, and in food. As an agricultural product, wines from California and throughout the world contain trace amounts of arsenic as do juices, vegetables, grains and other alcohol beverages. There is no re-

> search that shows that the amounts found in wine pose a
> health risk to consumers.
>
> Source: Trader Joe's. "A Note to Customers About Arsenic in Wine." March 20, 2015.
> http://www.traderjoes.comannouncement/a-note-to-customers-about-arsenic-in-wine

Unlike Trader Joe's other communications, which use the brand's distinctive tone of voice, this letter was written in a straightforward manner. It logically informed readers of the facts and simultaneously affirmed the brand's commitment to providing its customers only with quality products. In not trying too hard, it confirmed Trader Joe's trustworthiness.

In November of 2016, *The New York Times* reported that Thomas Nagel, a former employee at the Trader Joe's on the Upper West Side of Manhattan, had filed a complaint with the National Labor Relations Board regional office. Dismissed for an overly negative attitude and not having a "genuine" smile or demeanor, Nagel described hazardous stockrooms, abusive managers, and employees considering unionization—all things very much at odds with TJ's reputation and brand persona.[37] Trader Joe's employees—called Crew Members, Merchants, Mates, and Captains—are known for their warmth, friendliness, individual pride, and company spirit, as dictated in the company's mission.

Working at Trader Joe's isn't right for everyone. After all, part of an employee's job is to appear happy and even lively at work. John Shields, Trader Joe's CEO from 1988 to 2001, is known to have told Crew Members at the opening of each store to resign if they were not having fun after thirty days.[38] In return for embodying the TJ's spirit, taking customers on culinary journeys across the seas, and, perhaps most importantly according to Shields, "having fun," Crew Members are well paid relative to other retail workers, given their schedules at least two weeks in advance, have health and vacation benefits, and are trained across multiple positions.

Based on my research, Nagel's complaint received little media coverage apart from *The New York Times*, even though the paper notes that other Crew Members in the Northeast and Mid-Atlantic have confirmed his description. It's easy to imagine if a former Walmart—or even Chipotle—employee filed a similar complaint, the news would be more widespread. Because fans trust the brand in a deep way, similar to how they do a best friend, Nagel's claim hasn't resonated and was likely easy for people to dismiss as a one-off—at least for now. With a reputation as a neighborhood store that delivers great food at a great price to ME, a sincere, friendly corporate character, and a reputation for caring about its employees and WE issues, more so than many retailers Trader Joe's understands you have to create and maintain a strong customer rapport.

RECIPROCITY:
RECIPROCATE AND GIVE AS WELL AS TAKE

Like our most trusted friends, the most trusted brands give as well as take. Free giveaways are the most basic forms of reciprocity, yet they are not always meaningful. The most common giveaways are often tied to giving a reward purchase (two-for-one deals or promotional packs) or allow for a trial (seven-day free subscription), while the most powerful are more altruistic or make a statement about what a brand believes. For example, from November 7 through 9, 2016, *The New York Times* suspended its paywall for NYTimes.com for 72 hours, allowing for free, unlimited access to its digital content for the crucial days before and after the presidential election on November 8. When announcing the promotion, Arthur Sulzberger Jr. stated: "This is an important moment for our country. Independent journalism is crucial to democracy and I believe there is no better time to show readers the type of original journalism *The New York Times* creates every day."[39] While the promotion was developed in part to draw in new subscribers, Sulzberger Jr. tied it equally to the paper's raison d'être, which states: "The core purpose of *The New York Times* is to enhance society by creating, collecting and distributing high-quality news and information. Producing content of the highest quality and integrity is the basis for our reputation and the means by which we fulfill the public trust and our customers' expectations."[40]

When brands use them as an opportunity to thank customers, loyalty programs are also a form of reciprocity. Programs that are more like lip service or one-sided data collection tools can do more harm than good in building trust, though. Think about all the loyalty programs you've registered for and the number of fobs on your key chain or the cards in your wallet or in the bedside table drawer that resulted from doing so. Can you even remember all the programs you're a member of? And how do you feel about the airlines that allow you to collect miles and never use them, as compared to Bloomingdale's or another department store that offers loyalists free shipping with no minimum purchase, points for every dollar spent, double points for cosmetics, and more?

Or what about the cash-back rewards from credit cards, such as Discover? Do these programs enhance your trust in credit card brands more than supermarket ones, which may reward you with an unexpected coupon at the register? According to Colloquy, a publishing, research, and education practice for loyalty professionals, loyalty memberships are fast on the rise, having grown from 973 million in 2000 to 3.3 billion in 2014.[41] Yet a study from Kitewheel (a company focused on creating real-time personalized customer journeys) showed 66 percent of marketing executives believe loyalty programs are a way for consumers to demonstrate their loyalty to the brand, not the other way around, that is, a means to foster trust between the brand and its customers.[42] The time has come that brands must rethink this equation and show consumers they understand that loyalty goes both ways in relationships characterized by trust.

Farrow & Ball: A Space for Color and Creativity

The digital world has expanded the opportunities for brands to give relatively freely. One of the most powerful methods for demonstrating reciprocity is content that offers value to customers beyond the product. Content that is relevant and effectively delivered fosters trust and goes one step further into Step 2 of Brand Citizenship by providing knowledge that helps people more easily accomplish tasks, more effectively choose or use products and services, or add inspiration to everyday routines. Farrow & Ball's *The Chromologist* is a fun example of this. As its name implies, *The Chromologist* "translates the meaning of color." Through this blog, the seventy-year-old UK-based paint-and-wallpaper supplier offers a deep dive into the world of color in art, decoration, food, fashion, literature, and more.

With its name included only at the very bottom of the page, with a small endorsement that clicks through to the company's site, Farrow & Ball is nearly invisible. While the content *The Chromologist* features can be tied to Farrow & Ball's business, the purpose of the blog is clearly not to sell product or even teach people how to use it. The Farrow & Ball website itself does this by offering valuable content, including sample rooms for decorating ideas, style trends, tips on getting started, and more.

The Chromologist is more about inspiring people with common interests, heightening awareness and confidence, and connecting people based on shared enthusiasms. I can imagine Farrow & Ball using this blog to develop a community of people with shared interests that move it to Step 4 of Brand Citizenship, Community. Discussion on topics among readers would be encouraged, and participants would be offered opportunities to submit content as guest bloggers, which *The Chromologist*'s staff would then review and curate. In expanding the role of *The Chromologist* in such a way, Farrow & Ball would create devoted, loyal fans.

SunTrust Bank: Giving a Voice without Judgment

SunTrust Bank's onUp Movement takes reciprocity one step further. Stemming from and expressing the brand's purpose, "Lighting the way to financial well-being," onUp is a multiplatform program developed to help people gain control over their financial well-being. The output of insights SunTrust gained from conversations about financial stress and anxiety with 190,000 people and 8,000 businesses, onUp places the bank's finger firmly on the pulse of what many people feel.[43] Through onUp, SunTrust gives voice to how the average person thinks about personal finance. In recognizing that everyone has his or her own relationship with money—and that this relationship isn't right or wrong—the bank validates a wide range of perspectives and experiences, in part, by simply acknowledging that the range exists. Equally important, onUp helps SunTrust move across the ME-to-WE continuum of Brand Citizenship.

Reaching Out in Support of Economic and Financial Empowerment

To increase the visibility of the impact of financial stress on our health, SunTrust launched the program in January of 2016, with its first-ever Super Bowl ad. In a press release, SunTrust Chairman and CEO William H. Rogers Jr. said, "We are starting the conversation to encourage people to gain control over their finances. Similar to physical fitness, people need motivation and support to improve their financial well-being." He continued, "Across all income levels, people who are financially confident report being three times more satisfied with their lives."[44] The Super Bowl advertisement, which was phase one of the initiative, resulted in more than ten million social media impressions and 38,000 site visits on game day.[45]

With a script and imagery that potently portray the financial anxiety and stress many Americans are coping with, it's no wonder so many people viewed the site after seeing the Super Bowl ad. The narrator says it all:

Hold your breath. Hold it. Hold it. Keep holding. . . . At first you feel fine, then panic sets in. What you're feeling now is just like the financial stress that millions of us feel. It's like you're drowning. Meanwhile, big things. Little things. The moments that matter. Slip away ... SunTrust is about to help America catch its breath, by lighting the way to financial confidence. To help you to make smart choices to move forward, onward, and upward. So now, let go and breathe. . . . Feel that relief? Take the first step and join the movement, at onUp.com.[46]

Just after it launched onUp in February of 2016, SunTrust pledged to donate up to $250,000 to Operation HOPE. For each person who joined the movement through onUp.com, $1 was donated in support of HOPE's mission of economic empowerment. Operation HOPE is "the nation's first nonprofit financial services network for the underserved." Its founder, John Hope Bryant, has "rais[ed] and direct[ed] more than $2.5 billion in capital in urban, inner city and underserved communities since the 1992 Los Angeles riots." [47] In a press release, Bryant was quoted saying:

We commend SunTrust for raising awareness of financial stress in America, and doing something positive about it. ... This issue affects people of all income levels, and everyone can take action to better manage their finances. We are pleased that the initial sign-ups—up to a quarter million—will benefit the programs of Operation HOPE, where we work to advance financial literacy every day.[48]

In May of 2016, SunTrust launched a financial fitness program for businesses. Targeted to employees of companies, the initiative is a signature element of the onUp movement. SunTrust piloted the program internally with its own employees, a majority of whom did not feel financially confident themselves, despite working in a bank. The bank then bought the intellectual property for the program it had developed for its employees, offering it to other companies at no cost for the first year.[49]

Anyone—not just customers of the bank—can join onUp. While many things in life are out of our control, the program guides those who join the movement to see that many things are in their control—particularly becoming a good steward of their own money, no matter how modest their means. Since it launched in 2016, more than one million people have registered on onUp's website.

Wealth Management for Everyone, Regardless of Income Level

Incorporating things like quality of life, giving back, and creating meaningful moments and life experiences, onUp positions wealth in its biggest context. Its tone of voice avoids jargon and is very real: warm, conversational, intimate, understanding. After signing up online, you receive a friendly affirmation stating: "Nice work! You're one step closer to financial confidence." The site's tools are segmented by life stage or event—making it super simple for users to find resources and solutions. Even the Mental Wealth Quiz subtly invokes a paradigm shift, hinting that "wealth" may be less about money and assets and more about your individual perspective on money, coupled with your quest for things that bring you fulfillment, including peace of mind. Importantly, onUp doesn't shy away from potentially sensitive issues—such as paying down credit card debt—which it tackles in an open, nonjudgmental manner. Together, these elements endow the program with more relevance and resonance than traditional wealth management.

Consulting for a number of financial services firms over the years, I've conducted related qualitative and quantitative research with countless numbers of people. I don't recall many people trawling through traditional financial services collateral or websites to find the information they were seeking with any gusto. The "Real Stories" tab of the onUp website, for example, encourages just this. It opens with the subheading "Money Bloggers Get Real and Tell All: Bloggers share real stories that provide real-world tips you can apply to your financial picture. For. Real." It thereby motivates members of the movement to stick around, look around, read, interact, think, investigate more, and reflect.[50]

The onUp and SunTrust ethos is best summarized in a quote on the SunTrust Foundation's website:

> Our motivation of Lighting the Way to Financial Well-Being goes beyond our clients. We have a responsibility as community leaders to help drive those communities, and the people who live in them, forward to a life of financial strength. We're committed to using our position to help people start along their path to financial confidence— helping create flourishing, financially literate citizens across our footprint. This purpose is what drives us. It focuses our actions. It sets our goals. We believe that everyone can achieve the financial confidence to pursue a life well spent. We believe we can help them get there.[51]

Through onUp, SunTrust has engendered trust and brought the second part of its name to life. The program delivers a listening ear and empathy, placing SunTrust in the role of a trusted advisor to those who join their movement.

ACTIVE LISTENING:
TUNE IN TO WHAT PEOPLE WANT—AMAZON

SunTrust reaped great benefits from its conversations with 190,000 people and 8,000 businesses. The brand was genuinely interested in getting to know its customers holistically and better understand their hopes, dreams, and fears. Brands that invest time listening to customers, employees, and other stakeholders, and then acting on what they learn, more readily foster trust. Listening requires more than monitoring people's response rates to campaigns or new product and service initiatives and then using algorithms to determine what to send them next. Listening necessitates a human touch and empathy in order to build faith. It helps a brand appreciate customers and employees as individual people, not just members of market segments or niches with similar metric profiles.

The idea of listening is not new. However, it has received newfound attention over the past few years with the focus on big data. *Big data*, as a term, has become muddled as it's permeated the media. Although big data simply means pedabytes or huge amounts of data, it has come to symbolize analyzing these large volumes, the information technology and processes used to do this, and/or the business intelligence that comes from it, with the aim of such endeavors being to reduce—if not eliminate—risk in decision making. Without a doubt, big data expands a company's knowledge of its customers. It helps develop products and services that match a brand's current and potential customers' needs and behaviors and can provide insight to more meaningfully connect with stakeholders.

Even with big data, though, people are needed, at least for now. People develop the programs that process the information, analyze and predict behaviors, test hypotheses, and determine the final decisions that make big data science successful—or not. And people, not machines, understand the context for the psychological and cultural factors that influence our lifestyles and relationships with brands. Context is essential to identify patterns and understand the interconnectedness of trends. Without an understanding of the social and cultural context at the end of 2011, as a smaller-scale example, we would never have seen the emerging model of Brand Citizenship when analyzing our *CultureQ* data. Without context about your customers and the environment in which they're interacting with you, big data will fast become "dumb" data.

Human Intuition and Connecting the Dots

Through online analytics, brands now have enormous amounts of knowledge about who we are. Yet a large majority don't use this access to cultivate deeper relationships with their customers. Participants in our *CultureQ* research project expect brands that track them to know more about them, as a close friend would—the quirks and idiosyncrasies that make them unique individuals, not members of market segments, no matter how niche-oriented or small these groupings may be. Knowing marketers are collecting enormous amounts of personal data, and people's expectations for how brands should interact with them are growing. They expect more than products, services, and customized banner ads. They expect free content based on their interests that, like SunTrust's onUp, helps them achieve their goals or do things in new ways.

Give to Give—Not Give to Get

Amazon is the largest e-tailer in the United States. A ME brand, it made e-commerce trustworthy in its early days as a bookseller by providing a straightforward shopping experience and reliable customer service through big data analysis. Amazon knows what types of books we like, movies we watch, and products we buy, and, I'd bet, it would likely be better able than Facebook, for example, to profile what type of consumer each of us is. Whereas most of us carefully curate what we post and like on Facebook to reflect the things we want friends and colleagues to know about us, we filter what we buy on Amazon based on preference, price, and delivery time rather than how we wish to be perceived. Yet with all its knowledge about our habits and an excellent reputation for trustworthy service, Amazon serves customers mostly on a functional—not an emotional—level. To embody both ME and WE sensibilities and to move forward and back along the five steps of Brand Citizenship, Amazon should apply its expertise in analytics to foster more personal relationships and establish itself as more of a benevolent friend, not just as a boundless utility.

Jeff Bezos, Amazon's founder and CEO, is widely known for being obsessed with customers and continually demonstrates how listening is a successful long-term loyalty strategy. In July of 1994, Bezos launched Amazon with the mission "to be Earth's most customer-centric company; to build a place where people can come to find and discover anything they might want to buy online."[52] It was a clear value proposition that set the stage for Amazon's growth. In 2000, when the Internet 1.0

bubble was bursting, Bezos was repositioning Amazon from a seller of books to a seller of everything from A to Z and, alongside this, rebranding the company with a new logo—one designed to include a smile. Happy employees. Happy customers. Happy investors. They all add up to the Amazon Smile.

Using Big Data to Interpret Customer Needs

Nine years later, shortly after Amazon purchased the shoe retailer Zappos, Bezos emphasized the importance of listening to customers in a video posted on YouTube. As Bezos sincerely and passionately tells us, obsession over customers "is the only reason [Amazon] exist[s] today in any form. We've always put customers first. When given the choice of obsessing over competitors or obsessing over customers, we always obsess over customers." He went on, "We really like to start with customers and work backwards. . . . [I]t will cover a lot of errors." He then continued, "It's not a customer's job to invent for themselves. You need to listen to customers. It's critical. If you don't listen to customers, you will go astray. But they won't tell you everything and so you need to invent on their behalf." And Amazon is famous for listening to its customers and inventing on their behalf in large part through its usage of big data.[53]

Although Amazon's rationale for purchasing Zappos was never made perfectly clear, Zappos is legendary for its customer service, supported by a happy-employee culture. In an article deconstructing the purchase, Mashable hypothesized that Jeff Bezos was attracted by Zappos's customer centricity, unique culture, and people—its leaders and its employees.[54] When comparing Zappos's core values with Amazon's leadership principles, it's easy to agree with Mashable's assessment. Zappos's core values suggest a more human, friendly, and unguarded culture, whereas Amazon's leadership principles represent a more hard-driving, almost mechanistic data orientation.

AMAZON'S LEADERSHIP PRINCIPLES VERSUS ZAPPO'S CORE VALUES

AMAZON'S LEADERSHIP PRINCIPLES[55]

- Customer obsession
- Invent and simplify
- Leaders are right—a lot
- Learn and be curious
- Hire and develop
- Insist on the highest standards
- Think big
- Frugality
- Bias for action
- Earn trust
- Dive deep
- Have backbone
- Deliver results

ZAPPOS'S CORE VALUES[56]

- Deliver wow through service
- Embrace and drive change
- Create fun and a little weirdness
- Be adventurous, creative, and open-minded
- Pursue growth and learning
- Build open and honest relationships with communication
- Build a positive team and family spirit
- Do more with less
- Be passionate and determined
- Be humble

Prime. Prime Now. Prime Day. Prime Pantry. And thirteen-minute drone delivery. For all its convenience and listening to the customer, seven years after it acquired Zappos, Amazon still seems to be more of a public utility than a close brand friend like Zappos—even for its most loyal users. Participants in our *CultureQ* research chose Amazon as a leadership or favorite brand for more functional reasons than they did other leadership or—most especially—*favorite* brands, even including Walmart. For the majority who named Amazon, their reasons included reliability, serviceability, and scope. A smaller number also recognized it as inventive and pioneering. They said:

> Amazon is a leader. It was the first to revolutionize online shopping and gets me things in two days, although a lot of people do that now.

Their model of business has revolutionized the economy, and is adaptable throughout the world.

They are the #1 online retailer. Their Kindle product is innovative.

On the rise for sales, shipping methods and excellent customer service.

Great service for an online company.

Challenges to Forging a Connection with Customers

Amazon's reported lack of responsibility toward employees dampened the more emotional connection a few participants desired to have with the brand. As one explained, "I love the ease, especially with my Amazon Prime account. But I am concerned with its ethics of warehouse labor after reading an exposé on it."

In 2013, the British Broadcasting Corporation (BBC) exposed poor warehouse working conditions and an emphasis on efficiency over worker health and well-being.[57] Articles like this have had a lasting impact on a growing number of socially conscious shoppers' perceptions of Amazon, in the vein of similar negative coverage about Walmart, most notably because it was supported with additional evidence of a culture focused on outcomes at the expense of people. In August of 2015, *The New York Times* published a more controversial piece, "Inside Amazon: Wrestling Big Ideas in a Bruising Workplace," which detailed a white-collar workplace culture focused on pushing people "past their limits"—something that reportedly inspired some workers and relentlessly broke others.[58]

The article—and "An Amazonian's response," posted by a software developer named Nick Ciubotariu on LinkedIn—received so much attention that Jeff Bezos himself felt compelled to send a counterpoint to Amazon employees that he linked to *The New York Times*.[59,60] In his message, Bezos firmly stated that the "shockingly callous management practices" and "soulless, dystopian workplace where no fun is had and no laughter heard" are not part of the Amazon he knows. In the interest of full disclosure, I should also mention the people I've met who work for or with Amazon love the company.

However, after reading all the press, it's hard not to wonder if they're the exception or the norm. As Margaret Sullivan, who was Public Editor for the paper when the *Times* article was published, added in an opinion piece that was printed a few days later: "Many of Amazon's techniques and policies are common at other tech companies, and other companies in general. That kind of context was supplied later in an article on the front-page of the following Tuesday's *Times* about the 'relentless pace at elite companies' in America."[61] So why are people so keen to believe the negative perspectives on Amazon's culture more than the positive ones?

Barriers to Effective Listening: Secrecy and a Lack of Trust

One answer may be secrecy. While Google's corporate culture has become a benchmark for large corporations worldwide, the general public knows very little about Amazon's culture and campus. As Jodi Kantor and David Streitfeld, the coauthors of the "Inside Amazon" article themselves state, "Tens of millions of Americans know Amazon as customers, but life inside its corporate offices is largely a mystery. Secrecy is required; even low-level employees sign a lengthy confidentiality agreement."[62] Another clue may be found by reviewing *CultureQ* insights into how good Brand Citizens cultivate trust. Participants' comments about Amazon indicate that the brand exhibits lower levels of sincerity and reciprocity. While Jeff Bezos appears genuine in the numerous YouTube videos I've viewed, the Amazon brand experience doesn't include a personal tone of voice—his or anyone else's. Indeed, other than as a platform for effective purchasing, Amazon itself doesn't interact much with its customers, and it tends to give only to get.

Amazon customers pay to join Prime, the company's loyalty program, which motivates them to buy more from the company through free, two-day delivery and a streaming service of select movies, music, and other benefits. Forrester estimates that Amazon loses more than $1 billion in shipping charges to Prime customers who first pay $99 to join and then spend 240 percent more than nonmembers—an average of $1,200 per year in purchases per customer, compared to $500 per year.[63] Consumer Intelligence Research Partners further estimates that the company has 63 million Prime members in the United States, significantly more than the 1.4 million needed to break even on Prime, using Forrester's figures.[64] Given the scope of what it sells, Amazon has countless opportunities to offer free content beyond product reviews. Alongside the free movies and music, Amazon could potentially offer Prime customers select free news through Bezos's purchase of *The Washington Post*.

An Attempt to Recognize the Greater Good

Amazon rolled out AmazonSmile in October of 2013 to help customers who register for the service feel as though their purchases are contributing to the greater good. Like everything at Amazon, AmazonSmile is easy, offering an automatic way to support your favorite charity every time you shop. As both a brand consultant and consumer, I was enthusiastic when I first read about its launch and registered for it immediately. I quickly discovered, however, that the experience, including my Amazon Prime delivery time, was identical to the base Amazon brand. The only difference was an AmazonSmile logo in the upper right-hand corner. Most notably, Amazon didn't include the amount I "donated" to the organization I chose on my purchase confirmation. After I calculated the amount based on what I had bought, I realized this was probably because the 0.5 percent of the purchase price donated equals a very small amount. For example, only 25¢ would be donated from a $50 purchase and $5 from a $1,000 one. Later, I also grasped that I, as the purchaser, was not making the donation. Rather, Amazon was making it through its foundation and thereby taking the tax deduction.

A number of nonprofit experts criticized AmazonSmile when it was launched, noting that the positive feelings it creates among customers who use it potentially deter them from crunching the numbers and calculating the actual amount given to charity. Instead, most customers simply assume that a more substantial sum from their purchase is being contributed—likely deduced from their having previously, independently donated more to that same organization of their choice. Despite my reservations, I continue to use AmazonSmile when I buy things—that is, when I remember to. And each time I've forgotten, I think, "I should have typed smile.amazon.com instead of amazon.com" and am a little frustrated that Amazon doesn't always automatically redirect me to the AmazonSmile page. Every once in a while and by no means consistently, a message pops up reminding me to go to AmazonSmile when I haven't.

Amazon's advertising has been predominantly product focused. And, some have said, Amazon Echo with its artificial intelligence and virtual assistant named Alexa was developed to sell more products on Amazon, despite its not offering an Amazon.com shopping experience. So I was surprised to see Amazon's 2016 Christmas advertisement when I was in the UK. British Christmas ads are the equivalent of Superbowl ads in the United States. People anticipate their arrival, and many are "leaked" to the press or launched on YouTube in advance of being viewed on television. This specific ad, *A Priest and Imam Meet for a Cup of Tea*, which aired in the UK, the United States, and Germany, was centered on a sensitive subject—interfaith friendship between a Christian vicar and a Muslim imam—at a politically charged time after Donald Trump, then the U.S. president-elect, had promoted banning Muslims from entering America.

It opens with an imam visiting a friend—the vicar. As they sit on the sofa to enjoy a cup of tea, they joke about their aging knees, and as the imam prepares to leave, they laugh again knowing how painful it is to stand up. After the imam leaves, the vicar opens his Amazon Prime app, not knowing the imam is doing the very same thing. An Amazon delivery man then arrives at each of their homes with the identical gift of knee pads. The ad ends with each kneeling pain free, thanks to his new knee pads.[65]

Cognizant of the issues the ad might raise, a spokesman for Amazon told the British newspaper *The Independent*, they were sensitive in their casting. "[T]he gentleman playing the vicar is a practising vicar in London, the gentleman playing the imam is a devout Muslim and the principal of a Muslim school. We used an actual church and mosque for our scenes within the places of worship."[66] Like other Amazon Prime ads, *A Priest and Imam Meet for a Cup of Tea* shows how the brand helps us easily solve everyday problems. Unlike others, however, this one portrays an unexpected and selfless friendship, which makes it possible that Amazon was seeking to make a political statement to demonstrate that it has a heart and/or is concerned about a potentially divisive social climate.

In September of 2016, Walmart acquired Jet.com, an online shopping site that uses a mix of money-saving techniques to try to woo shoppers away from Amazon.[67] Having named Marc Lore, founder and CEO of Jet.com, as president and CEO of Walmart eCommerce in the United States, it's possible that Walmart may win back some of its customers who switched over to Amazon for convenience as it integrates Jet.com into its operations, especially if it more closely associates the Jet.com brand with the Walmart brand name and/or identity. As Lore states in the official notice announcing the completed acquisition, "Together we will be stronger and move even faster to reimagine the future of shopping."[68] Even though a notable number of participants in *CultureQ* research faulted Walmart for their treatment of their employees, our three years of research demonstrated that participants had a greater emotional attachment to Walmart than they did to Amazon.

Amazon's recent interfaith Christmas ad may however be signaling that the company recognizes it needs to be known as more than a big data behemoth looking to sell goods in every market category. It may demonstrate a cognizance that Amazon will win more fans and loyal customers by blending its commercial ambitions with a meaningful social mission. To enrich peoples' lives, a brand needs to do more than reduce delivery time. It needs to freely give more to its customers, the greater global community, and the greater good.

HIGHLIGHTS

CHAPTER 4:
Trust

► Trust is the starting point, not the endgame, for brand loyalty.

► Five characteristics are essential for earning lasting trust from customers, employees, and stakeholders: clarity, reliability, sincerity, reciprocity, and active listening.

► To nurture trust, mega-brands, like Walmart that have had reputational issues must be clear about why they exist and how they create meaningful social value to win trust with stakeholders.

► Reliability is a cornerstone of trust, and brands like Chipotle that strive to lead in the area of product development and delivery can face challenges as their ambitious goals benchmark them against higher standards.

► When a brand expresses a distinguishing character in everything it does, like Trader Joe's, it establishes a sincere connection with customers and reaps the benefits in terms of loyalty.

► Digital communications and information channels have made reciprocity a requirement for trusted brands. Farrow & Ball and SunTrust both discovered ways to give customers unexpected and worthwhile benefits that reflected their brand purpose and increased their brand strength.

► Brands that use big data to actively listen and establish emotional relationships reap the deep trust that characterizes true faithfulness; brands, like Amazon, that use analytics only to cross-sell are viewed more as potentially replaceable, albeit highly useful, utilities than as close friends.

CHAPTER 5

ENRICHMENT

Enhance Daily Life

*Make every day faster, easier,
better, and more inspiring.*

In an era of continuous technological innovation, being new and improved is not enough to capture market share. People take more notice of—and are less price sensitive to—brands that understand the things that are important to them individually, help them to simplify their routines, make mundane tasks less dull, and thereby make day-to-day living more manageable. Brands at Step 2 of Brand Citizenship understand that we're all stressed and therefore relish support and encouragement from others.

Advancing technology is overwhelming us with accessibility and information, even as it simultaneously simplifies how we do things. As machinery and equipment offer unlimited access to entertainment, knowledge, global communities, and more, they also escalate our need to be continuously connected, adaptive, and efficient. When we're disconnected, we fear we're missing out on something important—be it a news event, a friend's party, or something else. Just as we've mastered a new device, app, or software program, we're notified of an upgrade that requires us to learn a new way of doing things. And, nearly every day, our significant other, child, boss, or colleague tells us about a new tool that will help us to be even more productive at home or the office.

Despite how it sometimes feels, productivity is all about working smarter, not harder. In economic or business terms, it's related to output. In fact, productivity is defined by a simple equation:

$$Productivity = Output/Input$$

As technology has melded our personal lives with our professional ones, more and more people are looking to unite joy with productivity. We gain a sense of enrichment, contribution, and pride when we do something well. When we enjoy accomplishing a task, we are more productive. So it's no surprise that participants in *CultureQ* research told us they steadfastly rely on brands that help their daily lives flow more smoothly.

They're loyal to products and services that they trust to *efficiently accomplish daily tasks, achieve their goals,* and, as a necessary bonus, *make everyday life more joyful.* Brands positioned at Step 2 of Brand Citizenship improve and enhance our everyday lives, even in simple ways. Through their products and services, their communications, and/or their digital content, they integrate themselves into our routines and even help us to more willingly complete chores, thereby making everyday living more inspired. Brands at Step 2 recognize the things that are important to us, and make us feel more esteemed as individuals. Like Step 1, Step 2 is all about ME.

ENRICHING ROUTINES WITH LOVE

Brands at Step 2 of Brand Citizenship are characterized by self-awareness, appreciate the things we desire as people rather than view us as members of market segments, and use this insight to cultivate highly relevant and relatable products and services. They use their understanding of the tasks we are trying to accomplish and our lifestyle aspirations to deliver brand experiences, not just product features and benefits. Brands at Step 2 do not define themselves based on where they sit on a shelf or by their technical product category. They identify first and foremost with the experience people are seeking when using them.

I first learned the importance of this in the early 1990s working at a start-up marketing consultancy on the Instant Quaker Oatmeal brand. Instant Quaker Oatmeal is a trusted brand that has simplified routines for mothers since its inception. A ready-to-eat hot cereal, it often sits on a store shelf next to ready-to-eat—or what one might call cold—breakfast cereals. In the late 1980s, General Mills introduced a competitive cereal called Swirlers that gained a notable share of the instant oatmeal market. General Mills's Oatmeal Swirlers was a shorter-lived product that came with a packet of fruit-flavored jam you could swirl on the oatmeal before eating it. Although it was a lot of fun for children, our insight indicated that the novelty of swirling, or playing with, your oatmeal would wear off quickly. We guessed General Mills had created more of a promotional than a sustainable lift in sales. As Swirlers was discontinued, Instant Quaker Oatmeal's market share did not increase, as had been expected.

This was before today's big data analytics, and I personally spent countless hours combing through consumer tracking and store data, seeking to make sense of what was going on. After weeks of examining reams of reports, most of which compared Instant Quaker Oatmeal sales to those of cold children's cereals and cold healthy cereals, I had a hypothesis. What if Instant Quaker Oatmeal wasn't a substitute for cold cereal—either children's or healthy? What if Swirlers had picked up ready-to-eat cereal users who liked sweeter or novelty cold cereals, and these people were not even Instant Quaker Oatmeal users?

Having no budget for market research and a report due to the client in two weeks, my boss agreed to conduct a small-scale, anecdotal study to test my hypothesis. We interviewed about twenty-five pairs of mothers and children under six who were users of Instant Quaker Oatmeal, seeking to learn what breakfast time was like in their house on weekdays (for some people, it was on the go in their car), weekends, normal days, and special days. We also had them tell us everything they ate for breakfast—from Instant Quaker Oatmeal, to Wheaties, to Snickers bars, to fruit, pancakes, and scrambled eggs and bacon. Then, we separated the children from their mothers and had each tell us the things they ate for breakfast based on how they categorized them. They could have as many or as few categories as they chose. It quickly emerged that the experience of eating Instant Quaker Oatmeal was not at all like that of eating cold cereal, especially for the children. In the children's eyes, Instant Quaker Oatmeal's purpose truly was special. They told us things like:

Mommy makes it when daddy can't make me pancakes.

Mommy makes it because she wants to keep me warm.

Daddy makes it before he leaves on a business trip.

For the children we interviewed, Instant Quaker Oatmeal wasn't in the same category as other cereals. It was a meal that showed them their parents cared about their welfare and loved them. For the mothers, Instant Quaker Oatmeal was easier to make than traditional oatmeal, a healthy food, not a cereal, and a way for parents to care for their children and show them how much they loved them. Although General Mills's Oatmeal Swirlers incorporated product features that made a mundane ritual like eating breakfast cereal more fun for children, Instant Quaker Oatmeal enriched a family's day in a way other cereals did not. It was a trusted brand that fostered connection and faithfulness by adding greater meaning to a routine event, something Swirlers hadn't achieved.

Brands that deliver Step 2 of Brand Citizenship create holistic, integrated experiences. From a product's or service's look, feel, and communications to the user's experience with these things, they underpin relevance with more than product features. In this chapter, I'll explore Mrs. Meyer's Clean Day, Burt's Bees, Plum Organics®, and IKEA, brands that participants in my company's *CultureQ* research named as enhancing their daily lives. These brands, which represent products as diverse as household cleaners, personal care items, organic foods for babies and toddlers, and home furnishings, succeed in enriching and enhancing daily life while promoting deep brand loyalty.

MRS. MEYER'S CLEAN DAY: MAKING CHORES MORE ENJOYABLE

Monica Nassif founded The Caldrea Company in 1999 and began producing Mrs. Meyers in 2000. As the story goes, Nassif, who had been a marketing consultant for fifteen years, was frustrated by the toxic chemicals and harsh scents of standard cleaning products, as well as the mediocre performance of those with eco labels. During a visit to Atlanta, she had an *aha!* moment after seeing a pallet of household cleaners in a store. All the bottles were unattractive, and she suddenly realized that it didn't have to be this way. That "cleaning products could be created and marketed much like personal care and cosmetics—delightfully fragranced, earth friendly, hard-working and beautifully packaged." Nassif wrote a one-page business plan on her plane ride home from Atlanta.[1]

Named for her mother, Mrs. Thelma Meyer, who is described as a practical homemaker and mother of nine, Mrs. Meyer's Clean Day products were initially conceived as a more affordable brand of aromatherapeutic cleaning products than Nassif's signature Caldrea line, which includes home and body care products. With scents reminiscent of Mrs. Thelma A. Meyer's garden, the brand is folksy, eco-friendly, retro, and hipster all rolled into one. Mrs. Meyer's quirkiness stands out in the overcrowded household products aisle, even in more niche, socially conscious markets like Whole Foods Market. Beginning with its theme, "Hardworking Homekeeping," the brand's packaging captures you with engaging copy that balances content and information.

Bringing the Past to the Present

Simple, supportive line drawings look almost as if they've stepped out of a bygone era, one that in an age of automation is comforting to connect with. With a brand purpose centered on the idea that caring for our homes should be as enjoyable as spending time in them, the Mrs. Meyer's brand could potentially be seen as old-fashioned. Yet, even with its focus on making housekeeping more delightful, its nostalgia is decidedly modern. Reflective of Nassif's wishes when founding Caldrea, the packaging is beautiful, simple, and chic—more like a desirable cosmetic than a household cleaning product. As perfumes, Mrs. Meyer's scents—basil, lavender, lemon verbena, geranium, rosemary, baby blossom, honeysuckle, apple, parsley—might come off as dated. However, in household cleaners, they're decidedly ecological. *CultureQ* participants who used the dish soap, all-purpose spray cleaner, or laundry detergent described a level of clean they didn't initially expect from an earth-friendly brand, something that excites devoted fans. Mrs. Meyer's speaks to users in an emotive way that inspires them not to mind as much the scrubbing, mopping, and sweeping that are a part of weekly chores. One Millennial participant aptly summarized a number of participants' perceptions: "Mrs. Meyers Clean Day is sassy, classy and young. It makes cleaning fun, and doesn't smell like traditional cleaning products. It has an artisanal feel."

Mrs. Meyer's design and marketing communications agencies—Werner Design Werks and Hanson Dodge Creative—developed a voice, values, and story for the brand based on Mrs. Thelma A. Meyer herself. Although the Mrs. Meyer's brand is not unique in crafting communications with a person in mind, its agencies were very fortunate to have an actual individual for inspiration rather than a fictional one contrived in the studio. Like the people who buy the products carrying her name, Mrs. Thelma A. Meyer genuinely cares about her home, her family, and the environment. She's a decidedly real, likable mother and grandmother—a nonperfectionist homemaker who balances the need for cleanliness with a happy, lived-in home—whose story is told across the brand's marketing communications.

Like many of the brand's fans, Mrs. Thelma A. Meyer is practical. She knows "cleaning is something that just has to get done, so there's more time to enjoy family and friends."[2] Mrs. Meyer's Clean Day was developed for people who are looking to make a chore just a bit more pleasant. They know cleaning is necessary and love the idea that Mrs. Meyer's scent compels them to feel better about it. They don't want their family exposed to harsh chemicals and love that Mrs. Meyer's gentler formula is efficacious. They care about the environment and animals and love that Mrs. Meyer's products don't hurt the earth and aren't tested on animals. The small percentage of synthetic product ingredients don't trouble Mrs. Meyer's fans. They trust that the brand is doing its best on their behalf and is upfront about the purity of its ingredients, despite some activists' claims otherwise. Like Mrs. Thelma A. Meyer and the brand's target audience, Mrs. Meyer's Clean Day is responsible, balancing the pros and cons of natural ingredients with the efficacy of its products.

Products are made of naturally derived ingredients when possible, and the brand chooses safe synthetics when it is not. Their liquid cleansers don't contain ammonia, chlorine, or phosphates, and they are biodegradeable.[3] The packaging is recyclable, and Mrs. Meyer's is a member of the Leaping Bunny program, an international campaign focused on eliminating testing on animals for cosmetics, personal care, and household products.[4] The brand can be summed up by words like *hard work*, *generosity, neighborliness, sincerity*, and *appealing*. Fans are indifferent as to whether or not the brand's voice and backstory were retrofitted or whether the brand is becoming too commercial as it broadens its distribution in mass merchandisers. They love the holistic experience that speaks to them in real ways on many levels. As Kim Chisholm, the company's former vice president of marketing, told *Fast Company* in 2011: "We add a bit of delight to the rituals that take place in your home."[5]

In 2008, SC Johnson acquired Caldrea and added the Mrs. Meyer's line to its portfolio of brands that includes well-known consumer brands such as Ziploc® bags, Windex®, Pledge®, Raid®, and Kiwi® shoe polish.[6] In 2014, after doubling in size over five years, Mrs. Meyer's operations were further integrated into SC Johnson when it relocated from its longtime headquarters in Minneapolis, Minnesota, to Racine, Wisconsin.[7] Importantly, the move was transparent to Mrs. Meyer's users and did not result in a shift in the brand's purpose or persona.

Fostering Community Through Social Media

Although Mrs. Meyer's has a ME-oriented purpose, its personality has a social conscience that easily enables it to move back and forth across all five steps of Brand Citizenship. In 2013, the brand began to effectively use social media initiatives to further enrich its fans' lives, fostering community based on celebrating two things the brand holds dear: our homes and nature.

MRS. MEYER'S INITIATIVES CELEBRATING OUR HOMES AND NATURE

▶ It launched Grow Inspired, a content-oriented campaign developed to celebrate hardworking, generous people committed to helping others develop special and essential bonds with nature. The campaign included a national tour, a grant program to fund neighborhood community gardens, and a film series honoring real, caring people with vocations rooted in Mrs. Meyer's core values.[8]

▶ Hunt for a Homemaker was a 2015 contest that played off Mrs. Meyer's do-it-yourself (DIY) site, featuring experts such as Grace Bonney of Design Sponge, Maxwell Ryan of Apartment Therapy, and Paul Lowe of Sweet Paul. It encouraged entrants to "DIY something. Bake something. Grow something." The winner received a $75,000 prize and was featured alongside the experts.[9]

▶ In spring of 2016, Mrs. Meyer's joined forces with 800 people in Chicago and Minneapolis to celebrate Plant Something Day and make the world "a greener place" by gardening. To complement rolling up their sleeves and getting dirty, Mrs. Meyer's donated $10,000 to the American Community Gardening Association to support local community gardens in Minneapolis, Tulsa, St. Joseph, and Denver.[10]

▶ On Saturday, December 17, 2016, the brand celebrated Make Something Day. (Make Something Day has sometimes been associated with Black Friday, as an antidote to commercialism.) While the outward face of the initiative was craftwork, the bigger idea was to give people confidence in their own creativity and to help them experience childlike playfulness again and the wonder and joy that come from making things. The brand encouraged people to participate and submit their photos and projects—accompanied by the hashtag #makeandtell—a large number of which are featured on the DIY section of their website. Mrs. Meyer's Facebook page included video sessions to help kick-start fans to do projects.[11]

In March of 2014, Target introduced Made to Matter—Handpicked by Target, a collection of trustworthy brands designed to help customers more easily choose products that are "better" for them, their families, and the planet.[12] In February of 2015, Target added Mrs. Meyer's products to its list of featured brands, which also included Annie's Homegrown, Burt's Bees, Clif Bar, Seventh Generation, and others. Kathee Tesija, executive vice president and chief merchandising and supply chain officer at Target, told the Associated Press that brands featured in the program experienced a 30 percent increase in sales.[13] The number of people interested in eco-friendly products is clearly growing, as is the number of credible eco-friendly brands to choose from. With a ME-oriented brand purpose and a WE-oriented brand personality, Mrs. Meyer's stands out among such products as effectively bridging the best aspects of standard and eco products. It's no wonder its fans quickly became faithful and escalated the brand to the number three position in the eco category.

BURT'S BEES: THE IMPORTANCE OF AN ICON

With a company founder who is the subject of a 2013 documentary film and a brand purpose "to make people's lives better every day—naturally," Burt's Bees is a trustworthy ME brand that moves more determinedly across the five steps of Brand Citizenship than Mrs. Meyer's. Like Mrs. Meyer's, Burt's Bees has a homespun character reflective of the man whom it is named after. With a genuine, 1960s-era hippie, Burt Shavitz, as its founder, Burt's Bees offers natural, eco-friendly and highly efficacious products and has sustainability embedded in its core. Recyclable packaging made from recycled plastic. Responsible sourcing. And more. Today, the company's The Greater Good philosophy, which it publishes on its website for everyone to see, is central to how the brand behaves and engages users and other stakeholders, as well as to shaping its company culture.[14]

Built from Burt's Bees' triple-bottom-line-reporting focus on people, profit, and planet, The Greater Good forms a virtuous circle that frames how the brand plans to change the world: *Good for you. Good for us. Good for all.* Like the bees Burt Shavitz cared for, Burt's Bees is focused on "working hard on natural products that people love—and leaving only goodness behind."[15] It's easy for fans to be faithful to the brand and to feel good about buying its products.

The Role of Message and Design in Connecting People with Products

Incorporated in Maine in 1991, the year its famous lip balm was introduced, founders Burt Shavitz, a New Yorker turned beekeeper, and Roxanne Quimby, an artist and single mother of two, began selling candles made from leftover beeswax. Seven years earlier, Burt met Roxanne in 1984 while she was hitchhiking. They quickly became a couple and started selling a range of homemade products at craft fairs.[16,17] Roxane commissioned A. C. Kulik, a wood engraver who had a stall next to them, to design the company's labels, all of which the company continues to use today.[18] Although the brand's product line varied significantly—from honey, to dog biscuits, to candles, to Christmas ornaments—once introduced, the lip balm (which was a blend of beeswax and sweet almond oil) laid the foundation for the company to establish a niche in personal care products. Before organic and eco were a fixed part of popular culture, and long before brand stories were part of a marketer's arsenal, Roxanne clearly understood the role that simplicity of message and beauty of design played in connecting people with product narratives. With his beard and hat, Burt had a trustworthy—if not stereotypical—face of a granola-loving hippie. It was an authentic persona that would help to sell products and establish credibility. Envisioning this, Roxanne asked Kulick to carve Burt's image, which she then integrated into marketing materials. And, even more so than Mrs. Thelma A. Meyer, became a role model: Burt the icon was born.

In 1993, with sales greater than $3 million, the company moved to North Carolina to better handle its growing operations and that same year made the decision to focus only on personal care products. Burt and Roxanne soon had what's assumed to be a lovers' dispute of some sort. Burt returned to Maine, and Roxanne bought out his share of the company.[19,20] Within the next few years, the company grew significantly in size. Distribution channels for its personal care products expanded from Whole Foods Market and Cracker Barrel Old Country Store to more mainstream stores, such as Publix and Winn-Dixie, and internationally in Japan, Canada, and Europe. By 2003, the line included toothpaste, shampoo, and Baby Bee® baby products. At the same time, Roxanne chose to honor the company's roots and emphasize its brand purpose by preserving 185,000 acres of forest land in Maine through The Nature Conservancy.[21] In November 2003, AEA Investors bought an 80 percent share in the company, and three years later, in 2007, Clorox acquired Burt's Bees.[22, 23]

Instilling a Philosophy Across the Business

John Replogle, the company's CEO between 2006 and 2011, introduced The Greater Good to officially operationalize the company's purpose—and instill Burt's green philosophy across the business. Ensuring The Greater Good was more than words on a page, Replogle set policies that demanded follow-through on the company's green goals.[24] For example, employees' bonuses, in part, were based on how well the company met energy conservation goals, and the best parking spaces were reserved for hybrid cars and carpools. The company also bought offsets for 100 percent of its carbon emissions and set a goal of sending no trash to landfills by 2020. Under Replogle, Burt's Bees began to slide back and forth across the ME to WE continuum of Brand Citizenship, behaving responsibly while enriching users', employees', and stakeholders' lives alike.

The brand prioritized animal rights, responsible trade, employee benefits, and the environment alongside the natural origin of its ingredients and product performance. In a move to further live its purpose, Replogle established The Burt's Bees Greater Good Foundation in 2007. Dedicated to sustaining charitable grassroots initiatives supportive of human and honeybee health, the Foundation helps employees to do more, or "be bigger," than they can alone through funding and volunteer time in the local community of Durham North Carolina, and beyond. Replogle, who has since become CEO of Seventh Generation, saw Clorox's acquisition of the brand in 2007 as more than a financial opportunity. It was a means of scaling The Greater Good and a way for "Burt's Bees' 380 employees to influence the direction of Clorox, a company with influence that generated $4.8 billion in sales last year and employs 7,800 people."[25]

Since its acquisition by Clorox, Burt's Bees has remained highly responsible toward both the environment and its employees. The brand teamed up with the Natural Products Association and like-minded companies in 2008 to create a natural standard for natural personal care products that included a "Natural Seal" to certify items that are at least 95 percent natural and contain no ingredients known to be harmful. Actress Julianne Moore, a North Carolina native, mother, and proponent of natural products, raised awareness of the issue as part of Burt's Bees Voting Day, when she cast the first vote for natural on September 15,

2008. Moore encouraged Burt's Bees fans across the United States to make a conscious choice to use natural products and support the Natural Seal by voting online.[26] Anyone could vote, and voters also had the chance to win a limited C&C California for Burt's Bees T-shirt or a year's worth of product.[27]

Committing to Volunteerism

In 2009, Burt's Bees enriched its employee's lives, as well as the communities in which it operates, when it pioneered an employee volunteer program that fulfilled the company's goal to have 100 percent employee engagement in sustainability by 2020.[28] The company now holds an annual Culture Day to engage new and existing hires in the brand's values. Each year the event has a new theme that promotes community outreach and fraternity among employees and between employees and the local community.

In its marketing and advocacy efforts, Burt's Bees continues to use the same elements of storytelling that Roxanne first employed to captivate people. Like Mrs. Meyer's campaigns celebrating people who share the brand's values, the brand uses interactive Facebook programs featuring user-generated posts, photography, and video content. Ads that have featured real users, how they use Burt's Bees products, why they like them, and how long they've been buying them further engage loyal users to collaborate with the company and co-create the brand.[29]

Today, Burt's Bees maintains high levels of integrity, and Burt Shavitz, who passed on in 2015, continues to be a strong presence. The company is saving the converted turkey coop that Burt lived in in Maine, which it will move and display at its North Carolina headquarters.[30] Its Baby Bee and Mama Bee® lines have recently met the rigorous quality standards of Healthy Child Healthy World, a nonprofit focused on educating and motivating consumers to create cleaner, greener, safer environments for children and families. The Baby Bee line, which now contains only natural fragrances, is pediatrician- and dermatologist-tested. Baby Bee and Mama Bee and are both listed in the Healthy Child Healthy World's Shop Healthy guide, alongside brands such as The Honest Company, Plum Organics, Seventh Generation, and Way Better Snacks.[31] For Clorox, Burt's Bees is an iconographic and signature brand that adds to its product portfolio. As Jim Geikie, a longtime marketer for the company who became the general manager in May 2016, stated: "The whole purpose of the business is to reconnect people with the wisdom, power and beauty of nature. We think that's particularly important now as things become more urbanized, tech-driven and hurried."[32]

PLUM ORGANICS: BY PARENTS, FOR PARENTS

Like Monica Nassif of Mrs. Meyer's, Gigi Lee Chang had an *aha!* moment that later led her to create Plum Organics®. In 2004, Lee Chang was on holiday with her son, Cato, who was eight months old at the time. Cato, who had only been served homemade food until that time, wouldn't eat the packaged products his mother had brought for him. Curious to learn more, Lee Chang began to investigate the issue, uncovering two essential facts: (1) Our food preferences are formed by the time we're two years old, and (2) baby food had evolved very little since it was first developed, more than fifty years ago.

Coming from an advertising agency, with a strategic planning background, Lee Chang naturally began to ask deeper questions about the baby food market and to research the broader consumer perspective. As she spoke to people, she discovered it wasn't only about the flavor, texture, and integrity of the food. There was a whole psychology around parenting, confidence in the kitchen, and the relationship parents themselves have with food. Working women told her things like, "I don't make my own food, so how can I trust myself to make food for this most precious being?" They also openly admitted they thought the baby food sitting on store shelves was inferior and wouldn't even taste it themselves. Armed with this knowledge, Lee Chang set out to change the way that baby food was made at the time and the way that children eat—all in service to parents seeking to do the best they can for their children.[33]

How Values and Attributes Shape a Brand

Eventually connecting with someone in the natural food industry, Lee Chang jumped on the fast track and launched Plum Organics in five and a half months, including validating her initial suppositions in research.[34] Plum Organics was introduced at a trade show in March 2006, and by August of that year, the brand's frozen baby food products were being distributed in national stores like Whole Foods Market and smaller natural and organic grocery stores. In December of that same year, Plum Organics was named on *Entreprenuer's* 2006 Hot List of trends under the category of "healthy food."[35]

Lee Chang attributes much of the company's fast success to having a clearly defined brand purpose and personality from the start as she crafted her product offering:

> When I look back on it, the biggest success for me was the brand.... Today, when people learn I founded Plum and tell me all the things they love about it, I can ladder what they say back to the initial work I did with my brand agency putting down the values and attributes for Plum.[36]

By 2007, when Plum Organics became a B Corp, Lee Chang committed wholeheartedly to being a mission-driven company. (As discussed in detail in Chapter 2, B Corps—short for "benefit corporations"—are companies that adhere to the mandated regulations that come with certification in order to use the power of business to solve social and environmental problems.) For Lee Chang, B Corp certification was a natural step. It offered Plum the opportunity to be part of a community of like-minded brands. Lee Chang explained that being part of a movement that represented the evolving landscape for business was important to Plum. As a B Corp, the company gained access to partners that shared its values, supply chain innovations, and evolved thinking on the future of workplaces.

Late in 2008, the Nest Collective, an accelerator for wellness food brands for children, acquired Plum Organics. Sheryl O'Loughlin and Neil Grimmer founded Nest Collective (Nest). (Neil eventually became the president and CEO of Plum, Inc. and is now chairman of Plum PBC.) Like Lee Chang, O'Loughlin and Grimmer were food-conscious parents searching for food for their children that resonated with their own tastes and lifestyle. At the time of the Plum Organics acquisition, Nest had launched its own healthy kids snack portfolio under the brand name Revolution Foods. The two businesses were founded on similar principles and produced complementary product lines. Revolution products included organic lunchbox snacks and meals for children, and Plum Organics's line centered on organic, culinarily inspired baby food for three stages of development and sustainably produced meal and snack solutions for toddlers. For Lee Chang, Nest was "a place to nurture a larger vision, while staying true to the heart and soul" of Plum Organics.[37]

Innovation in Packaging, Ingredients, and Education

Nest's philosophy for Plum Organics's success was simple: meet the needs of the modern parent through innovative packaging and ingredients. By partnering with Nest, Plum Organics contributed to the progress of the entire industry when it introduced spouted pouches, which are convenient, portable, and better for the environment. Lighter and smaller than jars, pouches use less fuel for transport and thereby have a smaller carbon footprint.[38] Founded in part on the notion that food is critical to a child's development, since its inception, Plum Organics has gone beyond the standard offerings—like carrots, green beans, and pears—of traditional baby food lines. The brand offers ingredients and culinary combinations unique to packaged baby and children's foods. Offerings include things like Greek yogurt, purple carrots, roasted pumpkin, and coconut rice, all of which aid in developing an infant's palate and appreciation for a wide range of healthy food. This is what Plum calls "nutritional intelligence," which helps to cultivate an appreciation in young children for a wide range of foods.[39]

Based on their own experiences, Lee Chang, O'Loughlin, and Grimmer all felt that most pediatricians—when discussing phases of early childhood development—talk with parents about milestones such as when their baby sits up, walks, and talks; when parents introduce solid foods into their baby's diet; and what a child is eating when she is too heavy or too thin. However, many pediatricians fail to also discuss the role that food nutrition plays in human development. Created for parents, by parents, Plum strives to teach parents that food nutrition and variety are essential to early childhood development. The brand takes the fact that food nourishes our bodies and minds very seriously and does everything it can to make products better—which means great tasting and more nutritious, so babies and children want to eat Plum meals at all stages.[40]

Today the company's food philosophy continues to be central to product innovation. When developing new offerings, traditional consumer-packaged-goods companies often "know" what consumers are looking for and what they're willing to pay. Their business models aim to maximize product margins by delivering the expected value to consumers—and not more than that. Plum's Senior Vice President of Brand Marketing and Innovation Ben Mand passionately declares Plum Organics is *different*. Mand says:

> We approach it totally differently. Parents don't always know what's important for their little ones. They're really confused, and ask, "What do I need to feed my child?" It's very hard, especially for first-time parents, to know if they're doing things right. It's our job to know what's important for their little ones: What their nutritional needs are. How this impacts their development. Which nutrients to include. Which flavors to bring together. We call this knowledge nutritional intelligence. Even if some consumers don't know this is important, it's our job to get it in there. And then it's our job to help make them aware of the importance through education and marketing.[41]

Profitability Through Purpose

The year 2013 was a turning point for the Plum Organics brand in many ways: At the end of the first quarter, the brand introduced its social impact program The Full Effect®, and, by the end of the second quarter, it had been acquired by a multinational corporation. Through The Full Effect, Plum Organics bettered society and simultaneously enriched its users' experience with the brand by enabling them to be part of an initiative that reflected something that mattered to them: enhancing the lives of less fortunate children. After a private screening at Plum's headquarters of *A Place at the Table*, Participant Media's critically acclaimed 2012 documentary on food insecurity in America, Plum CEO Neil Grimmer was moved to do something. Alongside Plum's pediatric advisor Dr. Alan Greene and various organizations in the nonprofit, antihunger community, Plum developed a Super Smoothie specifically as an in-kind donation for babies and toddlers who don't know where their next healthy meal is coming from—the technical term for which is food insecurity. Food-insecure families also contributed to the creation of the Super Smoothie.

Filled with nutrients and super fruits, the Super Smoothie was the central feature of The Full Effect. Partnering with Perseus Books Group, Magnolia Pictures, and Participant Media, Plum first invited consumers to help them in nourishing food-insecure babies and toddlers. During the film's opening weekend, March 1–3, 2013, Plum donated one organic Super Smoothie pouch to a baby or toddler in need for every movie ticket sold, every online download of the film purchased, and every copy of the companion book and ebook sold. The campaign, which was meant to simultaneously raise awareness about food insecurity, while providing a solution, generated 100,000 pouches donated in total.[42] In April of 2013, Plum announced that it would distribute 500,000 Super Smoothies to communities in need. Since then Plum has continued to evolve the program and has united with parents who buy its products to help solve food insecurity across America. Plum partners with a number of nonprofits, including Baby Buggy, Conscious Alliance, Convoy of Hope, and Homeless Prenatal Program, among others.[43]

Between the launch of The Full Effect in 2013 and 2015, Plum donated a total of 10 million products and 1.6 million Super Smoothies. United with parents and fans, the brand continues to evolve the program and the foods it covers with the aim of solving food insecurity in America and, ultimately, across the globe. As it shares in its *Mission Report 2015*, The Full Effect helps Plum foster a more meaningful relationship with employees:

> Donating large volumes of the same organic food we sell costs something, but yields much more in return (the love and loyalty of our team and consumers top that list). As Neil says, business is personal. We count ourselves lucky to get to work every day on a mission we're each personally invested in (and to challenge "business as usual" a little along the way, too).[44]

In June of 2013, Campbell Soup Company (Campbell), which owns brands such as Campbell's®, Pepperidge Farm®, and V8®, completed its acquisition of Plum Organics, then the number two brand of organic baby food and the number four brand overall. Like Burt's Bees when it was acquired by Clorox, Plum saw joining Campbell as a real opportunity. "We have a mission centric core: nutrition and solving hunger with our benefit corporation status our secret sauce and innovation driving the entire process. Campbell has a dual mandate: strengthen the core Campbell business while driving new consumers and innovation. It's a perfect marriage," Grimmer explained to CSRwire.[45]

Mand expanded on Grimmer's statement:

> Campbell's really understands that things are fundamentally changing. I see it as an opportunity to have such an amazing impact and influence on a bigger, broader organization. If you look at their core, if you look at their product positioning and the changes they're making in benefits and policies, many of those things are a direct result of the Plum influence. Now we impact an organization that employs so many more people.[46]

Confirming it valued Plum for its socially driven purpose as much as for its financial potential, Campbell supported the brand as it became the first public benefit corporation (PBC) to sit within a public company in 2013. As Grimmer told *Fast Company* in an interview in January 2014, "We believe that profitability can be because of our purpose. We believe that's really been the hallmark of our success."[47]

THE ROLE OF THE PBC

Easily confused with B Corp certification, which Plum Organics had since 2007, a PBC is a legal entity that helps to align a company's mission and value creation. Whereas B Corp status is available to all businesses, regardless of legal structure or location, public benefit status is available only to corporations in the thirty states that recognize the structure and Washington, D.C. B Corps undergo the rigorous assessment process of B Lab, the nonprofit organization that certifies B

Corps, and must be recertified every two years, and PBCs commit to incorporating a public benefit into business decision making, and to annually report on their social and environmental impact.[48]

Public benefit corporate status legally safeguarded the company's mission for the long term as it integrated into Campbell's. It further reaffirmed that doing good is as important as doing well for Plum—the two things that have most likely helped to maintain and even grow trust for the company with the brand's fans. Importantly, though, neither B Corp certification nor being a public benefit corporation is the ultimate driving force for decision making. Like many other principle-centered companies, the brand's purpose and founding principles are Plum Organics's definitive guideposts.[49]

In 2016, Campbell launched a Public Benefit Corp internally, the Soulful Project, with regional food banks with a one-for-one model: "For every serving purchased we donate a serving of our Four Grain Hot Cereal to a regional food bank," The Soulful Project echoes—and seems directly inspired by—the Full Effect.[50]

A Quick Response and Community Outreach

In October of 2009, Plum proactively recalled a batch of its apple and carrot pouches that was possibly contaminated with the bacteria that causes botulism.[51] Acting when they first learned about the problem, before anyone became sick, the brand avoided a crisis and demonstrated its deep commitment to quality in all its products. In November of 2013, Plum again voluntarily recalled some of their baby food products for spoilage. Similar to Chipotle, Plum's efficacious supply chain is complicated and more prone to risk than industrialized, mass-produced foods. Grimmer said in a press release: "We started this company with the mission of providing the very best food to little ones from the very first bite. Because of our unwavering commitment to that mission, I'm writing to inform you that we are conducting a voluntary recall." More significant than the recall that took place in 2009, in this later recall, parents whose children had eaten the products took to Facebook to report their illnesses.[52]

As in 2009, Plum's voluntary recall and their handling of it emanated from their philosophy that doing the right thing supersedes making a profit, rather than following a legal dictate. When navigating a potential crisis like the one Plum faced—for a second time—acting quickly, honestly, and sincerely is essential to maintaining trust and brand equity. Issues of foodborne contamination were detected among only four UPCs in their product line of more than 100 food-pouch items. Unable to incontrovertibly rule out contamination with additional products, Plum called back close to forty products to eliminate any potential risk. As part of its crisis management, the brand also placed an alert about the recall on its website homepage, including images of the recalled products and easy-to-understand instructions on how to identify them by the UPC codes on their packaging.

To ease the situation for customers, Plum made the reimbursement process as hassle-free as possible. Parents could apply for product replacement vouchers via their website, email, and a toll-free number. The brand issued vouchers to anyone who said they had an item from one of the recalled UPCs—without asking for a receipt as proof of purchase. After all: *What parent holds on to their grocery store receipts?*[53]

Anne Westpheling, a mother of two boys—one four years old and the other four months—who has fed both her children Plum Organics, posted a message about the recall on her Facebook page for her friends "who weren't as social media savvy as I am and may have missed the announcement." She further explained her loyalty to the brand deepened because of how they handled the recall:

> I love them, I really do. Parents who, if they had all the time in the world would hand make all these custom baby puree, and do everything all organic and sustainable—but don't have the actual time to do that. . . . The honesty about their ingredients, and the purity of what they are selling to you, which is mostly true, is so built into the brand DNA that you felt like the recall and the issue that caused it, was a one-time mistake. . . . [F]or me [they] did enough in terms of maintaining

my confidence in them, that it didn't really bother me all that much. . . . They've had recalls since and managed each one well.[54]

In 2016, Plum rolled out its Grow Well™ Organic Infant Formula, further strengthening the brand's profile as a provider of holistic nutrition by providing an efficacious and convenient alternative to breastmilk. Based on five years of research, the formula is USDA Certified Organic and made with organic, plant-based oils, organic nonfat milk, and organic whey protein. It also contains no genetically modified ingredients. For nursing mothers who are unable to produce enough breastmilk on their own or who have chosen to alternate between breastmilk and formula, selecting a formula that is as comparable to the nutritional profile of mother's milk is extremely important. Grow Well soothes this concern for new mothers.[55] In 2017, mommyhood101 named Plum's infant formula number two in its ranking of Best Organic Baby Formula Options for 2017.[56]

Through the Eyes and Voices of Parents

In 2015, Plum launched its first advertising campaign, *Parenting Unfiltered*. The content, format, and objectives were refreshingly honest and sincere, further humanizing the Plum brand. Plum's senior management and innovators know parenting inside out: They're in constant dialogue with their parent consumers—and a majority of Plum's staff are parents themselves. As they surveyed their competitive marketplace, they saw an upbeat, shiny version of parenting—one that was a little too unrealistic based on their personal experiences.

Parenting Unfiltered embraces all of parenting by revealing the *real*: the joy, the tears, the funny moments, and the embarrassing times. Through it, Plum strengthens its relationship as a peer with customers. The lead-in content to parentingunfiltered.com explains: "This is parenting. It's about taking a chance, living unscripted, admitting uncertainty along the way. It's complex, but that's the best part. Why put a filter on it?" Successfully cultivating and engaging loyal fans across social media channels, *Parenting Unfiltered* was awarded a Shorty Award in 2016 for the best of social media in Family and Parenting.

PARENTING UNFILTERED'S 2015 PERFORMANCE METRICS

4-plus million total video views

3.5 million video views on Facebook

500,000-plus views on YouTube

82,000-plus shares

23,000-plus comments

90,000-plus likes on Facebook

25,000-plus Tumblr views

100,000-plus influencer impressions across Instagram and Twitter

11,000-plus individual holiday cards and 100,000-plus views of shared cards

Source: Shorty Awards, "Plum Organics: Parenting Unfiltered." http://shortyawards. com/8th/plum-organics-parenting-unfiltered-3

Confirming Its Commitment

As part of the Campbell Soup Company, Plum has access to resources previously unavailable to them as a small, independent firm. Using Campbell's in-house experts who specialized in multiple disciplines, including nutritional regulatory issues, Plum audited its entire product line. The audit revealed Plum had an opportunity to be more transparent in its naming architecture. As the brand proactively began to modify the names of its baby and toddler pouches and tots snack bars, the Center for Science in the Public Interest (CSPI), a watchdog and consumer advocacy group focused on safer and healthier foods, created a media stir about Plum's naming conventions. CSPI then delivered a letter to Plum, directly challenging them on their plans. As the number one organic baby brand, owned by a multinational corporation, Plum was a prominent target for an activist group like CSPI.[57]

Naming hierarchies are often very complex for food brands, and inconsistent practices were not unique to Plum Organics. Nonetheless, representatives flew out to Washington, D.C., to meet CSPI staff. Working collaboratively with the group, the brand adopted a new naming architecture based on the order of ingredient predominance and standardized this on their front and back labels. The revised naming was part of a larger rebranding that centered on increasing transparency overall. Refreshed graphics and reshot photography pictured ingredients as the new names indicated, based on their relative content in the product recipe rather than visual appeal. For instance, if raspberries were 10 percent of the product ingredients, Plum's new product label would not show a cornucopia's worth of raspberries in the visual.[58]

Everything Plum does is fully immersed in its social mission and commitment to children, parents, the greater community, and the world. The brand's human-centered design process ensures its products are the best fit for families' needs.[59] Their iterative process builds learning and progress into the brand's DNA. Employees continuously ask essential questions like: *What do we need to know? How will we learn that? What do parents want or need from us?* From the start, Plum's emphasis is on being parent-centric.

In 2015, Plum sold 59 million organic snacks and meals and launched twenty-nine new products in those categories. In 2015, they also donated 4 million organic meals and snacks, including over 700,000 Super Smoothies as part of The Full Effect program. Plum has partnered with the Homeless Prenatal Program (HPP) to "support some of the most vulnerable moms and young children in San Francisco" and with the Conscious Alliance to aid children living on the Pine Ridge Indian Reservation in South Dakota. Through its alliance with the Convoy of Hope, the brand has helped 81,000 people in need in 300 American communities and donated baby meals and snacks for disaster relief domestically and internationally, a total of 3,845,160 organic snacks. [60]

Striving to do whatever it takes to do right for every parent, Plum has the potential to be the number one baby food one day. Today, it is the number one organic brand and the number three brand overall, fast gaining on number two. Plum does everything possible to maintain the high bar that earned its status. And if Anne Westpheling's faithfulness to the brand is representative of the level and quality of relationships the brand has nurtured with parents, then Plum is succeeding on every level. As Westpheling observes: "If there's a continuum of baby and toddler food, [and] on one end you have the jars that our parents fed us, and on the other end you have purees that you've made yourself with organic vegetables you bought at Whole Foods, Plum is closer to the second one. . . . Plum feels like a mom and pop shop. Like a *friend*."[61]

IKEA: CREATING A BETTER EVERYDAY LIFE

Seemingly born in the 1980s for many Americans, IKEA introduced its first furniture store in 1958 in Älmhult, Sweden. The brand had opened the doors to its first showroom five years earlier and had begun as a mail order catalog in 1943.[62] The name IKEA, which has come to represent Scandinavian values to many people outside that geographic region, is in fact an acronym derived from its founder's initials, the farm he grew up on, and the village that was his hometown: Ingvar Komprad Elmtaryd Agunnaryd. [63]

Today, IKEA's global reach is greater than Walmart's and includes Korea, China, India, and Morocco. The IKEA brand unites nearly 183,000 employees across 340 stores in twenty-eight countries through its strongly defined culture that is centered on a common purpose: "to create a better everyday life for the many people."[64,65] IKEA is in tune with how people live and intrinsically senses that large-scale change is best achieved through collaboration among customers, employees, and suppliers. Participants in *CultureQ* studies perceived the company as follows:

> Their products are both really good, and yet fashionable or edgy.

> They understand I want my home to look good, but my life is stressful enough that I don't want to worry about protecting and nourishing expensive furniture.

> I am enjoying spending my free time with my friends ... having breakfast in IKEA.

A Joyful Experience

For more than half a century, IKEA has extended the experience it delivers across all five steps of Brand Citizenship's ME-to-WE continuum. Like Walmart, the brand is focused on accessibility—on offering a wide range of products at famously low prices. Yet unlike Walmart, IKEA is almost a religion centered on the mission of bringing well designed, functional home furnishings to "the many," developing enthusiastic employees, and respecting natural resources. The company is expert in how we interact with and relate to our homes. Without a doubt, since it started selling furniture, IKEA has taken its commitment to making every day better very seriously.

Well-known for their one-way system, IKEA stores engage all the senses. They're places where people can "touch, play, try and dream." Shoppers are welcome to lie down on the beds, open drawers, climb on the furniture, or simply sit on a sofa and watch other shoppers go by. Without question, IKEA stores provide a no-shaming, democratized shopping experience made simple, convenient, and straightforward: lockers to store your belongings, pencils to write down what you want, childcare, and a beloved cafeteria.

IKEA is designed as a furniture exhibition, a place for a family to have a fun, leisurely day out shopping. Signs direct you around the store and inform you of the economic and environmental benefits of the company's business concept. Model homes help shoppers visualize new, inspiring ways of enjoying life at home. The store's marketplace has more accessories than you'll ever need. And since April of 2016, customers can design their own kitchen, using virtual reality technology.[66]

For a number of *CultureQ* participants, even deciphering IKEA's unusual product names, which are evocative of what they perceive as an enviable Scandinavian lifestyle, makes shopping there more joyful: IKEA relates to its customers as guests or visitors, welcoming them into its home. And for those who opt to skip the store experience, shopping online or on the IKEA app provides them with new decorating, entertaining, and living possibilities. IKEA is a master at making the mundane interesting and at helping people to furnish their homes in an accessible, simple, and life-enhancing way.

IKEA's success stems in part from its restlessness to continually find new ways to improve and inspirit life for "the many" as our relationships with our homes evolve alongside culture. In 2014, the brand implemented two initiatives to engage customers and fans of the brand: *Life at Home* and *IKEA Home Tour* in the United States.[67,68] The brand's *Life at Home* website enlightens us on how people across the globe wake up. Incorporating a "data mixing board," the site enables users to mix and compare data to better understand how similarly and differently people in Berlin, London, Moscow, Mumbai, New York, Paris, Shanghai, and Stockholm live.[69] Each year, new research highlights a different feature of our relationships with our homes helping users to learn more about themselves by gaining insight into other cultures.

Possibly modeled after home improvement television shows, the IKEA Home Tour project brings together home furnishing and design experts from within the company as the IKEA Home Tour Squad. Working with fans preselected from video applications, the Squad solves universal challenges by offering "smart ideas and inspirational tips ... that can be helpful for anyone."[70] The makeovers reflect IKEA's design philosophy and feel more like manageable facelifts than complete refurbishments. Short yet comprehensive videos featured on the Home Tour YouTube page are complemented by live updates using the hashtag #IKEAHomeTour via social media.

What is good for our customers is also good for us in the long run.[71]

Ingvar Kamprad wrote this in *The Testament of a Furniture Dealer* (*The Testament*), also known as the IKEA concept, in December of 1976, around the time he migrated to Switzerland from Sweden for tax reasons.[72] Much more than a corporate manifesto, this book is the IKEA bible. Reading it, you sense Kamprad sought to ensure that IKEA's purpose reverberate strongly as the company expanded geographically. *The Testament*'s nine chapters underline the brand's product range, price philosophy, rules, and methods, which, taken together, make—and continue to make—IKEA a unique company centered on enriching our lives through appealing, well designed home furnishings.

In the introduction, Kamprad proudly informs readers that IKEA has helped to democratize Sweden, a country with a reputation for being a world pioneer in design, more than "many political measures put together." Written in the same decade that Anita Roddick founded the

Body Shop, *The Testament of a Furniture Dealer* reflects more of the practical missionary spirit of today's conscious capitalists than the anger of activism that was prevalent in the Zeitgeist in the 1970s. Kamprad undoubtedly saw business as an opportunity to better lives, create social change, and simultaneously make a profit. He believed:

> Profit gives us resources. . . . The aim of our effort to build up financial resources is to reach a good result in the long term. . . . We must offer the lowest prices, and we must combine them with good quality. If we charge too much, we will not be able to offer the lowest prices. If we charge too little, we will not be able to build up resources.[73]

For Kamprad, a virtuous circle was simply good business. And good business was about creating sustainable value by enhancing IKEA, customers, employees, trade partners, communities, Sweden, and the planet.

Striving to create a more satisfying working environment, one in which employees understood that the IKEA concept had to evolve to be timeless, Kamprad saw only possibilities—a continuous journey to achieve his vision. He encouraged curiosity, which in turn he believed motivated people and progress:

> Happiness is not reaching your goal. Happiness is being on the way. . . . We will move ahead only by constantly asking ourselves how what we are doing today can be done better tomorrow. The positive joy of discovery must be our inspiration in the future too.[74]

More than sixty years before Plum Organics was launched, Kamprad built a socially conscious, learning culture that remains foundational to the IKEA brand DNA.

Focusing Outward

To continually deliver its brand purpose, IKEA has necessarily had to evolve alongside society's progressing definition of "a better life." Over time, the focus of its purpose has extended from enhancing lifestyles in the developed world to safeguarding our health and the environment to promoting more equitable living in the developing world. While the brand has helped to shape how we live in our homes, it has not always been able to lead from ahead in all respects.

Confronted by one potential public relations crisis after another, as "the many people" became increasingly concerned about the effect of toxic products on their health and the sustainability of the environment, IKEA faced numerous challenges in the 1980s and 1990s. In the mid-1980s, after Denmark regulated the maximum emissions allowed from formaldehyde released into the air from the production of particle board, a primary element of many IKEA products at the time, pressure began to mount. As one of the largest companies operating in Denmark, IKEA was a ready target for public scrutiny and government testing. Emissions higher than allowed were discovered in some of the brand's products. The company was sued and assessed a fine for violating Danish laws.[75] Although the penalty was minimal, the IKEA brand was damaged, and the company sought to regain lost trust through immediate action.

Acting swiftly, Russel Johnson, then head of the quality department, set up a large testing lab for the brand's products, which later became one of the most sophisticated environmental testing facilities in Scandinavia. After analysis confirmed formaldehyde levels exceeded Danish requirements, IKEA chose to go one step further than required by law, adopting a new, more stringent German standard (the German E-1 standard) across all its markets.[76] Investigating the company's supply chain for particle board, Johnson eventually uncovered that the glue was at fault. The company worked with suppliers to fix the problem but to no avail. Determined to find a solution, Johnson reached out to chemical manufacturers in Germany for the answer.[77] In doing so, he did more than solve IKEA's problem. He set a new standard that advanced the entire European furniture industry and thereby benefited people in general, not just the IKEA customer.

With environmental awareness increasing, consumers began to challenge the well established IKEA brand for producing its hefty brochure long before the digital age, and change.org posted a petition to get Restoration Hardware to stop mailing its wasteful catalogue. As envisioned in 1953, IKEA's catalogue was designed to entice people to visit and experience the brand's furniture showroom exhibit. By the late 1980s, however, activists and consumers alike began condemning the brand for its catalogue, which, with the largest catalogue circulation in the world at the time, was perceived as excessive and not aligned with the brand's philosophy.[78]

Around the same time, environmental groups were also calling for boycotts of IKEA and other European retailers who used tropical rain forest wood. Anders Moberg, then CEO, recognized that to safeguard the brand, the company needed to better understand which social issues were relevant to its business operations. Moberg tasked Russel Johnson to draft an environmental policy for the group, telling him, "Environment is not just a new fashion, it will not just fade away, it is the new reality and we have to adapt to it."[79]

IKEA further demonstrated its prescience when Johnson proposed an Environmental Day for group management and staff to engage with the issues. Johnson chose an outsider—Dr. Karl-Henrik Robèrt, a medical doctor and cancer researcher with a growing reputation as an environmental expert—to facilitate and expand management's perceptions about environmental issues. One year earlier, Robèrt had launched the Natural Step, a nonprofit organization established under the patronage of the King of Sweden to help businesses and communities adopt sustainable practices. In June of 1990, the company held its first Environmental Day to craft its environmental policy. At first skeptical, the managers accepted the situation was serious and acknowledged that IKEA could effect change that would enhance people's lives. They developed a one-year environmental trial policy, which was approved by the board in August of 1991.[80]

Turning Crisis into Opportunity—Worldwide

In 1992, after the environmental policy had been adopted, IKEA faced a second formaldehyde crisis. This time, with one of its most popular items—the "Billy bookshelf"—in Germany, which was the company's then largest market. Journalists from a sizable newspaper and television station conducted investigative tests and determined that formaldehyde levels in the lacquer IKEA used on the Billy bookshelf, not the particle board, were higher than the legislated limits. The news spread and IKEA became notorious around the globe. The company lost between $6 and $7 million recalling the product.[81]

Like Stephen Ells at Chipotle and Plum Organic's founding team, IKEA executives were reminded that issues arise even with the best intentions and policies in place. Purposeful brands are expected to be one step ahead, behave well at all times, and advocate for good on behalf of their customers. IKEA grasped it needed more than an environmental policy. It required a tangible plan with concrete action steps that would upgrade its supply chain and operations. And so its environmental policy evolved into an Environmental Action Plan. Once again the company formed work groups making managers across the business responsible for co-creating the plan. The collaborative process enabled IKEA to effect further cultural change. Through it, Moberg and Johnson emphasized that environmental sustainability was an essential part of improving "life for the many" and the responsibility of everyone across the business, not just one department. With heightened awareness of environmental issues, in 1993 IKEA, alongside Greenpeace, World Wildlife Fund for Nature ("WWF"), and more than 100 other participants initiated and founded the Forest Stewardship Council ("FSC"), an independent international network promoting responsible management of the world's forests.[82] In 2015, IKEA's catalogue, which was distributed to more than 200 million people worldwide, became the largest print production ever to be fully FSC certified.[83]

In 1994, two years after Harper's published Jeff Ballinger's exposé on Nike using child labor, IKEA again made headline news when a Swedish television documentary, *Mattan* ("The Carpet" in English), featured children in decrepit conditions working on rugs in Pakistan. Although the documentary wasn't shot at an IKEA supplier, IKEA was clearly implicated in the documentary.[84] Once again IKEA took fast action and saw the crisis as an opportunity to improve its business practices and ultimately children's lives. Rather than contriving an answer, the company sincerely stated that it didn't know how the rugs were produced. And, once again, IKEA sought the counsel of experts to effectively understand and address the root causes of the situation rather than craft a public relations campaign designed simply to win back trust. Working with UNICEF and Save the Children Sweden, IKEA determined that switching suppliers would not put an end to child labor. More was needed. And, as a result, since 1994, IKEA has tirelessly worked to end child labor through education and advocacy. Formed in 2005, in partnership with UNICEF and Save the Children, the IKEA Social Initiative promotes the rights of every child to a healthy, secure childhood and access to a quality education on a global level.[85]

With a goal to better the lives of children globally, as well as its customers' homes, in 2009 the IKEA Foundation expanded its charter from its founding focus on architecture and interior design to include improving children's opportunities.[86] Today IKEA continues to demonstrate the large-scale impact that global companies can have on effecting real change and enriching all people's lives when they practice good Brand Citizenship. The IKEA Foundation estimates that its program commitments with partners such as UNICEF and Save the Children have helped in the range of 178 million children.[87]

Further applying what it learned in the 1990s, IKEA launched a code of conduct for its suppliers—*The IKEA Way on Purchasing Home Furnishing Products*—in 2000. Three pages long, the IWAY, as it's known, introduces suppliers to the IKEA concept and defines the behaviors IKEA expects from them in terms of legal requirements, working conditions, active prevention of child labor, external environment, and forestry management. It also explains what suppliers can expect from IKEA and highlights how IKEA will support and monitor suppliers to ensure they comply with the guidelines.[88,89] Underlining its determined stance against child labor, the brand introduced *The IKEA Way on Preventing Child Labour* at the same time it created IWAY. To ensure that no child labor is used by suppliers or their subcontractors, the company specifies that each supplier "maintain documentation for every worker verifying the worker's date of birth" and "keep IKEA informed at all times about all places of production (including their subcontractors)."[90]

A Standard Bearer for Sustainability

Affirming the transformative role it intends to play in enriching people, communities, and the planet, IKEA released a new sustainability strategy in 2012, *People and Planet Positive*. The strategy reflects the brand's LAGOM philosophy. Rooted in its Swedish heritage, LAGOM stands for "just the right amount" and is all about balance—about living in a rewarding and responsible way, not denying yourself or sacrificing what you love, while not taking from the planet more than you need.[91] The

People and Planet Positive outlines the brand's holistic, three-point strategy to integrate sustainability into daily life and progress our lifestyles through 2020.

IKEA'S PEOPLE AND PLANET POSITIVE STRATEGY THROUGH 2020

▶ Inspiring and enabling millions of people to live a more sustainable life at home by offering products and solutions that help customers to save money by using less energy and water and reducing waste.

▶ Becoming energy and resource independent, which includes producing as much renewable energy as is consumed in IKEA Group stores and buildings, building on the €1.5 billion ($1.8 billion) allocated to wind and solar projects. It also includes improving the energy efficiency in IKEA Group operations by at least 20 percent and encouraging suppliers to do the same. Continuously developing the IKEA range and making products more sustainable by ensuring all main home furnishing materials, including packaging, are renewable, recyclable, or recycled.

▶ Taking the lead in creating a better life for people and communities, which includes supporting the development of good places to work throughout the IKEA Group supply chain. Also, encouraging suppliers to focus not only on compliance but also on shared values. It also includes going beyond the immediate reach of the supply chain and helping to support human rights.[92]

IKEA also aims for all its products to have "circular capabilities" by 2030. This intent includes a bold initiative to "support customers who care, repair, rent, share, bring back and resell their IKEA products." Customers who resell receive a voucher for use in-store, in exchange for used IKEA products. As part of its efforts to collaborate with customers to sustain the environment, the brand also offers in-store workshops where it teaches techniques to refresh or restore furniture. IKEA's evolving socially conscious strategy has been paying dividends. In 2015, sales of sustainable products increased by 29 percent, as compared to 2014.[93]

IKEA's wider worldview unequivocally contributes to the brand's success. Studying people's relationships with their homes across the globe, it has become highly cognizant that not everyone has the luxury of envisioning a better future—even in their own homes. In October of 2016, in partnership with the Red Cross in Norway, IKEA installed an exact replica of a Syrian home in one of its showrooms to raise awareness of the plight of Syrians living through civil war. The exhibit entitled *25 Metres of Syria*, attracted 40,000 visitors and raised £19 million GBP for Red Cross efforts in Syria. It focuses on Rana, a mother of four, who fled to Jamarana, a relatively safe suburb of Damascus that does not suffer from heavy rebel shelling. Even though her apartment is not in the war zone per se, it's unfinished. As *The Independent* reported, Rana told the Red Cross, "When we had to flee to this area to find safety, we did not have enough money to rent a better place. We have no money to buy mattresses and blankets, or clothes for the children." In placing a replica of Rana's home next to model kitchens, living rooms, and bedrooms, IKEA is telling a more powerful story than an advertisement would. The exhibit also featured more information about Rana's family and the war and calls for action, detailing how people can help or donate.[94]

On June 30, 2016, IKEA opened the doors to a museum in Älmhult, Sweden.[95] Befittingly, the main exhibition is in what was the first IKEA store. Sharing stories of both the good and the bad, it affirms IKEA's focus on a journey that's about continual progress. The brand's purpose to "create a better everyday life for the many people" has grounded how it has enriched people's lives through innovation, expansion, and responding to crises. In being intentional, IKEA has created a historical record in which the brand's future is framed and strengthened in part by its past mistakes—making history, for them, forward facing.

CHAPTER 5:
Enrichment

► Brands that deliver holistic, integrated experiences—from a product's or service's look, feel, and communications to the user's experience with these things—underpin their relevance to customers with more than product features and thereby position themselves for continued success.

► Mrs. Meyer's Clean Day and Plum Organics demonstrate how intuition can play as strong a role as market research in identifying ways to make daily routines more convenient and inspiring.

► Start-up companies that engrain their brand purpose across their operations, such as Burt's Bees and Plum Organics, can stay true to their mission even after being acquired by a multinational corporation.

► Burt's Bees launched its line by integrating its founder's iconic image into its brand narrative and design. The brand continues to grow a community devoted to its core value of respect for nature.

► Plum Organics recognized the desire of parents to feed their babies and toddlers authentic, wholesome foods packaged in innovative, environmentally friendly ways and built a committed following as a result.

► Like IKEA, all brands need to be restless and consistent in how they present themselves: staying true to their purpose and personality while continuously evolving and raising their standards to reflect changing social values and expectations.

CHAPTER 6

RESPONSIBILITY

Behave Fairly

Treat employees, suppliers,
and the environment well.

A company's employee policies, community impact, supply chain management, and environmental footprint matter more than ever. Corporate reputations are made and lost by how well a business addresses issues that matter to its stakeholders and society at large. Increasingly, even investors are insisting that companies be fair to employees, proactive in managing their supply chain, focused on reducing their environmental footprint, and open to acknowledging and fixing their mistakes before they are called out on social media. So it's no surprise that behaving responsibly—defined by participants in *CultureQ* research primarily as treating employees well, being honest and ethical, and adopting reputable operational practices and policies—is the transition point for brands as they move across the ME-to-WE continuum of Brand Citizenship.

Companies at Step 3 of Brand Citizenship—Responsibility—simultaneously deliver benefits to their customers and returns to their investors—a ME orientation—and hold a wider stakeholder view on value creation—a WE orientation. Many brands starting on the pathway of Brand Citizenship begin with one-off initiatives that embrace traditional definitions of social responsibility and philanthropy. Things like recyclable bags, supporting the rain forests, charitable donations to AIDS research, and sponsoring community marathons are conventional first steps. While these are often well-intentioned and can create short-term public relations opportunities and promotional lifts in sales, they're unlikely to have a longer-term impact on corporate reputation, employee engagement, or market share when they're not strategically rooted in delivering a larger brand vision or purpose.

Interestingly, participants in our *CultureQ* research did not identify a number of more traditional brands at Step 3 on the ME-to-WE continuum of Brand Citizenship as good corporate citizens. Yet many of these companies had received kudos for their efforts from sustainability and social responsibility experts and the media—something that made me pause as I reviewed our *CultureQ* research. Some of the brands not named, especially long established ones, are not boastful about how they conduct business and are thought of as conventional rather than socially innovative. For companies like the John Lewis Partnership, which fit in that traditional mold, behaving responsibly has forever been engrained in their purpose, and doing what's right is just part of how they operate—every day.

Others, often in notorious industries like oil and gas, concentrate on communicating their positive social impact by reporting figures as proof of their commitment to behaving responsibly. As the *Oxford English Dictionary* confirmed when it chose post-truth as the word of 2016, objective facts are now less influential in shaping opinions than stories that capture us emotionally and reflect how we feel about issues. And still other brands, which are evolving gradually and haven't necessarily established a meaningful purpose to guide their daily operations or transform their business model, fear being accused of having ulterior motives for doing good when they announce initiatives focused on responsible corporate citizenship.

As I reached out to companies in doing research for this book, I was surprised to discover how real that last concern is among large corporations. Knowing their company and their firm's management are not perfect, many executives and communications directors I spoke with were worried that cynics and activists would work hard to uncover what they were doing wrong, if I highlighted what they were doing right. Many

concluded that being cited as a successful case study in this book required their company to have fully developed processes and operational
policies that would incorporate all five steps across their business. They
also often thought it meant they should be ranked in the top ten for citizenship. This more traditional view of success is limiting progress and
part of the challenge businesses must overcome. Good Brand Citizenship reflects a new, more collaborative way of thinking. As IKEA clearly
demonstrates, a successful case study is in large part about the journey a
company goes on in partnership with its employees, customers, investors, and other stakeholders as public awareness of issues shifts. It's not
a command-and-control operation, where executives solve such challenges on their own.

As a brand strategist pioneering the model of Brand Citizenship, I'm
enthusiastic about companies that seek ways to create social and financial value, and, as a consumer, I look to support brands that are focused
on doing good while also doing well. The more we know about a company's priorities and the advancements it is investing in, the more we
can make smarter buying choices and choose products and services from
brands that mirror our values. Given global populist sentiments and the
volatile political climate, though, I understand the uneasiness companies
are feeling.

THE FINE LINE OF BRAND ACTIVISM

Anyone who may have questioned the rising influence of populism—or
the anger toward Washington, Wall Street, and corporate elitism—that
emerged after the Great Recession stopped doing so after Brexiteers won
the day in June 2016 in the United Kingdom, and Donald Trump became the president-elect in the United States the following November.
More so than ever, populism is a growing concern for businesses. As a
resurgent movement that's part of our social fabric in a politically
charged climate, it impacts what some people perceive as good and bad
corporate behavior. Healthcare. Gun control. Women's rights. LGBTQ
rights. Minimum wage. Outsourcing. The number of brands that have
taken activist positions on issues in the public debate has grown significantly since 2010, and current events indicate more businesses, espe-

cially large corporations, may be increasingly pressured to declare their political leanings and points of view on social justice and civil liberties. Taking a public stand can be polarizing. Companies that do so run the risk of losing more customers than they gain, as well as angering employees, investors, and other stakeholders. In addition, not everyone defines doing good in the same way.

Beginning with our study at the end of 2011, *CultureQ* research first demonstrated the careful line that brands must walk between supporting causes and being political. Unsolicited, a small number of participants named brands such as Chick-fil-A and Hobby Lobby, which have been known for incorporating their religious beliefs about gay marriage and contraception, respectively, into company policy, as good corporate citizens, and a slightly larger number named each as a bad corporate citizen. The side a participant was on clearly was dependent upon some combination of their social and religious views and political leanings. The comments made about each of these brands were similarly divisive. Some participants applauded Chick-fil-A's and Hobby Lobby's actions, stating they "show[ed] they stand upon their beliefs" and "[were] not afraid to not be politically correct today." A larger number, however, argued on the side of social justice, unfavorably and equally emphatically saying:

They discriminate.

They believe in religious extremism.

Exclusionary politics and branding.

Taking away income and benefits from retirees.

Awful food and forcing their morals on others.

Forcing their religious beliefs on employees.

Before being vocal about controversial issues, a brand must sincerely assess where it stands, so as not to violate Step 1 of Brand Citizenship—Trust. Importantly, Chick-fil-A and Hobby Lobby each strive to live their activism. Their company cultures and policies reflect their positions to the extent allowed by the law, and for people who are familiar with each company, neither's stance was unexpected. For Chick-fil-A and Hobby Lobby, making a definitive statement about an issue in the public debate was not a marketing ploy or a community-building tool. It was about taking a responsible position based on their point of view.

Since our earlier *CultureQ* studies, brand activism has been increasing. Legacy and newer brands alike, such as American Airlines, BuzzFeed, Honey Maid, Ketel One, MasterCard, Spotify, Target, and Uber, flew the rainbow flag for marriage equality in June 2015. Later that year, Airbnb, Alcoa, General Motors, Goldman Sachs, Microsoft, Monsanto, Walmart, and many others openly signed President Obama's climate change pledge.[1]

And others such as Allstate, EarthLink, Kellogg's, Nest, Target, and Warby Parker pulled ads from the alternative-right media platform, Breitbart News Network (Breitbart News), in November of 2016 because of strong racist and anti-Semitic views. Steve Bannon, who became chief strategist to President Donald Trump after serving as his campaign's chief executive, was a founding board member for Breitbart News. Bannon became executive chair of Breitbart News Network, LLC, the media platform's parent company, after the death of Andrew Breitbart, Breitbart News's founder.

While those companies that supported the Supreme Court's decision about gay marriage and Obama's climate change pledge were generally praised, those that ended their relationships with Breitbart News, most notably Kellogg's, faced repercussions.

On November 30, 2016, Breitbart News retaliated against Kellogg's by posting an inflammatory article with the headline, "#DumpKelloggs: Breakfast Brand Blacklists Breitbart, Declares Hate for 45,000,000 Readers." Highlighting Kellogg's and labeling the "war against Breitbart News as bigoted and anti-American," Breitbart News Editor in Chief, Alexander Marlow, angrily called for readers to sign a petition urging people to boycott all of Kellogg's products.[2]

In addition to disagreeing with Kellogg's stance, many were angered that Breitbart News's values hadn't troubled Kellogg's and other brands until after Steve Bannon was named then President-elect Donald Trump's chief strategist. For some, Kellogg's decision was less about the brand's absolute stance and more about the company's inconsistent behavior. On the day Breitbart fought back, Kellogg's share price dropped from $73.62 on November 29, 2016, to $70.96. The decline was short-term, however, and Kellogg's reputation remains untarnished. Within less than a month, the company's share price bounced back, and the brand's fourth-quarter cereal sales in the United States were flat.[3]

EMPLOYEES FIRST

While there are signs that brand activism may be growing in importance, companies practicing Step 3—Responsibility—today are more often concerned about modifying policies and practices so that positive behavior change becomes institutionalized across operations.

To become active citizens rather than passive spectators, many brands like Unilever have broadened their definition of value creation to include a wider range of stakeholders, not only shareholders, society, and the environment. Having no formulas for success, they are experimenting with new systems and models to identify what will work best given their individual company culture. These brand owners appreciate that wider involvement is needed to achieve real impact, effectively strengthen their reputation, and cultivate deeper loyalty with customers, employees, investors, and other stakeholders. They understand that the old ways of doing things no long work. Brands at Step 3 accept that nurturing people and the planet is crucial to growing loyalty and profit in the longer term. Incorporating these elements into their operations, they are tapping into the power of the virtuous circle and creating greater social value alongside financial returns.

Step 3 of Brand Citizenship emphasizes the importance of putting people first, before profit and even the planet. Over our three years of *CultureQ* research, participants ranked treating employees well and fairly as the number one characteristic of a good corporate citizen and the number two trait of a leadership brand (behind the characteristic "produces reliable, durable products and services and offers value for quality"). As Walmart and Amazon illustrate, whether true or false, brands perceived as treating employees poorly bump along the ME-to-WE continuum rather than deftly gliding across it. Since the oldest Millennials entered the workplace around the turn of the new millennium, employee engagement and satisfaction have jetted to the top of executive agendas.

Indeed, when the Supreme Court decision in *Obergefell v. Hodges* made same-sex marriage legal in all fifty states in the United States in 2015, numerous media pundits proclaimed that embracing the rainbow was smart business because Millennials were a more diverse and inclusive generation. A 2014 *CultureQ* study into how people define their ideal employer revealed that Millennials, more so than Baby Boomers and Gen Xers, seek a friendly, supportive work environment; opportunities for social engagement; a commitment to volunteerism; and good values and a leadership reputation. Deloitte, PwC, McKinsey & Company, and many others have conducted studies that have uncovered similar insights.

Wanting to be treated well and fairly by your employer is not new. Nor is cultivating a happy workforce. Since the height of the Industrial Revolution, employers have equated employee benefits with the output of higher-quality products and better employee recruitment and retention. Long before today's populism was on the rise or Millennials entered the workforce, nineteenth-century industrialists understood that happier employees were more productive workers. Building company towns to house workers, establishing pension plans, and providing the services of company doctors, they sought to increase output and encourage loyalty as labor demand began to surpass supply by bettering workers' social welfare. While some like George Cadbury, founder of Cadbury's cocoa and chocolate company in Britain, were sincerely motivated by principles and responsibility, others like George Pullman, an American engineer and industrialist who created the Pullman sleeping car and developed a business around it, were more paternalistic or even exploitative. In 1875, the American Express Railroad established the first private pension plan in the United States, followed by other railroads, utilities, large manufacturers, and banks.[4] In 1910, Montgomery Ward offered one of the first group insurance plans. And in 1914, Henry Ford introduced the $5 workday, which was more than double the average factory wage at the time.[5,6]

Post–World War II, companies offered perks as they sought to recruit and retain the most talented workers from a limited pool. As the labor force grew, workers became more dispensable. When companies began to lay off middle management in the 1970s, downsizing to distribute greater earnings to shareholders, the needs of employees shifted to a secondary concern. Today, however, the needs of employees are again being highlighted, but not because the labor pool has shrunk in size. Indeed, with Millennials in the workforce, it has grown.

So why are businesses so concerned about keeping Millennial employees happy? Because, based on Gallup estimates, they cost the U.S. economy $30.5 billion in turnover annually. More so than prior generations, Millennials are less loyal to companies and more focused on their own priorities. Gallup's 2016 study, *How Millennials Want to Work and Live*, reported that 21 percent of Millennials, more than three times the number of non-Millennials, say they've changed jobs within the past year. Similarly, a Jobvite study found that 42 percent of Millennials change jobs every one to three years. Gallup further uncovered that 60 percent of Millennials are open to a different job opportunity, as compared to 45 percent of non-Millennials. While sites like LinkedIn have made it easier for unhappy employees to look for new jobs and for companies to steal talent, many Baby Boomers and Gen Xers judge Millennials as having unrealistic expectations of work—with those expectations being ego driven.

In 2007, before the Great Recession, I gained an alternative perspective to the latter perception through an exploratory study we conducted with eighteen- to twenty-seven-year olds in the UK, the United States, Australia, and Central Europe for STA Travel, the world's largest travel company for students and young people. As part of the research, participants completed journals and a series of creative exercises over one month, in which they reflected on their friendships, self-definition, free time, personal development, work, and travel. A highly creative and achievement-oriented group, the majority were overstressed and yearned for more meaning in their lives.

Participants who were twenty-two years old or older shared that they had switched jobs already or were planning to do so within a year. Work wasn't as satisfying as they had expected, and the idea of "putting in their time" before being given more responsibility did not resonate with them. The story a twenty-two-year-old Australian woman told us illustrates the Millennial perspective:

> Back in Sydney, work was going well, but I felt I had learned all that I could and became bored in the role. I was offered a secondment [or a temporary assignment] for three months as Marketing and Communi-

cations Consultant for the City of Sydney. My boss thought it was a great opportunity and approved it straight away. When it was presented to the management team, all but one signed it off, so it didn't go through. I was really disappointed and lost all motivation to stay in the company. For me, work was the biggest influence on me leaving [Australia to travel instead] when I did.

The workplace has not been the nirvana Millennials were promised by their parents, teachers, coaches, and others. A number of participants in our study felt their parents had "set them up for failure not success." From early on, they were raised to believe if you work hard, do well in school, and get into the right university, you'll get the best job, earn a lot of money, and be happy. Scheduled from one activity to the next, most rarely experienced unstructured time even at a young age. For the oldest Millennials who had entered the workforce before the Great Recession, the promised pot at the end of the rainbow was missing something.

Since 2008, when the job market weakened and as more Millennials entered the workforce, this nascent trend of Millennials having a lack of job loyalty has become one of the defining characteristics of this generation that employers continue to wrestle with.

In this chapter, I'll explore how organizations from the retail, consumer goods, and fashion industries are addressing issues of employee engagement, social welfare, and the environment while being true to their purpose. Each of the brands operates in a responsible way, uniquely balancing who they are with the benefits they deliver across the ME-to-WE continuum.

THE JOHN LEWIS PARTNERSHIP: EMPLOYEES AS PARTNERS

Beginning with the *happiness of employees*, John Spedan Lewis set up an employee-owned partnership in 1928, when he inherited the John Lewis Store and Peter Jones, which he had already been managing, from his father. His vision for the John Lewis Partnership was to establish a *better form of business*. That same year he converted the firm into a public company, John Lewis and Company Limited, and published the brand's first constitution. When Lewis set up the first Trust Settlement in 1929, the John Lewis Partnership became a legal entity, and profits became available for distribution among all employees, who are called Partners. Nine years later, the Partnership added Waitrose, then a chain of ten stores, to its portfolio. In 1950, Lewis transferred his remaining shares and ultimate control to the trustees, and the second Trust Settlement was created.[7]

With 88,900 employees as of February 2017, a sense of collective responsibility is deeply embedded across the organization and guides supplier relationships. Participants in our *CultureQ* research identify John Lewis department stores and Waitrose as both ME and WE brands. Still governed by the constitution Lewis wrote, the Partnership's reputation is based on value, choice, service, honesty, and being a good citizen. It supports local suppliers and producers, as well as Fairtrade and other initiatives that contribute to the sustainable development of the communities where farmers and workers live. Fairtrade is an organized social movement that offers an alternative approach to conventional trade, based on a partnership between producers and consumers; it aims to help producers in developing countries achieve better trading conditions and promote sustainability. With British awareness of Fairtrade at 78 percent in 2013, the brand is more mature in the UK than in the United States.

Seven principles in Lewis's constitution form the basis of the business. They are supported by rights, rules, and responsibilities that guide Partners' behaviors with one another and other stakeholders. Five of these supportive elements characterize the brand's approach to responsible business:

Principle 1, Partners: The Partnership's ultimate purpose is the happiness of all its members, through their worthwhile and satisfying employment in a successful business.

Principle 5, Customers: The Partnership aims to deal honestly with its customers and secure their loyalty and trust by providing outstanding choice, value, and service.

Principle 7, Community: The Partnership aims to obey the spirit as well as the letter of the law and to contribute to the wellbeing of the communities where it operates.

Rule 96, Sourcing Responsibility: The Partnership's relationships with its suppliers must be based on honesty, fairness, courtesy. . . .

Rule 109, Environment: The Partnership must take all reasonable steps to minimise any detrimental effect its operations may have on the environment. . . .

As Partners, employees "share power," which includes direct knowledge of business performance, a say in appointing leadership at the helm, and—of course—profit sharing. Among the fruits of this proactive Partner model is greater accountability on the part of employee owners, as well as better customer service. Every employee in every sector of the business is driven by a singular vision and a shared passion, with a collective eye on outcomes. The Partnership is "not a panacea," nor is it "a quick win"—but management and employees feel it's "worth the effort."[9]

The company has not altered the constitution-based model John Spedan Lewis set up in 1928. However, the Partnership also knows that it must evolve to maintain a competitive advantage. After years of sliding profits, in the early 2000s, for example, the company reviewed its structure and committed itself to change. To ensure its values would remain relevant in Britain's intensely competitive retail market, the Chairman and Partnership Board created two divisional boards to run John Lewis department stores and Waitrose supermarkets at the operational level.

In 2016, the Partnership launched *It's Your Business 2028* in the run-up to the hundredth anniversary of John Spedan Lewis's taking the helm of the business from his father. Envisioning what the world and retail may look like in 2028, the plan aims to ensure the Partnership's long-term sustainability by setting out its next phase of business. In support of *It's Your Business 2028*, the Partnership also issued the *4Ps Manifesto for Change* as an evolution of its *Our Partnership Plan*. Built around the 4Ps of Performance, Pay, Productivity, and Progression, "the manifesto is not a 'to-do' list. It describes powerfully what we believe needs to shift in our culture to make better jobs, better performing Partners and better pay a reality, and to achieve the ambition outlined in Principle 1 [the happiness of all Partnership members]."[10,11]

Serving the Customer First

When you visit a John Lewis department store, the staff seems to be content and even happy at work, although not in the same animated way as Crew members at Trader Joe's. Partners are friendly and focused on their customers' needs in a way that I personally haven't experienced elsewhere. The first time I visited Peter Jones, the Partnership's department store located in Sloane Square, London, I was looking for a specific kitchen tool that was hard to find in the UK. Rather than presenting me with something that didn't meet my needs but that the store sold, the staff member—that is, Partner—I spoke with directed me to go to another store nearby—one not owned by the Partnership—to find what I needed. Having only recently moved to London from New York, I was taken aback and reminded of the holiday film *Miracle on 34th Street.*

In the film, a feel-good Christmas comedy-drama released in 1947, the store's Santa, who genuinely believes himself to be Kris Kringle, refers Macy's shoppers to other stores for the best items and prices. Seeing how the strategy works, Macy's management creates a reference book for all the store's staff. During my first visit and many others to Peter Jones and John Lewis stores in London and elsewhere in the UK, I often jested that staff had a similar reference tool on their computers. Their sincerity and transparency readily won me over, in the same manner that it has built trust between John Lewis Partnership and Britons for many decades.

As highlighted in Chapter 4, when discussing Amazon, Christmas advertisements are as greatly anticipated in the UK as Super Bowl commercials are in the United States. John Lewis Department Stores are particularly well-known in Britain for heartwarming Christmas ads that express the character of the brand. It's hard not to be moved, or even teary, by the end of one of their holiday spots. Their 2015 commercial, *The Man on the Moon,* showed the lengths to which a young girl goes to connect with a literal man on the moon—an elderly, solitary, and seemingly lonely man. It is sweet and whimsical, and it stretches the imagination. The spot, like most of their yearly holiday commercials, shows how a commercial object (in this case a handheld telescope, delivered from earth to the moon via a cluster of balloons) transcends its utilitarian function to demonstrate empathy and creates human connections and unforgettable memories. *The Man on the Moon* spot ends with the written words, "Show Someone They're Loved this Christmas."

Their advertisement for 2016, *Buster the Boxer* involved a young girl's delightful penchant for jumping on her bed, which led her parents to buy her a very large outdoor trampoline for Christmas. Her father works through the night on Christmas Eve putting it together in their backyard before morning. What no one except the family dog, Buster, notices is a menagerie of forest animals who take over the trampoline and gleefully begin to jump on it, while Buster looks on at them both longingly and jealously. The next morning, as the young girl goes out into the yard, thrilled at her new present, Buster outraces her to be the first one on the trampoline—a look of ecstasy on his face leaves the family wide-eyed and slack jawed. The ad ends with the typewritten words, "Give Someone the Christmas They've Been Dreaming of."[12]

While technically clever and cute, *Buster the Boxer* feels somewhat off brand. The overt sales pitch for the trampoline is somewhat in contrast to John Lewis's brand personality, which typically avoids overt manifestations of consumerism. A collection of tweets sent in reaction to the advertisement further indicated that some people felt it had political or multicultural undertones. They saw a disparate collection of animals—would-be enemies in the wild—jumping on the trampoline reveling together with zero discord representing a society with greater tolerance and goodwill. Others posted video footage of actual animals jumping on backyard trampolines to show that the concept was not a fantasy, after all. I suspect, however, that the narrative was developed with profit and sales pressure from online retailers—particularly Amazon—in mind.

While the intent of the 2016 Christmas advertisement can be debated, it still aligns with the brand's values. It is honest and sincere, and it reflects "a better form of business." Like the Amazon holiday advertisement previously described featuring the imam and the vicar, the John Lewis's holiday videos are consistently about the spirit of giving from the heart, which the brand further communicates in the experience it delivers. John Lewis's sales over the 2016 holiday season were up, which makes it clear that any brand dissonance in 2016's spot left loyalists unbothered.

Innovating for the Future

With its eye on progress and keeping the brand relevant, in 2014 John Lewis began collaborating with technology entrepreneur Stuart Marks to create JLab, a start-up accelerator program designed to identify and develop strategic technology innovations for the company. Chosen from among several hundred applicants, companies selected to participate are given the opportunity to work out of the Partnership's headquarters. There, they are immersed in day-to-day operations firsthand, receive mentorship from specialists, and gain real-commerce insights on how to commercialize their products and make them more viable in the market-place. Between June and September, 2014, JLab gave five technology firms support to develop products and solutions across three main areas: the customer experience across all channels, the Internet of Things, and how John Lewis can use data to drive real-time, in-store personalization for customers. At the end of the period, one of the five was chosen for a £100,000 investment. In return for funding, the Partnership got an equity stake in the winning start-up.

Since its inception, the program has evolved. In 2016, JLab entrant categories included "health & well being," "simplify my life," "effortless shopping," "tech for kids," and "surprise us." And competitor concepts varied widely, ranging from a fully programmable, customizable walking robot to teach children about coding, 3D printing, and robotics, to technology that enables people to visualize new home furnishings to wedding planning via a combination of an app and website.

Waitrose: Committing to Sustainability, Community, and the Shopping Experience

The Partnership's high-end grocery and food retailer, Waitrose, was founded in 1904. Among the vanguard of the locavore, sustainability, and Fairtrade movements in the UK before they became mainstream, Waitrose aligns with the Partnership's overall commitment and approach to sustainability. The Partnership's working farm, Leckford Estate, supplies Waitrose with fruits, grains, organic milk, and free-range chickens. Over the years, Waitrose has garnered numerous accolades for sustainability, including nine UK Compassion in World Farming awards, given to food companies across the globe that are meaningfully improving animal welfare:

- ► 2015 Best Retailer Award

- ► 2012 Good Pig Award

- ► 2011 Good Dairy Award

- ► 2011, 2010, 2006, 2004 Most Compassionate Supermarket

- ► 2010 Good Chicken Award

- ► 2008 Good Egg Award[13]

A Plan for Greener Systems

In April of 2007, Waitrose committed to greener farming systems, pledging that by 2010 all the conventional fresh, prepared, and frozen fruit, as well as the vegetables and flowers, it sells would be farmed to high environmental standards, using sustainable farming methods. All the brand's organic produce is certified by the Soil Association, the UK's leading organic and sustainable certification scheme across food, farming, catering, health and beauty, textiles, and forestry. Other Waitrose items carry the Leaf Marque, an environmental assurance system that acts as an imprimatur for sustainably farmed products.[14] Waitrose's impetus for the certifications was not just local, but global. As Mary Vizoso, then head of fruit and vegetable buying at Waitrose, told *The Guardian:*

> Many communities in the developing world rely on trade in fruit and vegetables for their livelihoods. . . . That is why we are working at grass roots level to raise environmental standards on farms and plantations around the world through widespread adoption of the Leaf Marque scheme."[15]

The Waitrose Foundation (Foundation) was launched in 2008 as a partnership between Waitrose, the company's suppliers, and the growers who produce, pick, and pack fresh produce in Ghana, Kenya, and South Africa. Each stage of the supply chain donates a percentage of its profit to the Foundation every time a farm's product is sold. The money is then invested back in the farming community. Operating under the premise that all people should influence their own future, the Foundation gives each community the freedom to decide how to allocate its funds to local educational, social, and healthcare projects. The Foundation logo is promoted on products from Ghana, Kenya, and South Africa.[16]

Launched in 2011, the Waitrose Farm Assessment (WFA) surveys all the brand's produce farms to understand how sustainability initiatives are progressing and to identify the challenges the farms face in bettering their practices. The Waitrose Agronomy Group—a consortium consisting of suppliers, academia, and Waitrose—founded WFA in 1999. The global initiative enables "suppliers to assess growers against a range of questions covering safety, sustainability and quality."[17]

Joining with Customers and Suppliers to Support the Community

Waitrose's collaborations for good extends to customers, as well as suppliers and other business partners. Embracing Step 5 of Brand Citizenship—Contribution, where a brand embodies commitment to the greater good—the brand launched Community Matters in 2008. Receiving a token after they've shopped in-store, customers choose between one of three local causes they'd like to support by placing the tokens in the box of their chosen cause. Each month every Waitrose branch donates £1,000 (£500 in convenience shops) between three local good causes, based upon the percentage of tokens the cause has received. The three winning causes its shoppers voted for, nationally, online at waitrose.com split a £25,000 prize. Since Community Matters began, the brand has donated more than £14 million to organizations chosen by its customers.

Beginning in 2012, Waitrose launched The Waitrose Way awards for suppliers. In the same way that their shoppers choose the charities that the brand donates to for Community Matters, customers vote for the supplier they "think is doing the most to change for the better the impact their company is having on both people and the environment."[18]

In 2013, Waitrose expanded The Waitrose Way to include a sustainability framework. Embodying the brand's ethos and the Partnership's principles, The Waitrose Way framework outlines twelve sustainability goals under four key pillars: living well, treating people fairly, treading lightly, and championing British.[19] Waitrose partnered with a number of nonprofits over its four-week, multichannel launch. Prince Charles's Responsible Business Network, whose members collaborate to address issues that will help build a fairer society and a more sustainable future, awarded Waitrose with a Big Tick Award, one of the most respected endorsements of responsible business in the UK.[20]

THE *WAITROSE WAY*
SELECT PERFORMANCE METRICS

Social Impacts

▶ 1,005 customers switching from traditional energy supplier to British green-energy supplier Ecotricity

▶ 25 percent increase in the number of customers charging their electric cars at Waitrose

▶ Donation, by Waitrose branches, of enough food for 260,000 meals, which were distributed through the Trussell Trust food bank

▶ Increase in sales of British watercress of 400 percent after it was featured in the *Championing British* TV advertisement

Business Impacts

▶ 25,020 views of a Living Well Q&A on Waitrose.com

▶ Over 200,000 people reached with Facebook activity

▶ 20,000 entries submitted for a joint competition by the myWaitrose loyalty program and Ecotricity, with a grand prize of a year's supply of green energy

Source: Business in the Community. "Waitrose—The Waitrose way." June 2014. http://www.bitc.org.uk/our-resources/case-studies/waitrose-waitrose-way

In addition to the Big Tick award, a 2013 *Which?* supermarket report named Waitrose "the most environmentally and socially responsible supermarket and the supermarket that cares most about its customers."

Shaping a Modern Shopping Experience

Waitrose's emphasis on sustainability does not preclude the brand from enriching the experience it offers shoppers. With iPads at the front of stores that provide digital concierge services, mobile payments, and beacons (location-based services), technological integration has become a hallmark of the brand. In 2014, the company set up an incubator program, Waitrose Hot Ideas, to innovate new ways to create a *uniquely modern* shopping experience. The initiative is designed to make experimentation central to its proposition, from working collaboratively with customers at the early stages of product development to cultivating a more exploratory and interactive companywide culture.[21]

The incubator's first product to market was developed with the Silicon Valley–based entrepreneurs behind the Hiku device. Hiku "lives in your kitchen, scans barcodes and recognizes your voice" to create a shared shopping list on your phone. It's akin to Amazon's multipronged digital shopping system, which has multiple components, including the Amazon Dash scanning device and the Amazon Dash Button.[22,23]

Meeting Stakeholder Needs: Hard Choices, Responsible Choices

Despite turbulence resulting from Brexit, the John Lewis Partnership posted £435 million in earnings for the fiscal period ending January 30, 2017—a 24 percent rise in annual profits before taxes. Higher pension charges and lower property profits, however, resulted in pretax profits before exceptional items falling to £305.5 million, from £343 million the prior year. With trading profits under pressure from an increasingly competitive retail market, the Partnership made a tough choice and chose to cut bonuses for the fourth consecutive year. The tradition, which began in 1920, was suspended during World War II and again during a recessionary period in the 1950s. Bonuses peaked at 24 percent of salary in the 1980s, and the highest payout in recent years was 18 percent in 2011.[24] It was exceptional for the Partnership to reduce bonuses when profits rise.

While the Partnership's decision to cut bonuses was exceptional, it should not come as a surprise. As Chapter 2 outlined, for companies that seek to do good, their success is dependent on meeting the needs of a wide range of stakeholders. As I also discussed in that chapter, such companies are part of a symbiotic virtuous circle, which includes customers, employees, suppliers, communities, society at large, and even the planet. While preserving bonus levels would have benefited the Partners directly in the short term, as co-owners of the company, they ultimately know they have a vested interest in cutting bonuses if this helps to sustain the Partnership over the long term. Making tough choices is part of what it means to be human, and also what it means to be a responsible brand.

KIMBERLY-CLARK:
COLLABORATING FOR GREATER SOCIAL IMPACT

With Essentials for a Better Life as its brand purpose and sustainability as an integral part of its business, Kimberly-Clark's products are purchased by nearly one-quarter of the world's population every day. As of January 2017, 42,000 employees worked at the company's manufacturing facilities in thirty-seven countries. And the company sells products in more than 175 countries, with its brands like Kleenex®, Scott®, Huggies®, Pull-Ups®, Kotex®, Poise®, and Depend®, placing Kimberly-Clark in the number one or two slot, in terms of market share, in eighty countries.[25]

Social responsibility and sustainability have been central to the business since it was founded in 1872. Yet, as with many other corporations, social responsibility sat somewhat apart from day-to-day business operations; sustainability was largely an environmental compliance function—and Kimberly-Clark didn't shout out about its accomplishments. In 1994, Kimberly-Clark set its first environmental improvement goals with a five-year time horizon—its VISION 2000 program. Since then, it has raised the bar every five years. In the early days, the company had commitments around specific raw material inputs, such as fiber and the role of sustainable forestry, and outputs, like minimizing industrial waste. When it issued its 2015 sustainability goals in 2010, it marked a significant shift in its thinking. More recently, its Sustainability 2022 strategy commenced a more epic journey for Kimberly-Clark. The overarching goal is to integrate doing good across its entire value chain and positively impact macro and systemic issues, such as deforestation and climate change.[26,27]

Introducing the framework of *People, Planet and Products* in 2010, the company's intent for sustainability broadened significantly to include sustaining and building healthy working environments, addressing global commitments such as the United Nations Millennium Development goals, centering social programs on global issues, reducing the business's environmental footprint, and innovating products and business models to reach new consumers.

PEOPLE, PLANET AND PRODUCTS GOALS FOR 2015

People

▶ Zero workplace fatalities

▶ Socially focused programs in Kimberly-Clark communities

▶ 100 percent compliance of key suppliers with Kimberly-Clark's social compliance standards

Planet

▶ 25 percent reduction in water use and maintaining quality of discharge

▶ 100 percent certified fiber

▶ 5 percent absolute reduction in greenhouse gas emissions

▶ Zero manufacturing waste to landfill

Products

- ► 250 million new consumers touched

- ► 25 percent of 2015 net sales from environmentally innovative products

- ► 20 percent reduction in packaging environmental impact

- ► 25 percent net sales shipped in environmentally innovative primary packaging

Source: Kimberly-Clark, Building on Our Vision for a Sustainable Future, 2010 Sustainability Report.

Through the Kimberly-Clark Foundation, founded in 1952, Kimberly-Clark has contributed philanthropically to social causes for decades. Today the Foundation's work is divided into four primary areas:

1. Matching gifts, volunteerism, scholarships, and employee giving programs

2. Local community grants, including disaster relief assistance

3. Environmental grants, in support of Kimberly-Clark's global sustainability initiatives

4. Strategic mission-driven global partnerships driven through internal collaboration between Kimberly-Clark's sustainability team, its brands, and the Foundation[28]

The Challenge of Building Consensus

Not a top-down organization, Kimberly-Clark's local businesses and regional markets are free to make decisions that will impact their marketplace and employees. To achieve its 2015 goals, a new collaborative

approach among the Foundation, the sustainability group, and regional, business-line and product brand champions was required. Like
IKEA when it decided to develop its environmental plan, Kimberly-
Clark opted for a process of consensus that included soliciting input
from people company-wide. Conducting focus groups and discussions
across the organization, management initially sought a single overarching idea to guide its social goals—one that would resonate with everyone.

After several months of discussion and debate, it became clear that
leaders in different regions and those in the company's business-to-busi-
ness (as compared to consumer) divisions couldn't agree on the one social goal to motivate broad-scale participation. Tom Falk, Kimberly-Clark
Chairman and CEO since 2003 and the company's number-one advocate for sustainability and social responsibility, called for a timeout. In
that moment of tension, the idea to bring the company's billion-dollar
brands to the forefront of social initiatives emerged. Prior to that time,
the Foundation and even to some degree the sustainability group had operated independently from Kimberly-Clark's brands.[29] As Jenny Lewis,
vice president of the Kimberly-Clark Foundation, reflected in an interview:

> Tom [Falk] said we needed to go away and we needed to figure this
> out. And that's when we came back and said it's not just one thing.
> There is not just one place to play. We need to look at our biggest and
> best. And we landed on some of our million-dollar brands and began
> to figure out how we bring them more into the forefront to play a role
> in solving social problems. By 2014 we were ready to launch some pi-
> lots and get things going.
>
> Key stakeholder relationships were the key to success. Our CEO
> helped us start the conversation, and we had some strategic internal
> champions that helped me share the story. We worked diligently to
> find the intersection points of business and social value. Now we have
> a proof point we can share with other regions and brands to encourage
> them to engage with the programs. We are slowly being able to dem-
> onstrate that what's good for society is good for business.

The Next Step:
Aligning a Brand with a Social Cause

Without a doubt, the Andrex® team is one of the champions Lewis referred to. And the Andrex Toilets Change Lives program is an example of a successful collaboration among the Kimberly-Clark Foundation, a brand team, and the sustainability group. The Andrex brand, which launched in 1942 and now includes toilet tissue and toilet tissue wipes, is Britain's biggest non–food grocery brand.[30] In 2014, the brand pivoted from focusing on product attributes in its market communications to centering on higher-order benefits that were in alignment with Kimberly-Clark's brand purpose, *Essentials for a Better Life*. Andrex's new aim was to talk to consumers about how they elevate the standard of clean because cleanliness is fundamental to our physical and emotional well-being. Adopting the tagline, "How Andrex do you feel?," the brand began a new advertising campaign that contrasted adults awkwardly discussing "wiping" habits with children openly doing the same.[31] To expand the conversation on feeling clean and confident, the campaign included a partnership with the online parenting community, Mumsnet.[32]

In September of 2014, Andrex teamed its new consumer campaign in a pilot program with a social mission to help bring the dignity of clean and safe toilets to people everywhere: *Toilets Change Lives*. Tom Berry, head of sustainability, EMEA, explained the reasoning as follows:

> It made sense for them to "elevate the standard of clean" not just for
> UK consumers who use Andrex, but also some of the 2.5 billion glob
> ally who don't even have access to a safe, clean toilet. There hadn't
> been that alignment with this kind of social cause historically. The
> kind of social causes supported in the past were things like guide dogs
> for the blind. This was still an emotionally relevant charity for a lot of
> our consumers, so people liked it, but there was no connection be
> tween guide dogs, the product people were buying or what we wanted
> to do as a brand. That's why we started *Toilets Change Lives*.[33]

As part of the program, the Kimberly-Clark Foundation made a donation to UNICEF to help 60,000 people in Angola have the dignity of a clean and safe toilet. Inviting Andrex loyalists and others to participate and working with UK retailer Sainsbury's, Andrex set a goal to raise £600,000 and impact over 180,000 lives in Angola over three years. Twenty-five pence from every promotional pack of Andrex Classic White 9 roll sold in Sainbury's supermarkets from September 2014 for three months was donated to UNICEF to help communities in Angola improve sanitation.[34] Berry believes the partnership with Sainsbury's helped to make the program successful. He explained:

> Sainsbury's is a strategic partner for us in the UK for a long time. We have a good, close working relationship with them. Also, from a values perspective they have a strong sustainability strategy focused on "delivering value with values" to their customers. This alignment between both organizations' sustainability strategies helped change the conversation—rather than just having transactional discussions, we were able to raise it up within the organization to higher levels because it was more about company and corporate values.[35]

The campaign expanded in 2015 and again in 2016 to include Kimberly-Clark's toilet tissue brands in Switzerland, the Netherlands, and Spain (Hakle, Page, and Scottex) and also to support work with UNICEF in South Africa, as well as Angola. For every promotional pack of Andrex Classic Clean 16 roll toilet tissue and Andrex Classic Clean Washlets® sold in Sainsbury's for three months, beginning in May of 2016, Andrex donated 15 and 5 pence, respectively, for each product to UNICEF.

A year before IKEA encouraged Norwegians to experience a Syrian's home through its in-store installation, Andrex and UNICEF drew attention to the sanitation crisis in West Africa and to the fact that one in six people in the world don't have access to a toilet. In November of 2015, the brand featured an "Angolan option" among luxury marble, chrome, and glass suites in Just Add Water, a bathroom store in London King's Cross rail station.[36] Arranged to reflect rural Angola, the tin shack had a dirt floor and was piled with garbage. Working in partnership with UK agencies Salt and Mindshare, J. Walter Thompson used hidden cameras to capture shoppers' reactions to the Angolan option and released a film on World Toilet Day, November 19, 2015, to increase awareness of the issue.

Andrex's *Toilets Change Lives* added value to the business through three sources: improved customer relationship, increased sales, and brand equity and influence. Berry detailed this further:

> We've driven significant value from it in terms of our customer relationship. We already had a good relationship with Sainsbury's, and the program built on that. In partnership with them we were able to get better visibility in store and subsequently incremental sales. This wouldn't have happened if we weren't running a good social cause campaign. In the first year we sold 1 million extra rolls of Andrex. [And the program also enhances] brand value.. . . . The campaign helps us get more share of voice on social media because it's an area where people are emotionally engaged, which is difficult to achieve when just talking about bath tissue. We're talking about the brand in an interesting and engaging way, which helps our brand accomplish both its business objectives and its social mission. . . . It's a virtuous cycle, the better [business] return we get the more [money] we can put back into the program, and the more we can invest back in partners like UNICEF to do more good on the ground.[37]

Andrex's successes have inspired other Kimberly-Clark brands and regions to implement their own *Toilets Change Lives* programs. In 2016, several lines of business in the United States, Switzerland, Spain, South Africa, the Netherlands, Brazil, Bolivia, and India implemented initiatives. The Cottonelle® brand in the United States, for example, launched a campaign with *Water for People* to raise funds and awareness around the lack of basic sanitation for families worldwide. And in India, Kimberly-Clark is partnering with Charities Aid Foundation to fund sanitation programs in schools and early child development centers.[38]

To complement the more consumer-facing *Toilets Change Lives* program, Kimberly-Clark cofounded the Toilet Board Coalition in partnership with Unilever and other companies, government agencies, sanitation experts, and nonprofit organizations. Working with entrepreneurs globally, the purpose of the coalition is to innovate commercially sustainable and scalable solutions that will improve sanitation. In addition to financial support, Kimberly-Clark contributed to the development of an accelerator program to mentor businesses with the most viable ideas and take them to the next level. Bringing business acumen, resources, and expertise, they help these entrepreneurs maximize their supply chains, train employees, learn to sell, develop marketing materials, and more. Through the accelerator model, Kimberly-Clark enables a sanitation entrepreneur to be well equipped to ask for capital funding and expand its program to serve those most in need around the world. In addition to the financial support, Kimberly-Clark helps accelerate the coalition's agenda and long-term effectiveness through capacity building—contributing everything from marketing, sales, and finance, to research and engineering through the skills of its employees.[39]

Harnessing Innovation and Breakthrough Solutions

Kimberly-Clark both taps into existing innovation in the environmental space and independently develops breakthrough solutions that create advantages for their business, in addition to shaping consumer behavior and evolving the industry overall. Bilateral relationships with organizations such as FSC (Forest Sustainability Council), WWF (World Wildlife Fund), and WRI (World Resources Institute) boost the company's expertise to develop healthier supply chains and more sustainable forest management systems in the world. And the company's own technical and economic knowledge has created businesses such as GreenHarvest, launched in 2015 by Kimberly-Clark Professional. A substitute for tree fiber that incorporates agricultural waste, such as wheat straw and bamboo, into Kleenex® and Scott® Brand towel and tissue products, Green-Harvest reduces the natural forest footprint, lessens energy usage (recycled paper is actually fairly energy-intensive to manage), and creates a new income stream for farmers.[40] Better for the environment. Better for farmers. Better for people. GreenHarvest is exemplary of the combined forces of sustainability, Brand Citizenship, and conscious capitalism at their best—which is better for business.

In June of 2016, Kimberly-Clark issued its 2015 Sustainability Report and announced Sustainability 2022, new goals to coincide with the company's 150th anniversary. As Tom Falk stated in a press release, "In 2015, we achieved or surpassed our 5-year sustainability goals and will continue to set aggressive goals for ourselves to make a positive impact in the world around us." Sustainability 2022 aims to set new standards in the company's four main areas of focus.

KIMBERLY-CLARK'S SUSTAINABILITY 2022 GOALS

► Social Impact: Improve the well-being of 25 million people in need through social and community investments that increase access to sanitation, help children thrive, and empower women and girls.

► Forests & Fiber: Innovate Kimberly-Clark's tissue products to reduce their natural forest footprint by 50 percent, while increasing their use of environmentally preferred fiber.

► Waste and Recycling: Extend Kimberly-Clark's zero waste mindset to all solid wastes and deliver innovation to help keep product and packaging material out of landfills.

► Energy and Climate: Achieve a 20-percent reduction in absolute greenhouse gases, versus a 2005 baseline.

► Supply Chain: Uphold Kimberly-Clark's values through proactive environmental and social programs that address material risks and sustain our commitment to human rights, worker safety, anticorruption, and environmental protection.

Source: Kimberly-Clark. "Kimberly-Clark Corporation Concludes 5-Year Sustainability Program, Unveils New Strategy and Goals." Kimberly-Clark Corporation. June 30, 2016. http://investor.Kimberly-Clark.com/releasedetail.cfm?Release ID=977859

Director of Global Sustainability Strategy and Business Development John Federovitch explained the company's progressive journey to good Brand Citizenship as follows:

Corporate entities, including Kimberly-Clark, have historically given back to communities through traditional philanthropy. Examples such as disaster relief or partnering with a local shelter was typical. This is all good work, but does it really have a sustainable impact?

Five years ago, we started to partner on bigger, thornier global issues with NGOs like Malaria No More and UNICEF ... in an attempt to drive larger scale change and impact. We recognized an opportunity to deliver the promise of our brands while tackling relevant issues within the supply chain. This has proven to be an effective way for Kimberly-Clark to raise awareness around social issues while impacting the lives of billions of people.

In the career section of its website, Kimberly-Clark shares:

Throughout our history, we have been committed to improving the environment and making the communities where we work better places to live. We do this because it is the right thing to do—not because we seek awards or recognition. But sometimes our work is noticed by local, national and international organizations.

And, indeed, the company's work has been noticed. The brand's numerous accolades include being number twenty-four among Vietnam's 100 Best Places to Work in 2013, winning top honors with a number one ranking among the Great Places to Work Institute's 2014 Best Multinational Workplaces in Latin America. The same institute also named it number four on the 2012 list of the World's 25 Best Multinational Workplaces and number two on its 2010 Best Company to Work for in Brazil ranking. The equity advocacy 2020 Women on Boards also recognized Kimberly Clark, as part of the organization's "national campaign to increase the percentage of women on U.S. company boards to 20 percent or greater by the year 2020, as a Winning Company for our commitment to board diversity." In 2012, 25 percent of Kimberly Clark's Board of Directors (three members) were women. These are just a handful of its well deserved honors—among many more. [41] Without a doubt, Kimberly-Clark is a large corporate brand that demonstrates good Brand Citizenship enhances reputation, strengthens relationships with suppliers and partners, and grows sales.

H&M: THE ETHICAL SOLUTION

The fashion and textile industry is notorious for polluting the environment and practicing unethical behavior. In Chapter 1, we explored the events at Rana Plaza in Bangladesh and saw how it was a tipping point for consumers who had previously turned a blind eye toward—or were totally ignorant of—the mistreatment of garment workers globally. However, even if all garment workers were treated with esteem like the Partners at John Lewis, fashion and textiles would still be called out for irresponsible and unsustainable behavior: Water usage. Pesticides. Toxic waste. Fossil fuels. Greenhouse gases. Body image. Animal cruelty. Cultural appropriation. Consumerism. Waste. And more. There's no way around the numerous challenges the trade faces.

The call for ethical fashion is on the rise. And alongside it, the number of new and existing fashion brands that are incorporating fair labor practices, ethical supply chains, and sustainable production processes is increasing. The Ethical Fashion Forum (EFF), the industry body for sustainable fashion that represents more than 10,000 members in over 100 countries, defines ethical fashion as "an approach to the design, sourcing and manufacture of clothing which maximizes benefits to people and communities while minimizing impact on the environment."[42] Like IKEA, members of the EFF believe ethical businesses must do more than mitigate harm. They must actively play a role in advocating for the fair treatment of workers and sustaining communities and the environment.

With the rise of fast fashion, this is a tall order. To keep up with peoples' cravings for all things new, even leading fashion houses have increased the number of collections they introduce each year. In 2016, people kept clothing for about half as long as they did in 2001, and in 2014, the average person purchased 60 percent more garments than in 2000.[43] Simultaneously, donating clothing for resale or reuse has become more complex. Although the global thrift retailer Savers, also known as Value Village, reported that 59 percent of North Americans donate their reusable items to thrift stores or nonprofits, much of the clothing that's donated to nonprofits ends up in a landfill or the developing world.[44] In February of 2016, five East African countries announced they were considering banning the import of secondhand garments to develop their own domestic clothing industries. In Uganda, for example, secondhand garments account for 81 percent of all clothing purchases.[45]

In 1947, Erling Persson opened the first Hennes ("hers" in Swedish) women's clothing store in in the town of Västerås, just outside of Stockholm. Persson acquired the hunting and fishing equipment store Mauritz Widforss in 1968, adding men's and children's clothing to the product line. The brand's name was changed six years later in 1974 to H&M when it was listed on the Stockholm stock exchange. Two years later, the first store outside of Scandinavia opened in London. In 2000, after expanding in Europe and establishing an online presence, H&M launched in the United States on New York's Fifth Avenue.[46] Arriving at a time when Target and Old Navy had made it chic to pay less, H&M attracted bargain hunters and socialites alike.

In 2008, H&M began to sell home furnishings. And in 2009 and 2010, the company expanded to the Middle East and Asia, and opened concept stores under five new brand names: COS, & Other Stories, Monki, Weekday, and Cheap Monday. Today, the H&M group has more than 4,300 stores in sixty-four markets and e-commerce in thirty-five markets. In 2017, the group will build stores in Kazakhstan, Colombia, Iceland, Vietnam, and Georgia—and roll out online in Turkey, Taiwan, Hong Kong, Macau, Singapore, and Malaysia. Most of the new stores will be H&Ms.[47]

H&M stores are known for long lines and sellouts of celebrity collaborations, which began in 2004 with Karl Lagerfeld. These partnerships give budding fashionistas, who otherwise couldn't afford to purchase clothing by high-end designers, the opportunity to buy fashion designers and brands like Karl Lagerfeld, Jimmy Choo, Kenzo, Victor & Rolf, Balmain, and many more at mass-market price points. They also help to keep the H&M brand fresh and in the forefront of fashion—albeit disposable fast fashion.

Sustainability: Much More Than a Trend

In response to the growing movement of people seeking to make more sustainable fashion choices while still being fashionable, H&M introduced its first dedicated Conscious Collection in 2011. In doing so, the brand aimed to use its "scale to bring about systemic change to [the] industry and across [its] entire value chain." Through H&M Conscious, the brand delivers on seven commitments:[48]

1. Provide fashion for conscious customers.

2. Choose and reward responsible partners.

3. Be ethical.

4. Be climate smart.

5. Reduce, reuse, recycle.

6. Use natural resources responsibly.

7. Strengthen communities.

According to SMART (Secondary Materials® and Recycled Textiles— The Association of Wiping Materials, Used Clothing and Fiber Industries), 95 percent of textiles worn or torn can be recycled.[49] As the leader in fast fashion, H&M began to "close the loop" in 2013 by using old clothing to make new clothes. In February that year, the brand launched in-store collection points worldwide for customers to deposit old clothes.[50] I:Collect, a clothing recycling firm that reprocesses the materials and makes them available for new use, sorts and manages the clothes H&M collects.[51] Given the timing of this recycling initiative, shortly after the Rana Plaza disaster, a number of activists focused on the fashion industry—ecouterre.com, a website that focuses on sustainable fashion design, is one example—criticized the brand's concentration on recycled clothing as "damage control" for the tragic factory collapse in Bangladesh. In raising awareness of poor worker conditions in the fashion industry, Rana Plaza put a microscope on the sector overall, ultimately increasing the public's consciousness of the problems associated with fast fashion.

Reflecting the shifting Zeitgeist, H&M's recycling initiative was an important first step to changing industry behavior and practices. In 2015, the brand went one step further, rolling out a sixteen-piece denim collection made from recycled cotton from items collected in-store. Like IKEA, H&M is aiming for its products to have circular capabilities.

In 2013, the company created the H&M Foundation (Foundation), which receives private funding from the Stefan Persson family, the company's founders and largest shareholders. Since it was founded, The Stefan Persson family has donated 1.1 billion Swedish kronor ($154 million/€123 million) to the Foundation. With a mission "to drive long lasting positive change and improve living conditions by investing in people, communities and innovative ideas," the Foundation focuses on four areas—achieving impact in each through partnerships with prominent global organizations:[52]

1. **Education:** Working with UNICEF, H&M focuses on providing quality education for all children.

2. **Clean water:** In partnership with WaterAid, it invests in clean water and sanitation in schools to offer children a better future.

3. **Equality:** Through a partnership with CARE, it provides women with seed capital and skills training to start up or expand businesses.

4. **Protecting the planet:** In 2015, H&M introduced the Global Change Award, an annual innovation challenge to progress the circular fashion movement. Five winners split a €1 million grant and become part of a one-year accelerator program provided by the H&M Foundation, Accenture, and the KTH Royal Institute of Technology in Stockholm. Similar to Waitrose's Community Matters and The Waitrose Way awards, the global public is invited to distribute the €1 million grant between the five innovations through an online vote.

With the aim to educate people to care for clothes more sustainably and reduce their personal environmental footprint, H&M launched CleverCare at the 2014 Copenhagen Fashion Summit.[53] CleverCare is a collaboration between H&M and the Swiss company, Gintext—the international association for textile-care labeling, which is responsible for the ubiquitous clothing maintenance symbols. A garment-labeling system that H&M introduced on all its products in 2014, CleverCare advises consumers on "How to reduce climate impact, effort and money caring for fashion the clever way" through five specific actions:[54]

1. Don't wash your clothes too often.

2. Lower the temperature when machine washing.

3. Think about reducing the amount you tumble dry.

4. Think of ironing only when necessary.

5. Use dry clean only when necessary.

When H&M issued its 2014 *Conscious Actions Sustainability Report*, the company's thirteenth sustainability report, CEO Karl-Johan Persson linked the brand's purpose more closely with sustainability in his opening statement:

> Our business idea is to offer fashion and quality at the best price. It's about the best value, not the cheapest prices. Sustainability is an important part of this.

The brand's sustainability vision builds on this further:

> H&M's business operations aim to be run in a way that is economically, socially and environmentally sustainable. By sustainable, we mean that the needs of both present and future generations must be fulfilled.[55]

Anna Gedda, head of sustainability at H&M, went even one step further in the 2015 *Conscious Actions Sustainability Report*, declaring that a closed-loop is the brand's ultimate goal, saying, "We want to use our size and scale to lead the change towards fully circular and truly sustainable fashion."

As the report also notes, "At H&M, we have set ourselves the challenge of ultimately making fashion sustainable and sustainability fashionable."[56]

With a mission to make sustainability the norm, not the exception, H&M rolled out its 2015 Conscious Exclusive collection—the brand's third elegant collection—to fanfare. Exclusively made from materials such as organic silk, leather, linen, and cotton, recycled polyester and lyocell, the collection launched at a dinner party in New York City's West Village, where its spokeswomen, actress Olivia Wilde, also celebrated a new pop-up store in H&M's Times Square flagship store.[57]

Hosting a cocktail party for reporters and bloggers in its New York City showroom, H&M further underlined its focus on circular fashion with the 2016 collection. Wilde was present here as well, along with Barbara Burchfield, who cofounded the Venice, California–based company Conscious Commerce with Wilde. Conscious Commerce is a creative agency and incubator whose mission is to integrate conscious consumerism into every commercial market and retailer. Highlighting H&M's sustainability efforts and the brand's upcoming, first World Recycle Week initiative, cocktail party attendees were greeted by unwanted clothes piled to the ceiling, accompanied by the T.S. Eliot quote, "In my end is my beginning." Deliberately designed to provoke thoughtful debate, the display stood in stark contrast to the glamorous Conscious Exclusive collection, which was inspired by the archives of the Musée des Arts Décoratifs, in the Palais du Louvre in Paris. H&M simultaneously was acknowledging the wastefulness and ugliness of fast fashion and the opportunity that exists to minimize it by turning it into something beautiful.[58] Ultimately, though, for circular fashion to be successful, H&M's customers must be as accountable as the retailer itself.

Committed to Changes Since Rana Plaza

On May 31, 2016, The New York Times published an article titled, "Retailers Like H&M and Walmart Fall Short of Pledges to Overseas Workers," which collectively took these retailers to task for the slower than anticipated change in garment-labor practices and standards that such retailers had promised in response to the Rana Plaza collapse in Bangladesh.[59] While the pace of change for factory labor practices may not be fast enough for some, H&M remains committed to its goal to have an impact.

Particularly notable are its measures against the use of child labor. As it states in the portion of its website covering sustainability, "We take a clear stand against all use of child labour and it is a minimum requirement for all factories producing for H&M."[60] The company continuously monitors compliance of its requirements in the factories that make its clothing. It also works with local doctors who help auditors to judge how old a worker is. The first time that a manufacturer is found to be noncompliant and using underage labor, H&M works with the supplier to rectify the problem. If there is a second violation, H&M stops working with the supplier entirely.[61] This is good work that should not be dismissed. H&M can go one step further, however, by being more transparent about its supply chain and open about the issues it's working to fix.

Activism fueled by social media and global interconnectivity led some of the planet's biggest retailers to make sweeping changes in response to the Rana Plaza tragedy. As we all expect more of brands, our relationships with them, especially large corporate brands, are increasingly resembling those between constituents and politicians. While symbiotic, mutual accountability is essential for success for both types of relationships. We all are the constituents of brands, and while we applaud the responsible actions companies take, we must also play our part. Like all brands, fashion brands can go only so far if people don't change their behavior alongside them. As highlighted previously, Brand Citizenship is a journey, one that requires collaboration, co-creation, and constant rethinking—and potentially reconfiguring—business practices afresh.

HIGHLIGHTS

CHAPTER 6:
RESPONSIBILITY: BEHAVE FAIRLY

▶ Well-intentioned, one-off philanthropy or socially responsible programs that are not strategically designed to deliver a brand's purpose are unlikely to have a long-term impact on corporate reputation, employee engagement, or market share.

▶ Good Brand Citizenship reflects a new, more collaborative way of thinking; it cannot be achieved with a command-and-control mentality where a board or executives solve problems without input from customers, employees, and other stakeholders.

▶ Increasingly, brands are required to walk a fine line between supporting causes and taking a political position or public stance that runs the risk of angering customers, investors, employees, and other stakeholders.

▶ Brands that take a political stance on issues that don't align with company culture and policies run the risk of losing trust, violating Step 1 of the model of Brand Citizenship.

▶ Demographic and attitudinal shifts have led to employee engagement and satisfaction rising to the top of executive agendas. Emphasizing this, being perceived as treating employees well and fairly is the pivot point on the ME-to-WE continuum of good Brand Citizenship.

▶ From the beginning, The John Lewis Partnership put employees (partners in the business) at the center of its success as a retail brand. It continues to balance the needs of customers, partners, and stakeholders as it adapts to remain relevant in a fiercely competitive marketplace.

▶ Recognizing that divisions and regions had different priorities, Kimberly-Clark brought its billion-dollar brands to the forefront of delivering social initiatives, tackling relevant issues in their supply chain and raising awareness of social issues. Equally as important to achieving its ambitious social goals, the company's CEO is the number one advocate for embedding sustainability and social responsibility across the business.

► Andrex's *Toilets Change Lives* program, which is aligned with Kimberly-Clark's brand purpose, confirms that collaboration across traditionally siloed departments—and with other companies—helps innovate impactful and scalable social initiatives that increase sales.

► In an industry known for poor environmental and ethical practices, H&M has learned the lessons of sustainability and the need for social justice, thereby building brand loyalty and creating a reputation for leadership. H&M is focused on educating and collaborating with consumers to make an inherently wasteful industry circular.

CHAPTER 7

COMMUNITY

Connect Me

*Bring people together through shared values
and common passions.*

Belonging: The American psychologist Abraham Harold Maslow labeled belonging as one of our five basic needs, after physiological requirements (under which fall physical survival, including food, water, and shelter) and safety demands (including feelings of security and stability, living free of fear, and safe from harm). In the *Theory of Human Motivation*, he shows that our identity is connected with—and even dependent upon—our feelings of belonging. Maslow explains that once a man's physiological and safety needs are met, he will

> hunger for affectionate relations with people in general, namely, for a place in his group, and he will strive with great intensity to achieve this goal. He will want to attain such a place more than anything else in the world and may even forget that once, when he was hungry, he sneered at love.[1]

As Maslow further describes in his paper, we only achieve self-esteem, the respect of others, and self-actualization once our need for belongingness, love, and affection is fulfilled.

Maslow's hierarchy of needs clarifies that our identity—our sense of self—is in large part defined by the social networks and communities we belong to—and equally those we opt out of. Traditionally, our social identity was formed by circles such as our family, neighborhood, nation, education, religion, political party, profession, and so on. Forces in modern society, however, have broken down many of these classic conventions, which have defined and labeled who we are to others for decades, if not centuries.

Today, the emerging generation is a visible composite of long-established distinctions. Our multidimensional lifestyles mix and match education and class, religion and politics, neighborhoods and professions in the same way that we mash up the clothes we wear and the music we listen to. And while many in the populist movement may yearn for more linear self-definitions from the past, it's hard to imagine Millennials and Gen Zers enabling this over the long term. More diverse than Baby Boomers and Gen Xers, a significant number of each generation are children of interracial, interethnic, or interfaith marriages. Many identify with more than one label from traditional categories or choose to reject labels altogether—including, sometimes, even traditional gender norms.

Technology has opened all our eyes—not only those of Millennials and Gen Zers—to new cultures and new lifestyles. And in doing so, it has widened everyone's opportunities for belonging to global communities, alongside local ones, and to virtual groups side by side with physical cliques. Our technologically facilitated interconnectedness naturally promotes more fluid self-definition. Although some people have always broken out of their social group or taken on multiple personas, they historically did so cautiously—and, societally, not at such a large scale. Today, however, we have more freedom to choose whom we affiliate with and to adopt different personas for the various communities we interact with. For example, childhood friends versus coworkers, classmates versus online friends, or those in a women's mastermind group versus friends from church, temple, or mosque. As one Millennial *CultureQ* participant succinctly and confidently stated, "I feel my identity is fluid and that people who know me only know aspects of my identity."

This sense of ME and WE intertwined comes to the fore in Step 4—Community—of Brand Citizenship. In Step 4, brands facilitate connections to a larger collective: people who buy the same products and services, share ways of living, or are united through common purpose and values. In a consumerist culture, our social identities are in part wrapped up in the brands we choose. The labels we buy, wear, eat, and even work at symbolize who we are to ourselves and to others. They represent our affiliations with certain lifestyles, social groups, attitudes, and ideals. Consciously and subconsciously, we decide whether or not to become a member of, for instance, the Apple, Google, Chipotle, and Burt's Bees communities, and so forth. Those who opt for lesser known or unbranded products and services sometimes are making more determined statements about who they are by declaring who they are not.

Brands positioned at Step 4 are often perceived as extensions of our own personas, in sync with how we define ourselves today and who we aspire to be. In the same way we're drawn to people who are similar to us, demonstrate an understanding of the things we care about, or are part of a group we yearn to join, we're attracted to brands that share our personal values and connect us emotionally, virtually, or physically to like-minded people—or represent something aspirational that we desire. With a clearly defined attitude or passion at the center of their brand purpose, brands at Step 4 frequently engender fierce loyalty from customers, employees, and other fans. Only brands that behave sincerely and are masterful at "listening" persuade us that they understand our inner emotions. All brands, however, have the opportunity to foster greater affinity by demonstrating a firm belief in, or commitment to, the things that matter to the people they aim to engage—whether they be customers, employees, shareholders, or other stakeholders.

In this chapter, I explore how brands as diverse as Giffgaff, IBM, Ellevate Network, and Natura build brand strength by creating and supporting communities of customers, staff, and stakeholders.

CERTIFYING PRIORITIES

Like people, brands too have a social identity. They belong to WE brand communities that badge the things that matter to them and certify the ethos behind their operations to customers, employees, supply chain partners, investors, and other stakeholders. CECP. Certified B Corp. USDA Certified Organic. Fairtrade. CleverCare. FSC. The number of communities for like-minded brands is growing, and as it grows, the number of labels on product packaging that help shape a brand's identity for consumers is increasing.

The Forest Stewardship Council: Advancing Sustainability

The Forest Stewardship Council (FSC), for example, is a WE brand founded in 1993, after the 1992 Rio Earth Summit. It became a legal entity in 1994 after its secretariat was established in Mexico. Deforestation was one of the issues that remained contentious among governments after the 1992 Summit. So a number of nongovernmental organizations, including World Wildlife Fund and Greenpeace, joined forces and crafted an innovative nongovernmental, independent international forest certification scheme. Today, approximately 31,000 companies in about 150 different countries are certified, and FSC represents approximately 475 million acres of working forest lands, which is about 10 percent of the total working forest in the world. Balancing the interests of different stakeholders, FSC is governed by three chambers, representing environmental, economic, and social interests, each with equal voting power to ensure triple-bottom-line decision making. Each chamber is further subdivided into North and South, to safeguard equity among the different interest groups, geographic regions, and economic power. The United States, for example, is in the North chamber.[2]

Companies typically have some combination of three primary motivations for engaging with the FSC community: (1) values alignment, (2) supply chain risk mitigation, and (3) brand enhancement. Even companies known for doing good, such as Patagonia, Ben & Jerry's, New Leaf Paper, and Seventh Generation, work with FSC to some degree to decrease supply chain vulnerability and risk (political, environmental or manmade) and underline the credibility of their social identity.

As I discussed in the previous chapter, Kimberly-Clark is a brand that has been focused on doing the right thing since it was founded. Yet in 2004 when Greenpeace began its Kleercut campaign, targeting

Kleenex and Kimberly-Clark operations in Canada, the company didn't have a good response. As our knowledge of environmental factors increases and public sentiment shifts, brands—most especially those that have responsibility or doing good built into their social identity—must necessarily progress their operations. In 2009, after understanding the problem and researching solutions, Kimberly-Clark outlined a new sourcing strategy that specified the goal of 40 percent of fiber in North American tissue products be either recycled or certified by FSC. Although Kimberly-Clark's response was five years in the making, the brand became an industry leader in sustainable logging practices and ultimately encouraged less deforestation across the industry.

That same year, one year before it issued its *People, Planet and Products* framework and 2015 sustainability goals, Kimberly-Clark conducted market research to understand whether the FSC label on product packaging impacted perceptions of the brand. They found it positively did, even though people weren't necessarily aware of FSC. Thanks to Kimberly-Clark, demand for FSC-certified fiber increased across the tissue industry, and as demand outpaced production, logging companies themselves were forced to shift toward more environmentally friendly operations. Kimberly-Clark's relationships with retailers such as Walmart and Target, who were interested in developing more sustainable practices as well, were strengthened as they sought to learn about the company's new strategy.

If you include packaging and marketing materials, forest products extend well beyond tissues, toilet paper, and envelopes into virtually every product category. There are FSC Band-Aids®, FSC Ben & Jerry's, FSC Lego®, and FSC Ribena juice. FSC certifies brands with one of three product labels:

1. **FSC 100 percent:** Products contain only material from FSC-certified forests and meet FSC standards.

2. **FSC Mixed Sources:** Products with material from FSC-certified forests, recycled material, or other controlled sources.

3. **FSC Recycled:** Products contain only postconsumer material and may include some pre-consumer material.

While the different badges make sense to sustainability professionals, their distinctions are bound to confuse the average person who's
looking to help the environment through their purchases. With un-
aided-awareness scores for FSC hovering around 10 percent in the
United States and a global goal of 20 percent awareness by 2020, FSC
US is aware that it needs to educate shoppers about the meaning and
purpose of certification.

The Campaign to Save Our Forests

Kimberly-Clark, Proctor & Gamble, McDonald's, HP Inc., International
Paper, and Williams-Sonoma partnered with FSC US and the World
Wildlife Fund to create a campaign, called *One Simple Action, One Profound Impact*, to help people understand how purchasing FSC-certified
products helps sustain our forests. FSC US launched a video in October
of 2016, *FSC: One Simple Action*,[3] and primarily distributed it via social
media channels. FSC US followed the video with a digital brand guide
to make it easier for certified companies to use the label on packaging.
Sharing FSC's story and the meaning of certification at point of purchase (POP) is an important next step to educate consumers and encourage the purchase of FSC-certified products over noncertified ones. With
POP shelf space selling at premium prices, however, financial commitment from manufacturing companies and retail brands will be necessary.

Certified forests will soon come to life for everyone through an interactive, virtual experience that FSC US is working on with Google to
create. Using the Google Street View application program interface, the
digital initiative will transport people to one or more certified forests.
Viewers will be invited to explore a certified forest on their phone, at
their desk, and potentially in the store aisle. The site is being designed to
educate, inform, and encourage people to buy FSC products. In creating
a connection between individual people and the certified forests themselves, FSC US will foster a sense of being a part of something more
meaningful and "bigger than me"—the feeling of belonging to a larger
collective focused on sustaining the environment.[4]

GIFFGAFF:
SERVE THE PEOPLE, SERVE YOUR BRAND

Virtual groups naturally developed alongside our ability to connect with people across the globe, and as they did many brands were compelled to launch online communities for customers and for employees. Often, these communities were not founded with a strategy to cultivate meaningful connections. Instead, brands saw them as an opportunity to broadcast messages, collect personal data, and offer promotions. To successfully nurture trust and, even more so, faithfulness, online communities, like traditional ones, must serve the people first, not the brand. Brands must facilitate, not own communities—and enhance, not control ongoing conversations on these platforms by way of the content they contribute. For many brands, however, this act of giving to give, not giving to get, does not come naturally.

While affinity for a brand and what it stands for likely brings members of a community together, it's essential that the brand nurtures an environment that helps people to connect and belong. Importantly, people join communities to interact with other people who share a common social identity or a common goal, not to socialize with marketing and sales promotions. While brand purpose should sit at the forefront of a community, every member should be equally free to shape the conversation. Communities create shared meaning only through the interplay of their members. And they remain relevant only when they continually morph with members' evolving needs, interests, and rituals.

Giffgaff—a mobile virtual network in the UK focused on enriching its customers' connections with the brand through building community—piggybacks on the network of its parent company, O2. A WE brand with ME sensibilities, the mobile phone provider launched in 2009 as "an experiment." Determined to start a different type of mobile network, Vincent Boon, a member of the start-up team, looked to crowdsourcing to find out what his potential customers really wanted when he set out to build the company. He created an online forum, the input from which directly informed the brand's pricing and packages. Gathering feedback from its customers and altering its practices accordingly constitute one of Giffgaff's hallmarks. Going one step further, the brand is transparent when explaining to customers which changes it adopts—and why it has done so.[5]

Giffgaff's appeal comes from its low prices, no contracts, and fair treatment of customers. Each month, the brand texts customers telling them how reduce the cost of their mobile package. Leapfrogging 160 mobile virtual network operator (MVNO) competitors for a top-3 slot, Giffgaff became the UK's third-largest mobile carrier in 2014.[6]

Building Community Through Engagement

Today, with its online forum sitting at the center of its community, the company outsources its customer service. Users go to this virtual space for help, posting questions—most of which are answered within five minutes—rather than contacting a call center. Unlike other community-board sites, where members help one another out of kindness or to demonstrate their tech prowess, Giffgaffers reap very tangible benefits: The company pays them each time they answer another member's questions. Members are rewarded through tariffs and the Payback scheme, which offers cashback, airtime credit, or a charity donation in return for friends activating SIM cards.[7] The community also offers customers opportunities to contribute ideas for product innovation and marketing and promotions.[8]

Giffgaff's newsletter, which focuses on the latest news, events, newcomers, and community activities, is also run by its community members. Members craft their own content and, also, publicly recognize one another. Using three levels of acknowledgment, they express their appreciation for one another and thereby enhance esteem:

▶ Kudos: Kudos are awarded when a member has helped someone out, given when someone has posted or shared something "great" or bestowed in affirmation of another member's idea.

▶ Best Answer: A graphic "tick" highlights a tech support solution or answer that has successfully aided other community members.

▶ Payback: Giffgaff's way of compensating community members for jobs well done: members earn payback helping others, getting involved creatively, sharing ideas, recommending Giffgaff, or just having fun in the community. Members claim Payback funds twice each year in the form of direct deposit to their bank accounts, a credit with Giffgaff, or as a charitable contribution.[9]

Nearly since its inception, Giffgaff has won numerous industry awards, including:

- ► 2010, Most Innovative Community Award at the Social CRM Customer Excellence Awards[10]

- ► 2010, the Forrester Groundswell Award for excellence in social marketing[11]

- ► 2010, Nominated for the Marketing Society's Brand of the Year, losing to the department store John Lewis Partnership[12]

- ► 2012, Best MVNO (mobile virtual network operator) in the Mobile Industry Awards[13]

- ► 2016, uSwitch Mobile Awards Best Network gong, Best for Data, Best for SIM only, and Best Customer Service[14]

In November of 2013, Giffgaff partnered with Ratesetter, a peer-to-peer lender, to offer its members credit lines of up to £700 to purchase Giffgaff mobile phones. In 2015, it expanded the program to include peer-to-peer microlending with loans of up to £7,500. The company's chief operating officer, Nigel Sudell, hinted that the brand might be re-shaping itself "from a community-led network to a community business" that uses the profits it generates to have a positive local impact.[15]

Connecting on a Deeper Level

Through communications that confirm it gets Millennials and older Gen Zers, Giffgaff demonstrates it, too, is a member of their community, not only the creator of it. In the brand's 2014 online film series, *We're all the boss*, for example, it unabashedly demonstrated it sympathizes with young adults "stuck" living at home with their parents. As the advertisements demonstrate, parents don't *intentionally* embarrass their young adult children. They simply do so by being themselves and going about their everyday lives. The problem isn't parents—it's the fact that *you're* living at home and have to bear witness to them. The somewhat ironical *We're all the boss* campaign points to the fact that, in Giffgaff's community-driven platform, no one individual is boss and simultaneously stirs both genuine embarrassment and empathy for our homebound Millennial.

As part of the campaign, in partnership with the UK radio station Kiss FM, Giffgaff sponsored a contest offering the prize of one year's rent to enable the winner to move out of their parents' home. Listeners entered by creating and submitting a short-form video or by posting why they deserved to win on Twitter or Instagram, with #KISSgiffgaff. Giffgaff Brand Director Tom Rainsford said of the campaign:

> We're aware that the financial future for many young people is unclear—so [we] wanted to give an ambitious individual the opportunity to have their rent paid for a year. That way, the money saved can be utilised on doing something they've always wanted—whether that be starting a new business, going to university or even just put towards saving for their own place one day.[16]

When a Kiss FM DJ and camera crew delivered the good news to the winner, genuinely shocked, she shared, "This is like the best thing that ever happened to me—I was thinking I could maybe move out when I was about fifty." Other young adults still living at home were invited to get involved in the conversation and vent their frustrations using the hashtag #alltheboss."[17]

In a 2016 KPMG Nunwood study, Giffgaff rose 45 places in the UK Customer Experience Excellence rankings, with its strongest scores achieved in Time and Effort, Personalisation, and Integrity. As reported in the study, the brand places its primary focus on its customer community—over its staff. This exceptional practice was noted in the study for cultivating a more emotional connection between members and the brand.[18]

An outgrowth of its community, Giffgaff's Run by You Awards were born out of a member's idea in 2013. Originally known as the GAFF-TAs, a play on the British Academy of Film and Television Arts (BAFTA) awards, they evolved into Giffgaff's first-ever online award ceremony for their 2016–2017 recognitions. For the fourth awards ceremony in

2017, Giffgaff pared its original ten categories down to four categories: Creative Genius, Bright Spark, Savvy Sage, and Lifetime Achievement. A video tribute, the verbal and visual equivalent of balloons and confetti, was made for each winner. The tributes extolled the reasons why other community members chose that member and even dove into metrics, including—for instance—the number of times other community members viewed the useful, problem-solving information that the member shared. In an interview with *The Telegraph*, Mike Fairman, Giffgaff's founder said, "We're driven by a belief that working with our members is better than trying to be a normal business. . . . We do it because it's the right thing to do." The etymology of Giffgaff befits the brand; it's a Scottish word that means "for mutual benefit." And in focusing on all things community, this is what Giffgaff offers.

IBM: JAMMING TO TRANSFORM ORGANIZATIONAL CULTURE

People can gain a sense of connection when a brand unites them for a day, a weekend, a month, or longer around a common purpose. In the same way musicians come together to interact with other players and make music for their own enjoyment, brands can connect employees, customers, and others virtually through the spirit of co-creation, innovation, and collaboration. A jam is an interactive session or collaborative event, designed to broaden thinking and hone solutions in a creative, experimental environment. Jams offer a safe way for bold, unexpected ideas to surface.

Through selective crowdsourcing, jams encourage social communities. Whether used to solve specific problems, innovate new products and services, or involve participants in brand and culture development, jams bring people together through focused conversation to create something they couldn't do alone. They foster a sense of belonging and mutual respect by soliciting and valuing participants' input. A jam enables a brand to create a secure community that encourages formulating new ideas, experimenting with new ways of working, and connecting people through shared purpose. The most effective jams transition participants into ongoing conversations that redefine their relationship with the brand and enhance loyalty.

Reconnecting to Core Values

IBM has used jams to involve its 400,000 employees in shifting corporate culture, strategy development, and innovation since 2001, three years before Facebook was founded and five years before the first tweet. Incorporated in New York in 1911, IBM's roots can be traced back to the 1880s[19] Today IBM operates in 175 countries and has twelve research labs on six continents.[20,21] In March 2002, Sam Palmisano became the CEO of IBM when Lou Gerstner, who had been running the company since April 1993, retired. Palmisano was named chairman in January 2003.[22] Palmisano retired in 2012, and Ginni Rometty has been president, CEO, and chairman since.[23]

Gerstner was brought in as an outsider to transform the mainframe provider to a modern hardware and information technology business and to make it financially sound. He did both. Yet, when Palmisano, a "true-blue IBMer who started at the company in 1973 as a salesman in Baltimore,"[24] stepped in, he noticed something was missing. As one former IBMer from the company's brand strategy and research team noted:

> Gerstner did what was needed to right the ship, but some of the baby was thrown out with the bath water. What made IBM great could still make IBM great. IBM had a focus on the individual. The individual contribution was valued. And that became sort of an entitlement mentality, which Gerstner got rid of. But then there was still some of the respect for the individual that may have gotten thrown away with that. And some of IBM's other values. So Sam really wanted to talk to people and say: What does it mean to be an IBMer, you know, right now, moving into the 21st Century? What does that really mean?[25]

In a speech at Columbia University in New York City in 1962, Tom Watson Jr.—then chairman of IBM—codified the three Basic Beliefs that had defined IBM's place as Big Blue in the world for decades:[26]

► Respect for the individual: Respect for the dignity and the rights
of each person in the organization

► Customer service: To give the best customer service of any company in the world

► Excellence: The conviction that an organization should pursue
all tasks with the objective of accomplishing them in a superior
way[27]

Asking the Tough Questions

Forty years after this speech, Palmisano felt something was missing. The
brand was financially sound, yet IBM's identity was culturally wounded.
He sensed that the Basic Beliefs, which effectively had guided decision
making for decades, could act as a foundation to revitalize the essence of
what it meant to be an IBMer. Indeed, two years earlier while at Interbrand, I learned something similar while researching whether the IBM
brand should update the iconic logo designed by Paul Rand in 1972. A
stealth team from the brand group and design lab wondered whether
modifying IBM's identity would more effectively signal the new, more
agile IBM to the world. One of the key insights from the exploration
was that current and potential customers were not looking for a clean
break with IBM's heritage. They wanted to know that levels of quality
and reliability historically associated with IBM coexisted with the company's new business model.

Employee's behaviors, not just products and communications, define
perceptions of a brand—when they are at the office, visiting clients, and
speaking about work at a dinner party. IBM was shifting from being a
traditional, hierarchical corporation to a more agile, knowledge-based
one. IBM employees themselves had to participate in reshaping the Basic
Beliefs to reflect this change. Like Anders Moberg and Russel Johnson of
IKEA and Tom Falk of Kimberly-Clark, Palmisano had the foresight to
know that creating an inclusive process would most effectively advance
the brand. As the former IBMer who was part of the team that conducted the research reflected, "It all started in Sam's office."

Palmisano first sought input from 300 senior executives, then
opened the discussion to a wider number of people through focus

groups. Insight from the research set the themes for IBM's ValuesJam, an online conversation over seventy-two hours in July of 2003. The ValuesJam was broadly centered on the theme, "What does it mean to be IBM today?" Fifteen to 20 percent of IBMers are estimated to have participated in the ValuesJam, including Palmisano himself.[28,29]

As I scanned a copy of one of the discussion boards available online, I was struck by how the same conversation could take place in a number of large U.S. businesses. Years of cuts focused on delivering shareholder value had eroded IBM's culture of belongingness and, in turn, employee loyalty. The first basic belief Tom Watson Jr. codified, "Respect for the individual," no longer resonated across Big Blue's culture. "Treating employees well and fairly," the first attribute of Step 3 of Brand Citizenship—Responsibility—was absent. One participant in the ValuesJam pondered if there was a way to link shareholder value to employee value:

> Actually, I think there is a way to link the stockholder value to employee value. How would the market react if at an announcement of quarterly earnings our senior executive team made a statement that earnings are down a cent a share because we chose to invest that value directly in our employees? We might get a positive market response— or not.[30]

The ValuesJam demonstrated that Palmisano's hunch that something was missing from IBM was on the mark. Over the next two months, analysts combed through the discussion boards and used analytics to mine the data and identify common words and themes. Alongside the analysts, Palmisano and other executives read through countless comments themselves so they could internalize sentiments across the business. A small team that included Palmisano then crafted a revised set of corporate values that were introduced to the company in an intranet broadcast in November 2003:[31,32]

- ► Dedication to every client's success

- ► Innovation that matters—for our company and for the world

- ► Trust and personal responsibility in all our relationships[33]

Shifting Culture and Building Community over Time

Demonstrating how the values translated into everyday operations was an essential next step. Palmisano charged the head of IBM's e-business hosting services for the U.S. industrial sector with identifying gaps between the company's practices and new values. He then instructed his fifteen direct reports to do the same. Nearly a year after the new values were announced, IBM hosted another jam focused on identifying organizational barriers to innovation and revenue growth.[34] Since then, IBM has hosted several other jams, including InnovationJam in 2006, which built a community that included external participants, seeded ten new IBM businesses with investment totaling $100 million and ultimately led to IBM's Smarter Planet agenda. It had a second InnovationJam in 2008 and one in 2013 centered on creating the best experiences for IBM clients. IBM also formed a jam-based consulting service that works with governments and other organizations to effect scalable societal change.[35, 36]

Importantly, for some IBMers, the company missed an opportunity to communicate the brand's new cultural narrative and more effectively create belongingness companywide after the ValuesJam in 2003. As one former employee shared:

> It created these things that were important that may have been the whole essence of what an IBMer was, but then no one held anyone accountable to act on them to build the community. It was like you set up the framework to build a bigger sense of community and connectivity across the organization through doing this ValuesJam. And there never were stories of IBMers that did these great things or that were really living up to the IBM values. All I got was like a mug and a pen that had the values on them.[37]

It was an important insight: Ongoing conversations alongside periodic event-based jams would have given the 80–85 percent of employees who didn't participate in the ValuesJam a way to become active contributors as IBM transformed its culture. And global stories or case studies exemplifying the brand's ethos in action would likely have fostered greater interconnectivity company-wide and imprinted the values into the brand's DNA more integrally. Although digital communities and social media were not a part of daily life in 2003, many companies less technologically advanced than IBM had intranets and shared databases. Yet this missing piece should not undermine Palmisano's prescience. Even today, many businesses don't facilitate interconnectivity between departments, offices, and regions beyond email. In hosting the ValuesJam, Palmisano took a risk that few CEOs have.

Shifting company culture and cultivating community across an organization as large as IBM is a journey that takes time and, in part, demands learning by trial and error. Palmisano understood that IBM's robust heritage was central to revitalizing the feeling of belonging across the organization. And he further recognized that shared identity and purpose would stimulate innovation, growth, and stability over the long term.

ELLEVATE NETWORK: "INVESTING IN WOMEN IS SMART BUSINESS"

The number of formal and informal communities has skyrocketed with technological interconnectivity and social networking. While many brands have offline and online presences, not many branded communities do—especially those with a global reach. Ellevate, a Certified B Corp focused on changing the culture of business from the inside out by investing in women, is one that has.

Originally founded in 1997, by Janet Hanson as 85 Broads, the Ellevate community has grown over twenty years from an informal group of female colleagues to a unique global network for women. With its original name a play on Goldman Sachs's address, 85 Broad Street, where Janet and the other founding members had worked, the network began as an alumni group for Goldman Sachs's women. Today Ellevate is a unique online network with chapters in more than forty cities across the globe and tens of thousands of members.

As Hanson tells it, she had "four different careers" at Goldman, and during her stints had sent letters to the executives she knew explaining that they could keep more women from leaving if they created a firmwide network to connect them. A few years after departing the company and starting her own asset management firm, Milestone Capital Management LLC, Hanson decided to bring Goldman women together herself. For her, facilitating this network wasn't about sharing bitterness or resentment; it was about collective experience and camaraderie with other intelligent, accomplished women—about fostering social identity and community through belongingness.[38]

In 1997, Hanson hosted a dinner at the Water Club in New York City, inviting all the women she had met during her tenure at Goldman. She gave out T-shirts that her sister had made with the 85 Broads logo on it: a woman climbing up the ladder and adding an S to the street sign that said, 85 Broad. As Hanson recalls:

> Everybody was like: "Oh, this is great. . . . " But there was no efficient way [for the founding members] to stay connected. . . . We knew after that first dinner it was going to be fun to do. We can get people together, but there's no way that we're going to be able to really scale this. And then, the Internet came along.

Two years later, in September of 1999, she launched the website 85broads.com; one month after that, on October 27, 1999, Reed Abelson at *The New York Times* wrote an article about the network, "Management: A Network of Their Own; From an Exclusive Address, A Group for Women Only." After this spotlight, 85 Broads, which had seventy members at the time, began to gain momentum.

In February of 2000, Hanson was giving a speech to the Harvard Business School's Women's Society about what it was like to launch her own firm after being at Goldman Sachs. She got halfway through the speech when she decided to pivot and divulge her enthusiasm for 85 Broads. Hanson remembers a student raising her hand and stating the obvious: "It's really great. Glad you did it. But look around this room." The student then pointed out that the number of women who were going into investment banking was tiny and that the number of women who were going into investment banking at Goldman Sachs was even tinier. The student finally concluded, "So you're talking about a network that the vast majority of women in this room cannot join." And Hanson had a grand *aha!* moment. On the spot, she decided the network would no longer be exclusively for current and former Goldman Sachs women. And then, it *really* took off.[39]

With business as its through line, the network, which Hanson personally funded and for which she did not charge a membership fee, initially attracted women with MBAs. In 2001, after seeing the impact 85 Broads could have for young women, Hanson introduced a co-mentoring program, which she called Broad2Broad, for women studying in MBA programs at leading business schools. The co-mentoring program recognized that women of all ages have something to offer one another. With this knowledge, 85 Broads began to welcome women studying in any graduate program and soon thereafter opened the network to undergraduate women. As women in college joined the community, it became apparent to Hanson, who read every potential member's application herself, that the top U.S. schools were also attracting smart women from outside the United States. Excitement around this growing awareness that women across all six continents were doing remarkable things with their lives inspired her to expand 85 Broads's scope and go global. The reach of 85 Broads extended to include professional women worldwide from all industries. "We became like flypaper for women who wanted to be part of a network of other very smart women, but it was women from different countries, cultures, regions, backgrounds."[40]

Hanson joined Lehman Brothers in 2004 and was working there at the time it collapsed in 2008. With her personal finances impacted by the firm's demise, she could no longer support the network herself. She raised just enough capital to keep it going and created a tiered fee membership structure in 2009. Confirming the belief that "women rock and have so much power, individually and collectively," the fee structure had little impact on the network's popularity. For members, 85 Broads was a trailblazer that captured and amplified what extraordinary women were doing internationally. It enhanced their sense of self and social identity. Every member of the community was connected online through shared personal stories, and chapters sponsored local events where members met, professionally networked, and engaged on a more personal level.

Passing the Baton to a New Generation

By May of 2013, when Sallie Krawcheck, formerly president of the Global Wealth & Investment Management division of Bank of America, and Ally McDonald, who became 85 Broads's global president, acquired 85 Broads from Hanson, the organization comprised 30,000 women, representing 130 countries with more than forty chapters and campus clubs. In selling 85 Broads, Hanson saw herself as securing the organization's future by passing the baton to a younger, highly accomplished professional woman who was focused on raising up women.[41] Krawcheck shared her reasons for purchasing the network in a LinkedIn post on May 13, 2013:

> Networks are beginning to operate alongside the traditional corporate structure, serving as a modern means for individuals to come together to exchange ideas and information. They enable their members to contribute to, and pull from, the network to accomplish more than the sum of the parts would indicate. Powerful connections can increasingly be made outside the C-suites, boardrooms and private clubs. . . .
>
> The next step is to move from advocacy to real investments in women, just as smart companies—and smart investors—are increasingly recognizing.
>
> I am becoming involved with and investing in 85 Broads because investing in women is smart business. And women investing in themselves and in others, as they do through the network, is even smarter business.[42]

By summer of 2014, 85 Broads had grown to 34,000 members, and Krawcheck rebranded the company to Ellevate Network, signaling the shift from advocating for women to investing in them. Along with the name change, the network also announced a joint venture with Pax World Management, a fund management company, called the Pax Ellevate Global Women's Index Fund. Reflecting Ellevate's belief that investing in women is smart business, the fund focuses on a selection of companies culled from a global index according to the gender diversity of their top ranks.[43] Companies in the fund had women in 31 percent of board seats and 24 percent of executive management positions, compared with a global average of 11 percent for each. A portion of Ellevate's revenues from membership dues and events are invested in the Pax Ellevate Global Women's Index Fund. And members of the network can invest in the institutional share class of the fund, which has a lower fee structure. As Krawcheck explained in an interview with CNBC, "When women are economically engaged, our community is much larger."[44]

B Corp Status:
Solving Social Problems Through the Power of Business

In February of 2016, six months after Kristy Wallace became Ellevate's new president, the network was certified as a B Corp. According to Wallace, who was the driving force behind certification, becoming a B Corp was a natural next step in achieving their mission "to close the gender achievement gap in business by providing women with a community to lean on and learn from." Wallace ties becoming a B Corp directly to the network's purpose:

> We're a mission-driven organization. A for-profit centered on closing the gender achievement gap in business, helping women get ahead, equal pay, paid leave, starting companies, raising money for their companies, getting on boards. All of this is very important to us, so we looked into being a B Corp for many reasons—one of which was to support that mission and ensure it remains a guiding principle for our business. Becoming a B Corp was also part of a bigger picture. When you become a B Corp, you go through a pretty extensive process of self-evaluation around: Are you good for your workers? Are you good for your community? Are you good for your environment? And particularly for us as a business: Are we good for the women in our community? Are we really all around doing the right things and thinking about them in the right way and staying true to our mission to drive impact for them? ... We wanted to ally ourselves with other organizations that were mission-driven and focused on solving social problems through the power of business. ... The B Corp community is focused on creating a more diverse and inclusive workforce, and Ellevate partnered with B Corp to create guides and resources.[45]

ELLEVATE'S SEVEN GUIDING PRINCIPLES: ALIGNED WITH THE B CORP ETHOS

Ellevate's seven guiding principles inherently align with the B Corp ethos:[46]

- ► **There is power in diversity:** We value different perspectives and recognize that they help us grow. We challenge the norm to make diversity a reality.

- ► **We work to make the world a better place:** We believe that the world can change for the better and we are making it happen. We don't wait for others to do it.

- ► **Community lifts us up:** We use the power of teamwork to solve problems. We communicate openly and work together to elevate each individual.

- ► **We practice gratitude:** We're passionate about the work we're doing and recognize that we're privileged to be doing it.

- ► **Honesty, integrity & respect, always:** When in question, we always default to the "most respectful interpretation" of a situation.

- ► **Be authentic:** We believe in the power of being accountable to our work as well as our personal lives. We work to make everyone comfortable presenting their genuine selves inside and outside of the workplace.

- ► **Action is important:** We get sh*t done—without freaking out.

Source: Ellevate Network. "Ellevate Network's Values & Guiding Principles." https://www.ellevatenetwork.com/articles/7677-ellevate-network-s-values-guiding-principles

Helping individual members achieve their aims—and thereby raising their self-esteem—is Ellevate's priority. The Network offers multiple ways to interact. It has an active and engaged social medial presence that is crafted to be a positive voice to lift women up, inspire them, and share relevant information. Its weekly podcast, which Ellevate launched in August of 2016, includes raw, true stories of women and how they navigated the business world. *Morning Boost* newsletter invites members to local chapter events, reminds them of upcoming jam sessions, offers targeted articles, and polls members on their opinions on key issues. Further appreciating that different women have different reasons for joining the community, Ellevate invested in an algorithm-based infrastructure to customize the experience for every user. As Wallace explained, "We want to help you, and we want to hand deliver to you the tools, the information, the resources you need to get ahead."

More than 500 events annually provide how-to advice, coaching, education, community support, and friendship, through seminars, online jams, casual get-togethers, mentoring, and formal networking. With closing the gender gap as central to its purpose, Ellevate's programs also aim to advance the workforce, educate employers, and progress laws and legislation to effect more scalable change. The Network partners with thirty to forty corporations to create internal women's networks and leverage the tools and resources it offers individual members. It also collaborated with the White House Council on Women and Girls and interacts with local politicians and legislatures regarding bills and laws and issues pertaining to women and girls, or women in the workplace.[47]

Twenty years after Janet Hanson sought to connect women alumni from Goldman Sachs, the Ellevate Network continues to galvanize women to support one another through the power of business and the power of community. When I think about Ellevate's purpose and the concept of how engaging women economically helps to progress society, I envision a rich future for the organization—and the potential to further broaden its social impact: Imagine, if in addition to the Pax Ellevate Global Women's Index Fund, the organization also created a microfinance fund or series of grants for woman-owned start-ups in disadvantaged communities, domestically in the United States and abroad.

Ellevate could even go one step further in supporting these fledgling businesses. It could connect them with members who would provide pro bono services in finance, strategic planning, marketing, design, or technology—the skills any new business needs to succeed. The network's social impact would grow, individual members' sense of belonging would be grounded in even more meaning, and the gender achievement gap in business would narrow. A win-win-win strategy.

NATURA: IN HARMONY WITH ONESELF, COMMUNITY, AND NATURE

Founded in 1969 as a door-to door operation by Antonio Luiz Seabra, the Brazilian cosmetics firm Natura has a global sales network of more than 1.4 million consultants and 7,000 employees.[48] Frustrated with brands that promoted eternal youth, Seabra envisioned "cosmetics as a means for self-knowledge and promoter of well-being, powered by human relations as a way to express life."[49] Natura, which sells premium mass-market products, launched its first line of men's products in 1970 and followed with women's cosmetics two years later. In 2004, the company went public and was listed on the Sao Paolo Stock Exchange.[50] In December 2012, it announced it was acquiring a 65 percent stake in the Australian cosmetics manufacturer Aesop for $71.6 million. In January 2017, it exercised its options and acquired 100 percent of the company.[51] And today, 53.5 percent of Brazilian households purchase the Natura brand at least once a year.

Natura perceives its present and future as part of an expansive and intertwined community that includes customers, beauty consultants, employees, the world, and nature. The brand's tagline, *"Bem Estar Bem,"* literally translates to "well-being well." Rodolfo Guttila, director of corporate affairs and government relations from 2001 through 2013, explained the company's definition of well-being as "the harmonious, pleasant relationship of a person with oneself, with one's body. Being well is the empathic, successful, and gratifying relationship of a person with others, with nature, and with the whole."

Natura's holistic, integrated philosophy is further summarized by four principles—humanism, balance, transparency, and creativity—which are framed through a series of core beliefs.

NATURA'S CORE BELIEFS

► Life is a chain of relationships.

► Nothing in the universe stands alone. Everything is inter-dependent.

► Natura believes that valuing relationships is the foundation of the great human revolution in the search for peace, solidarity, and life in all of its manifestations.

► Continuously striving for improvement, by developing individuals, organizations, and society.

► Commitment to the truth is the route to enhance quality of relationships.

► The greater the individual diversity, the greater the wealth and vitality of the whole.

Source: Natura Annual Report. 2008. PDF download.

Formulating products based on the "biodiversity of the Brazilian flora," connectivity, belongingness, and self-esteem are central to the Natura brand. Long before Dove began advocating for "Real Beauty," Natura started a conversation with women in 1992 to understand how their backgrounds impacted their individual perceptions of beauty. In 1996, Natura's Chronos brand, which was introduced in 1986, rolled out the manifesto *"Muhler Bonita de Verdade,"* which translates in English to "Truly Beautiful Woman." The campaign that supported the manifesto aimed to fight stereotypes by using real women, not models.[52]

Building Community Through Education, Training, and Social Outreach

With a presence in Mexico, Chile, Colombia, Argentina, Peru, Bolivia, and France, Natura's sales model is comparable to Avon's in the United

States. Consultants have the choice to sell products only or to sell products and recruit, train, and coach new consultants. Perhaps a direct result of the company living its ethos across its day-to-day operations, the brand has one of the lowest turnover rates of direct sales companies.[53] Cultivating a global community, Natura works closely with its consultants and supports them as they grow their businesses. It uses a Human Developmental Index, which accounts for health, education, and overall knowledge, to identify the best social investments to improve consultants' quality of life. In 2013, for example, the brand pledged to integrate its nearly 74,300 low-income beauty consultants in Mexico into a specialized job training program.[54] At the time, approximately 98 percent of consultants in Mexico were women who lacked formal education or prior work experience. In addition to strategic planning, direct sales, computer skills, customer service, accounting, and project management, the program also fostered self-awareness and guided the consultants to become agents for change in their own communities.[55]

Natura earmarks 3 percent of its profits for public education and community investment to improve quality of life for the communities in which it operates.[56] The Instituto Natura, which the brand started in 2000 to improve public education in Brazil and Latin America, further raises funds for investment in education through the *Crer par aver* ("Believe to see") product line, which is twenty years old. All the proceeds from the sale of *Crer par aver* are invested in educational projects throughout Brazil, many through Natura Movimento.

In 2006, Natura consultants formed Natura Movimento ("Natura Movement")—a community of friends of Natura Brasil, united by the belief that "the future of mankind depends on capacity for solidarity." Through this program, the brand fosters collaboration, creates a greater sense of belongingness, and scales its impact. Encouraged to participate in existing social and environmental outreach programs or develop their own initiatives, consultants are liberated to become "agents of transformation" themselves. More than 2.6 million young people and adults in Brazil have had the opportunity to learn to read and write thanks to Natura Movement.[57]

Amazônia:
Using Sustainable Business Practices to Improve Quality of Life

Natura and innovation have always been synonymous. On its website, the company reports that it renews 30 percent of its portfolio every year, with about 220 product launches. While the idea of offering customers the option of product refills is relatively commonplace now—Natura introduced the concept in 1983, cutting the impact of conventional packaging in half. It was certified as carbon neutral in 2007, and in 2015 Forbes hailed the brand "as one of 75 most innovative growth companies."

Valuing indigenous knowledge, Natura has tapped rural Brazil for product development for decades. As a result, the company has "signed partnership agreements" with thirty-six communities. Further relying on the Amazon's biodiversity as a platform for research and development, Natura launched an ambitious Amazônia program in 2011 to improve the quality of life not only in the communities it works with but in the region as a whole. Like its Human Development Index, Natura uses a Community Social Progress Index to measure quality of life and well-being in riverside communities along the Jurua River in Amazonas and thereby generate more than income for families in the region. Michael Porter's Social Progress Index, that uses fifty-two social and environmental indicators, forms the basis for the index.[58]

The Amazônia program also expands and reinforces the brand's long-term commitment to the area by promoting new sustainable business practices based on science, innovation, production chains, and local entrepreneurship. As part of the program, the company committed to achieving four goals by 2020:

- ▶ Purchase 30 percent of raw ingredients from sustainable sources.

- ▶ Invest one billion reals in the region.

- ▶ Build an interdisciplinary network of 1,000 researchers focused on the Amazon.

- ▶ Involve between 10,000 and 12,000 small producers in its supply chain.[59]

Leading with B Corp Status

In 2014, Natura made a move that many in sustainability circles and beyond judged as an important game changer for business: The brand became the first publicly traded company to be certified as a B Corp. Until Natura, B Corp firms tended to be privately held and relatively small. As I shared in Chapter 2, becoming a B Corp is a highly detailed process for any company, and applying the necessary performance standards and meeting the legal requirements for certification are even more complex processes for large, multinational public corporations. While other relatively large companies like Kickstarter and Green Mountain Power, a renewable energy company, also received B Corp certification in 2014, they are privately owned and don't even begin to approach Natura's size and global footprint.

Announcing the brand's B Corp status, Roberto Oliveira de Lima, Natura's CEO from 2014 through 2016, said in a press release, "Attaining this important certification strengthens our belief that, yes, we should seek profits, which is the basis of our activities, but that this shouldn't be the sole purpose of our existence."[60]

In December 2014, in a *Fast Company* article, João Paulo Brotto Gonçalves Ferreira, then Natura's vice president of sales and sustainability and CEO since 2016, directly addressed why the company sought B Corp status:

> We decided to become a B Corp after a study carried out in 2013 on sustainable business parameters to help build our Sustainability Vision 2050. From these studies, we found that some practices that are necessary for certification of a B Corp were already incorporated in our activities. . . . We consulted and received positive feedback from shareholders because triple bottom line management has always been in our business model. The certification strengthens Natura's aims to create value for all its stakeholders, a well known [sic] practice by investors.[61]

In recognition of Natura's long-standing commitment to sustainability, UN Environment awarded the brand its 2015 Champions of the Earth award, in the Entrepreneurial Vision category. The honor is bestowed on companies with outstanding track records in and continued commitment to sustainability. Through its eco-innovation life cycle approach, the brand has had an average annual growth of 26 percent from 2005 to 2010 and has doubled in size from 2007 to 2011. Natura achieved socioenvironmental benefits of more than $750,000 in 2012, alone, through selecting suppliers based on high sustainability performance.[62]

While Natura is decidedly a cosmetics company, since its inception it has been a brand on a more holistic mission to create a harmonious and fair future. Without a doubt, Natura is a member of an intertwined global circle that includes people, communities, and the environment. As Guilherme Leal, who joined Natura in 1979 and is now president of the management board and one of the primary shareholders of Natura Cosméticos S.A., states on a brand video on the company's website: "This notion of all things are interconnected, it was the foundation of our commitment to sustainability."

HIGHLIGHTS

CHAPTER 7:
Community: Connect Me

► The social networks and communities we belong to and opt out of in part shape the definition of who we are. All brands have the opportunity to cultivate loyalty and a sense of belongingness by demonstrating that they care about the things that matter most to customers, employees, and other shareholders.

► Brands, like people, express their social identities by joining communities of like-minded companies. For consumer goods, a company's associations are often identified by labels on product packaging that help shape a brand's identity for consumers.

► The Forest Stewardship Council certifies brands sourcing materials from sustainable forests, underlining the credibility of their social identity. Knowing that the number and type of certifications on product packaging is growing, it is working with major corporations to educate consumers on the meaning and purpose of these badges.

► Britain's Giffgaff built a highly successful brand in the competitive telecom space by creating a mobile community based on fair pricing, an online forum at the center of its network, and reaching out to customers in a variety of creative, entertaining, and practical ways.

► IBM learned that even the most cohesive cultures can become unglued in the process of becoming financially sound. Progressively reaching out to employees in a collaborative process to heal wounds and restore the consciousness of shared purpose, it learned how complex and challenging cultivating a sense of belongingness can be.

► Ellevate provides an example of how a network can grow from an informal beginning to an on- and offline global enterprise dedicated to bringing women together in support of one another through the power of business, community, and social purpose.

► Biodiversity, connectivity, belongingness, and fairness are central to Natura, the Brazilian cosmetics giant. Since its inception, it has embraced a holistic mission and viewed itself as part of an interdependent global community.

CHAPTER 8

CONTRIBUTION

Make Me Bigger Than I Am

*Galvanize employees and consumers to experience
giving or change of habits firsthand.*

In the postmillennial era, many of us are passionate about seeing positive change in the world—however we define it—yet struggle with the challenges of changing our behavior to effect this change. This even applies to Millennials. While the media has often painted Millennials as more altruistic than Baby Boomers and Gen Xers, my company's *CultureQ* research has not confirmed this. For example, when asked what type of job would be most appealing to someone entering the workforce, Millennials chose a corporate career over working in a nonprofit or NGO by 100 to 200 percent between 2011 and 2014. Many commentators point to surveys where Millennials report more than other generations that they would purchase products that support a good cause over one that doesn't. While I'm certain those participating in these surveys have good intentions, when confronted with purchase trade-offs concerning price, quality, flavor, and the like, Millennials, like most people, don't always do what they say. As one late twenty-something participant told us in exploratory research we conducted on "Millennial Misconceptions" in 2012: "The biggest misconception is that we are very different from other generations at this age."

Millennials were first labeled the Echo Boom to reflect that they were products of their Baby Boomer parents. Like many of their parents when they were younger, many Millennials hold—or once held—an idealist's desire to right injustices and help those in need. Despite their civic-mindedness and earnest desire for fairness and progress, however, Millennials are also products of a market economy that has morphed into a consumer culture, or market society. Through my company's *CultureQ* research project, I've learned that many Millennials define the boundaries of relationships to suit their needs. Like many Baby Boomers and Gen Xers, they do not readily compromise what they want for a group's, or the collective, betterment. Someone else must do this: a company, a figurehead, government, or other institution. Perhaps Millennials' inclination not to be self-sacrificial, blended with their desire to improve the world they live in, has, in part, led to conscious capitalism gaining traction, as I covered in Chapter 2.

Embracing the philosophy of conscious capitalists, brands positioned at Step 5 are all about unleashing the power of the collective WE to make a meaningful difference, while simultaneously delivering ME benefits to their customers. Well-known brands such as Patagonia, Seventh Generation, Method, TOMs, and Warby Parker are not activist organizations run by radicals angry at the system or nonprofits concentrated on developing programs around single causes. Rather, they are for-profit pragmatists selling awareness of social issues, behavioral modification, and progress as much as goods and services. Inviting people to help progress society or sustain our planet through their purchases, as well as inspiring and enabling employees to do good by working for them, many companies at Step 5 of Brand Citizenship are perceived as generous in spirit while equally focused on doing good and earning a profit.

Eco-friendly, supportive of employees, and advocates for suppliers and people in the developing world, brands positioned at Step 5 often embrace social entrepreneurship, seeking to earn money and simultaneously find integrative ways to solve social and environmental problems. Three years of *CultureQ* research confirmed brands at Step 5 are highly associated with delivering emotional benefits such as:

- ► Feeling proud when I use it

- ► Helping me to give back to society

- ► Making me a more responsible citizen

People who work for companies positioned at Step 5 and those who buy their products and services proudly badge themselves as advocates for the cause the brand is centered on. Both constituents also tend to be fiercely brand loyal. They perceive themselves as belonging to a community of people who care and often judge themselves to be doing good simply by association. That's because these brands distinguish themselves from their competitors through a purpose that is grounded in solving a social or environmental problem that their fans care about. Without this brand purpose defining who they are and what they do, each of these companies would likely just be another consumer goods, clothing, cosmetics, or optics company.

Many positioned at the ultimate end of the WE spectrum are trailblazers, and all have the characteristics of authentic leaders: They are self-aware and self-regulated. The most successful ones integrate Trust, Enrichment, Responsibility, and Community when doing good, and simultaneously serve their customer's ME and social identity needs. They use storytelling to convey the importance of their mission, and they inspire and motivate others to join them in fighting their cause. They are respected for their moral compass and transparent about their priorities and operations—and, through their focus on social or environmental issues, are also transformational. Like Plum Organics, Ellevate, and Natura, brands positioned at Step 5 that are Certified B Corps and/or benefit corporations sought these designations to join a community of like-minded brands and to guarantee that their principles, purpose, and ethos would remain central to their business as it evolved. Importantly, however, a brand does not have to be a Certified B Corp or a benefit corporation to be identified as a Step 5 contributor.

In this chapter, I'll examine how three companies—Lush, Seventh Generation, and The Kenco Coffee Company—succeed in running profitable businesses that are fully committed to a larger purpose.

LUSH: A FRESH PRODUCT, AN INSPIRING STORY

Lush is a perfect brand for the ME to WE era. Officially founded in 1995 in Poole, a city on the south coast of the UK, the brand's roots trace back to the 1970s, and its evolution reads almost like a hero's journey.

After working together in a hair and beauty salon, Mark Constantine, a trichologist, and Liz Weir, a beautician, opened the Herbal Hair and Beauty Clinic in Poole in 1977. They made henna hair colors and beauty products based on natural raw materials. Struggling to sell their products, which were ahead of their time, Constantine reached out to Anita Roddick, who founded the environmentally conscious brand The Body Shop in 1976. Roddick placed a small order for Constantine and Weir's products, and as the Body Shop grew so too did the size of their orders. With business blooming, they hired more employees and bought an herb farm in Cambridge.[1,2,3]

As contract suppliers to The Body Shop, Constantine and Weir developed mainstay products for the brand, such as Peppermint Foot Lotion, Honey Beeswax cleanser (Ultrabland), Herbal Hair Colors (henna), and Body Butters. From the start, Herbal Hair and Beauty Clinic and The Body Shop shared a joint passion for sustainable-ingredient sourcing and minimizing harm to the environment. Constantine even introduced the anti–animal testing policy to The Body Shop.[4] Eventually, Roddick was advised that it was too risky for Herbal Hair and Beauty to own the formulas for many of their best-selling products, so The Body Shop acquired them.[5]

Unable to open any shops for five years due to the specifics of their agreement with The Body Shop, Constantine and Weir sought a new channel for their passion.[6] They invested their funds in Cosmetics To Go, a mail order sideline business Constantine had founded with his wife.[7] Sales were hugely successful, thanks to innovative products such as bath bombs and shower jellies. However, the business model was unsustainable.[8]

In 1995, Constantine, Weir, and their Herbal Hair and Beauty Clinic team from their days supplying The Body Shop opened a store in their original factory in Poole and named it Cosmetic House. Using fresh ingredients from their local market, leftover soap flakes, and essential oils, they began making soap upstairs and selling it downstairs. They made soaps in the same way a restaurant kitchen makes daily specials, based on the ingredients at hand. With inventory changing on a day-to-day basis, Cosmetic House used chalkboards to announce product choices. A signature of the Lush brand, the chalkboards are still used today. Lush developed the signature font still used on their blackboards today from the handwriting of their first employee, Jo. And the concept of a beauty "delicatessen," or what I think of as more of a "farmer's market," where your senses of sight, touch, and smell are stimulated, and friendly people help you choose what to buy, continue to be part of the Lush brand experience.[9]

Dissatisfied with the name Cosmetics House, the team launched a competition among their customers for a new name. A woman from Glasgow, Elizabeth Bennett, suggested *Lush*, a word befitting the brand and the products it sold. The online *Oxford English Dictionary* defines *lush* as an adjective meaning:

> 1. (of vegetation, especially grass) growing luxuriantly...
>
>   1.1 Very rich and providing great sensory pleasure...
>
> 2. *British informal* Sexually attractive...
>
>   2.1 Very good or impressive.[10]

Alternatively, the word is a verb meaning "to make someone drunk," and anyone who's ever walked in—or even passed—a Lush shop will readily tell you how the fragrances and colors of the products may intoxicate your senses.

The Six Pillars

Today, Lush Fresh Handmade Cosmetics has 100 shops in the UK and nearly 950 stores internationally.[11] In addition to soap, bath bombs, and shower jellies, the brand also sells body butters and lotions, shampoo bars and conditioners, and more.

Decidedly distinctive in look and experience from competitive brands, both in-store and online, Lush is transparent about the six pillars that guide its business:

1. 100 percent vegetarian

2. Ethical buying

3. Fighting animal testing

4. Freshest cosmetics online

5. Handmade

6. Naked packaging

These six pillars are further supported in the brand's manifesto.

LUSH BRAND MANIFESTO

► We believe in making effective products from fresh organic* fruit and vegetables, the finest essential oils and safe synthetics.

► We believe in buying ingredients only from companies that do not conduct or commission tests on animals and in testing our products on humans.

► We invent our own products and fragrances. We make them fresh* by hand using little or no preservative or packaging, using only vegetarian ingredients and tell you when they were made.

► We believe in happy people making happy soap, putting our faces on our products and making our mums proud.

► We believe in the right to make mistakes, lose everything and start again.

► We believe our products are good value, that we should make a profit and that the customer is always right.

* We also believe words like "fresh" and "organic" have an honest meaning beyond marketing.

Source: Lush. "We Believe." 2017. http://www.lushusa.com/on/demandware.store/
Sites-Lush-Site/en_US/Stories-Article?cid=article_we-believe-statement

Lush's website, which was refreshed in 2013, blends storytelling with products to create a cross between an activist's or environmentalist's newslog and a stimulating artisanal product palette, which brings their cosmetics to life on-screen. The UK site features Lush Kitchen, where visitors can buy fresh, exclusive products that are sent the day they are made, and The Activist Toolkit, which includes everything from a history of grassroots activism to how-to guides. Simultaneously fun and sophisticated, headlines and photography underline the purity of the brand's handmade products, emphasize ethical buying and social responsibility, and portray natural beauty over unachievable glamour.

Lush is selling a confident belief system, not an image. And online, like offline, this has been a successful strategy. In the first year, sales for the new website were up 20 percent year-on-year, with Lush Kitchen contributing an average of 10 percent to total digital sales.

Lending Global Support to Humanitarian, Environmental, and Animal Rights Causes

From in-store samples to supporting the environment, to fair treatment of animals and people in need, Lush is one of those brands that *gives to give, not to get*. In 2007, it introduced its Charity Pot hand and body lotion, which it uses to raise money in support of humanitarian, environmental, and animal rights causes globally. I remember the first time I spied a Charity Pot in Lush's shop on the King's Road in London. Each product transparently featured a photo and language highlighting the mission of one of the nonprofit organizations Lush supported through the Charity Pot. After reading the labels, I was keen to support the causes, so I opted to buy two Charity Pots, instead of one. Although I didn't think I was "voting" for an organization with my purchase, the labels and highlights compelled me to buy more than I had planned. I strongly suspect I am not the only customer over the years who has done this.

Donating *100 percent* of the purchase price of the Charity Pot (minus taxes), Lush absorbs the costs of production, packaging, and distribution. Offering funding to smaller organizations that have difficulty finding support elsewhere, the brand has contributed more than $20 million through 5,500 donations to charities in forty-two countries. Charity Pot product labels are updated to reflect the charities supported by the fund, and in 2014 Lush reformulated the Charity Pot to include ingredients from its SLush—Sustainable Lush—Fund projects. Established in November 2010, the SLush Fund expands Lush's ethical buying practices from including solely the purchase of fairly traded ingredients to developing supportive partnerships with the communities that produce them. Lush donates 2 percent of the amount it spends on raw materials and packaging to the Fund. The money is then invested in sustainable farming and regenerative community projects.[12]

Lush is a brand that lives its beliefs to the fullest. In 2006, for example, collaborating with its customers, the company precluded the need to produce 3 million plastic bottles through customers' purchases of naked shampoo bars, instead of bottled liquid shampoo. Going one step further than IKEA or H&M as they seek to make their products circular, Lush is aiming to completely eliminate the need to close the loop.

Lush is also known for being political and outspoken, a tone that trickles down from Constantine. On July 12, 2007, for one hour beginning at noon, Lush staff made a bold statement when they went naked, literally. To compel people to buy more "naked" products and urge the press to raise awareness of the environmental problems caused by excessive packaging, Lush staff in fifty-five cities across the UK took to the streets to distribute leaflets wearing only white Lush aprons with the slogan, printed with "Ask me why I'm naked" on the front.[13] The campaign was timed to coincide with a program called, *The Insider: Packaging Is Rubbish*, which aired the next day, on July 13, 2007, on Channel 4 in the UK. On the program, Lush founder Mark Constantine joined forces with the Women's Institute, the largest voluntary women's organization in the UK, to show the public why eliminating packaging must become a strategic imperative to save the environment.

Some called the brand out for cashing in on the 2011 London riots in 2015, when it released a perfume Lavender Hill Mob—featuring an etching of a building aflame. Others saw the perfume as in line with the brand and Constantine's cheeky and even mischievous personality. Stephanie Boyd, Lush's PR representative, defended the decision, clarifying that the product was a celebration of the resistance, not the riots themselves:

> Lavender Hill Mob incense was created as a celebration of what people did and their resistance to the riots, not the riots themselves.
>
> ... It is scented with calming lavender for this reason.

To give back to the global community, while simultaneously pushing its agenda to stop animal testing, Lush began awarding the Lush Prize in

2012. As of 2016, it had awarded £1.5 million in prizes since 2012 with an aim to bring forward the day when safety testing will take place without the use of animals. Twenty winners representing eleven countries won a total of £330,000 in 2016. Of the 2016 winners, Lush noted, "We were especially pleased to have our first winners from China, South Korea and the Middle East."[14]

Putting Customers First While Serving a Larger Purpose

In 2014, the UK magazine for informed consumer choice, *Which?*, rated Lush the country's favorite high street shop because of its "try-before-you-buy offer" and "friendly and knowledgeable staff."[15] Lush had reclaimed its top spot in the poll after being rated number two in 2013. The 2014 annual survey's 12,504 customers who rated high street shops "on price, products, service and after-sales service or returns based on their last visit" gave Lush a total score of 83 percent.[16]

Lush placed at the top of KPMG Nunwood's 2015 Customer Experience Excellence rankings—rating as the number one customer experience brand in the UK. The survey credited Lush's "well-defined customer experience strategy" as helping it to ascend by six places since 2010. According to Nunwood:

> Much of this strategy is underpinned by the company's staunch moral and ethical values that protect the customer just as much as the environment. Lush adheres to this by creating products that shoppers truly need, and does not attempt to force purchases by discounting items. In turn, this helps in the reduction of waste, and therefore helps to protect the planet.

It also noted Lush's philanthropic work, providing legal aid to Guantanamo Bay prisoners, driven by a clever bath bomb offer inviting shoppers to "buy one, set one free." The funds benefited the human rights organization Reprieve—which succeeded in getting two prisoners released. Praising the brand the KPMG Nunwood reported:

> For some brands, it is an action that is easier said than done, but Lush ensures customer satisfaction by employing passionate people to look

after them. These employees are trained to understand customer needs, and to advise on the best products to suit their requirements, and not simply to hit sales targets. Moreover, these staff members are taught about the company's ethical values and manufacturing processes, and it is often the case that many of the people who work at Lush become devoted 'fans' of the products themselves, making them more enthusiastic about assisting the customer.[17]

Lush rolled out an app for both iOS and Android in 2016 that, like its website, reflects the brand's personality and ethos. Bridging the gap between its retail experience and the digital space, the app includes product ingredients, how they're meant to be used, and their efficacy. It also has a "Stories" tab that's a compendium of both beauty content and pieces focused on Lush's ethics, sustainability, philanthropy, and advocacy work. It includes a community aspect, connecting fans across social media platforms so they can interact with one another and also see trending products on Facebook and Instagram.

Underlining the activism that is an inherent part of the brand and seeking to scale its impact, in February of 2017, the brand sponsored its Lush Summit (Summit) in London, "Calling all activists, campaigners and like-minded people." The Summit brought together charities, speakers, and grassroots organizations from around the world and gave them a platform to talk about their work. Of course, it wouldn't be a Lush event without exclusive products too. The daylong summit featured several stages, rooms, and lounges, filled with informational booths, exhibits, and vendors, collectively covering topics ranging from climate change to digital ethics and animal slavery. The Summit further included art installations and a special area offering Lush Spa treatments. In celebration of the tenth anniversary of Charity Pot, Lush featured "donation videos, stories and a timeline," as well as oversized Charity Pot tubs, where attendees were encouraged to take selfies. The event was streamed online so people everywhere who share the brand's values could join.[18]

SEVENTH GENERATION: THE IMPACT OF DECISIONS ON THE NEXT GENERATIONS

Seventh Generation has had more than one life, although not as many as Lush did. Cofounded in 1988 by Jeffrey Hollender and Alan Newman, the brand is considered by many to be the first in the United States to build sustainability into its purpose, something it did at its inception. Hollender grew up on New York City's Park Avenue and from an early age was acutely aware—and unsettled by the fact—that he had more advantages than most people. An activist during the Vietnam era and serial entrepreneur, Hollander believed a nontraditional education could be more beneficial than the school system. He dropped out of college and started a nonprofit organization in Toronto—the Skills Exchange of Toronto. In 1979, he returned to New York City and founded Network for Learning, an adult education program and audio publishing company, which he sold in 1985 to Warner Publishing, a division of Warner Communications[19,20] Hollander always envisioned having a product that "makes a positive contribution to the world" rather than a "product that makes money that allows [him] to donate to a cause."[21]

While researching his first book, *How to Make the World a Better Place: A Beginner's Guide*, he came upon a mail order company called Renew America, which sold only green products. He soon discovered that the market for Renew America was too small to make it profitable. Nonetheless, in 1988, he acquired the company, which Alan Newman was running at the time, and he and Newman renamed it Seventh Generation. The name itself distinguished—and in many ways continues to separate—Seventh Generation from its competition, most of which use the words *green* or *eco* in their names. As a name with a story behind it, Seventh Generation communicates a WE value system: a desire to balance ME needs with sustainability.

A Commitment to the Future

As the story goes, there was a Native American woman who worked for the company after Hollender acquired it. Quoting the words of the Great Law of the Iroquois Confederacy, "In our every deliberation, we must consider the impact of our decisions on the next seven generations," she suggested the name Seventh Generation.[22] Although I was unable to find the exact phrase the employee recited in the Great Law of the Iroquois Confederacy,[23] I did find something similar in the *Kayanerehkowa* (The Great Law of Peace, also known as the Constitution of the Iroquois Confederacy):

> Look and listen for the welfare of the whole people, and have always in view not only the present, but also the coming generations, even those whose faces are yet beneath the surface of the ground—the unborn of the future Nation.[24]

While this doesn't reference the "seventh generation," one can imagine oral tradition modifying it or a Native American parent explaining the Great Law to a child with the lesson of being intentional about leaving a legacy for generations to come.

Having helped to develop many names and paraphrased parables, poems, myths, and so forth in the crafting of brand stories, there is a part of me that wonders, as others have, if Hollender reshaped the narrative himself to more readily convey (or even justify) a company ethos that was ahead of its time. Nonetheless, the message of the quote is genuine to the company's product offering and the way the brand behaves. I can easily imagine a brand launching today with the name Seventh Generation and explaining the meaning behind the name without quoting it as being from the Great Law of the Iroquois Confederacy. Less mystical, perhaps, but equally thought-provoking. Ultimately, the name Seventh Generation asks each of us to pause and consider the long-term implications of our actions before acting. And in doing so, the brand could be thought of as antithetical to a digital culture grounded in instant gratification and immediacy.

Between 1988 and 1991, Seventh Generation's sales grew 70 percent, from $100,000 to $7 million. Then in 1991, one year after 500,000 people requested the brand's catalog during the 20th Earth Day Celebration, the company ran into financial trouble. Under intense stress to cut expenses before they ran out of money, Newman took a leave of absence and ultimately left the company. In 1993, Seventh Generation issued an initial public offering with individual shares priced at $5.00. In 1999, the company bought back its stock to ensure the integrity of its purpose and to prevent a hostile takeover.[25]

Around 1996, after selling its catalog, which had been a financial burden on the business, to Gaiam Inc., Seventh Generation formed a relationship with Whole Foods Market. In an interview with Jessica Harris on NPR's *Scratch*, Hollender noted that Whole Foods was "responsible" for the growth of the organic and natural products industry. The partnership "propelled" the brand's success and was Seventh Generation's entrée to get on other retailers' shelves.[26]

Expanding Its Reach and Setting a Standard

Around the same time the company bought back its stock, Hollender observed the ME-to-WE continuum in action. With the presence of natural foods growing in mainstream retailers, he recognized that although people were concerned about the environment (a WE orientation), they were more motivated to buy organic and sustainable products because of the health and safety benefits these products offered them personally (a ME orientation). With this insight, he repositioned Seventh Generation as a ME and WE brand, changing the tagline from "products for a healthy planet" to "safe for you and the environment." Better mirroring its target audience's priorities, the brand grew over the next few years at an accelerated rate.[27,28]

In May 2007, B Lab certified Seventh Generation, making it a founding B Corps member, alongside Patagonia, King Arthur Flour, Method, and others. As a pioneer of social responsibility, Hollander had sought an opportunity to develop a vital rating system for corporate social responsibility in the United States, and B Lab offered this.[29] In 2011 alone, the brand "helped save 77,000 trees, 28 million gallons of water and enough energy to heat 1,700 US homes for a year." They also prevented 35,000 pounds of chlorine and 52,000 pounds of volatile organic compounds from being released into the environment. Between 2010 and 2011, "the company decreased normalized greenhouse gas emissions by 8 percent, a change whose impact is equivalent to the removal of 283 cars from the road for a year."[30]

Setting a high bar for other certified B Corps, in 2013 the brand was named a B Corp Rockstar, and in 2104 it won a B Corp Best for the

World award in the Best for the Environment category. In 2008, it was the first company to disclose ingredients on labels. Unlike food products, household cleaners are not required by law to disclose all their ingredients. All of Seventh Generation's products, raw materials, by-products, and processes are sustainable. Today, the brand lists every ingredient in its cleaning products, including fragrance ingredients, and explains all the materials contained in its feminine care, diaper, and paper products on the packaging. After the EPA revamped its environmental safety label in 2015, the company invested in having its chemical ingredients reviewed and earned the new Safer Choice logo on some of its products in 2016.[31] That same year, it won a Safer Choice Partner of the Year Award for Formulators—Product Manufacturers. Then, in January of 2017, Seventh Generation announced it would lobby state legislators and the U.S. Congress in support of legislation requiring companies to disclose chemicals in the products they make.[32]

In June 2009, having grown sales of the brand to $150 million, Jeffery Hollender stepped down as CEO of Seventh Generation and remained on the company's board through fourth quarter 2010. After a period of transition, John Replogle, who as you may recall was CEO of Burt's Bees between 2006 and 2011, was named as the new CEO.[33]

Under Replogle, Seventh Generation has matured yet remains true to the mission and principles Hollender set. Like Lush, the brand is political and believes in activism yet speaks with a reasonable, pragmatic voice. The mission section of the company's website quotes Replogle saying: "Now, almost everything we do affects everything else in unimaginable ways and business as usual cannot successfully lead us into a brighter beyond. We are in urgent need of a new and better business model." In advocating for this new and better model, the brand lends its voice to political issues related to climate change, to conserving natural resources, and to social justice. A further look at the mission section of their website reveals posts such as "Women March Nationwide and Prove Power in Unity, What Now?," "How to Stay Informed & Prepared to Take Action in the Wake of Election Results," "Voters for the Next Generation," "To Our Fellow Citizens . . . ," and "We Stand with Standing Rock."

From Engines of Destruction to Instruments of Regeneration

In 2012, Seventh Generation was the first brand to have its full line of home care, baby, and health and beauty products to be USDA-certified as biobased. (Biobased products are derived from plants and other renewable agricultural, marine, and forestry materials and provide an alternative to conventional petroleum derived products.[34]) That same year Replogle, who introduced The Greater Good to officially operationalize Burt's Bees purpose when he was that company's CEO, announced Gen2, the brand's 2020 sustainability goals, when it published its *Corporate Consciousness Report* for 2011. The company issued its first sustainability report in 2004. In the report, Replogle reinforced the brand's aim to make business in general better, not just its own:

> When I took the wheel at Seventh Generation, I thought I would be leading a green products company into its next era. Yet it quickly became clear that that was only part of the equation.
>
> The other half of the job, and the role that's arguably more important, is running a working business laboratory whose mission is to explore new and infinitely more sustainable modes of operation with the power to transform companies of every kind from engines of destruction to instruments of regeneration.

SEVENTH GENERATION 2020 SUSTAINABILITY GOALS

- ► 100 percent employee engagement in sustainability

- ► 50 percent less water in products

- ► 1 percent of employee time in service of the community (20 hours/year)

- ► 75 percent of consumer laundry loads in cold water to lower green house gas emissions

- ► 100 percent conservation of palm forests (conserve equivalent to the use)

► 100 percent virgin paper and pulp FSC certified

► 0 percent plastic waste

► formulated products 100 percent biobased or mineral[35]

Source: Seventh Generation. "Seventh Generation's 2020 Vision for Sustainability." The Seventh Generation Corporate Consciousness Report. 2011. PDF format.

By the time the company published its 2012 *Corporate Consciousness Report*, Seventh Generation had found a way to unify its 2020 goals with its mission. In his opening letter, Replogle states that a group of employees

came together to simplify our mission into four aspirational principles that define who we are and where we are heading. Articulating our goals in this way has unified us in their pursuit and enabled us to develop a 2020 Roadmap with cohesive year-to-year goals and business plans across all units in our company.[36]

SEVENTH GENERATION ASPIRATIONAL PRINCIPLES

Nurture nature

► Choose plants not petroleum

► All products and packaging biobased or recycled

► All agricultural materials certified sustainable by a credible third party

► All products and packaging biodegradable or recyclable

► All energy from non-fossil sources

► All Seventh Generation consumers wash their laundry in cold
  water

Transforming Commerce

► All ingredients, materials, packaging, and our supply chain are
  disclosed.

► Seventh Generation engages industry to create safer consumer
  products, reduce greenhouse gas emissions, and take responsibility for product packaging.

Enhancing Health

► All Seventh Generation products are not acutely toxic and are
  free of chronic toxicants; these and all other product benefits are
  clearly promoted to our consumers.

Building Communities

► Seventh Generation and its suppliers improve the quality of their
  business communities, exceeding social standards for health,
  safety, environment, and equity.

Source: Seventh Generation. "The 'Best Place to Work' in North America." "Our 2020
Goals," May 20, 2012. https://www.seventhgeneration.com/transforming-commerce/
our-2020-goals

Each year since, the company has reported on its progress in meeting the
sustainability goals and set new objectives to do so for the coming year.

In 2013, Seventh Generation created its own social venture arm, Seventh Generation Ventures, to scale the brand's impact by acquiring
smaller companies. Seventh Generation Ventures helps like-minded,
mission-aligned brands build capacity to accelerate their growth. In
speaking with FastCoExist in 2014, Replogle emphasized that Seventh

Generation Ventures would be mission driven and have a longer-term perspective than other acquisitive businesses:

> I think there's an insidious dilemma in the public markets today, that causes CEOs to not look at a longer timeline. Something that would be a sustainable investment with a five-year payback likely would not be pursued in most large public companies, but if it has a positive impact on consumer health and a positive environmental footprint, we'll look at that.[37]

Envisioning building a portfolio of mission-aligned brands focused on human and environmental health, Replogle told the media that Seventh Generation planned to remain a privately held independent company for the time being.[38] In May of 2013, Seventh Generation Ventures announced it would acquire Bobble, a maker of reusable filtered water bottles with an aspiration to make the single-serve water bottle obsolete.[39] And in 2014, after a cash infusion of $30 million from a London-based investment manager, Generation Investment Management Fund, cofounded by Al Gore, it acquired Gamila Company, a maker of gourmet coffee and tea brewing products.[40]

In spring of 2015, Seventh Generation kicked off a $15 million, two-year, multimedia advertising campaign—the largest in its history and only the second to use television spots as well as digital advertising.[41] Featuring the popular actress and comedian, Maya Rudolph—former *Saturday Night Live* cast member and one of the stars of the hit movie *Bridesmaids*—the ads appear to be aimed at the growing awareness of the natural category overall and at accelerating Seventh Generation's growth in the face of increasing competition in the green and eco category from manufacturers like Clorox and private label brand retailers such as Walmart. A mother of four, who is rumored to use Seventh Generation products "in real life," Rudolph focuses on how pure Seventh Generation products are compared with regular detergents, dish soaps, diapers and baby care items, and feminine care products. The ads are accompanied by the tagline #comeclean.[42,43,44]

Bringing Suppliers into the Loop

Also in the spring of 2015, Seventh Generation flexed its B Corps muscle—in a cooperative way—in an effort to *transform commerce*. As part of B Lab's Measure What Matters cohort, Seventh Generation reached out to its suppliers with an invitation to take the B Corp Assessment. Seventh Generation employees were so "enthusiastic" about the program they contacted everything from "local mom & pop shops and distant companies alike." One hundred percent of full-time Seventh Generation's employees participated, contacting 200 companies. Seventh Generation further used the initiative to both teach employees more about the B movement and have an opportunity "to volunteer with another B Corp." Replogle's goal was "to inspire all of Seventh Generation's suppliers to become B Corps by 2020."[45]

Three years after Seventh Generation Ventures started, Unilever announced it was acquiring Seventh Generation in September of 2016. Just days earlier, it had been reported that Unilever was looking to add Honest Tea Company to its portfolio of purpose-driven brands, which also includes Ben and Jerry's. Just as he had previously viewed Clorox's purchase of Burt's Bees and as Neil Grimmer viewed Campbell's acquisition of Plum Organics, Replogle, a Unilever alumni, believed the purchase was a way for Seventh Generation to scale its impact: "We look at this as having a multiplier effect for our business … ," said Replogle. "We always aspired to be a billion-dollar brand. We see this as a springboard as opposed to throwing in the towel."[46]

KENCO COFFEE COMPANY: SUSTAINABLY TRANSFORMING LIVES

According to the International Coffee Organization, the market price of coffee was $1.42 per pound in February of 2017. A Fairtrade Foundation report in 2013 noted that 25 million small farmers produce 80 percent of the world's coffee. Smaller coffee farmers are vulnerable to intermediaries and earn only a fraction of the market price. So it's no surprise that many face livelihood challenges and that the next generation of growers is forgoing the rural countryside for urban environments. Organizations like Fairtrade International are addressing some of these issues by eliminating the intermediaries, connecting farmers with importers and guaranteeing them a minimum price. Some coffee brands like Kenco Coffee Company, owned by Mondelez International and distributed by Jacobs Douwe Egberts (JDE) in the UK and Ireland, are also working to transform coffee farming, making it more sustainable.

In 1923, a group of retired coffee planters founded the Kenya Coffee Company to select and roast beans for the group's luxury coffee shops in London. After World War II, a food merchant, John Gardiner, purchased the company's roasting plant and coffee shops, which are known to be the UK's first branded chain of high street shops. In 1962, with the percentage of coffee beans from Kenya having declined, Gardiner rebranded the company Kenco Coffee Company. The company grew, and Truste House, a hotel group, took over the shops, continued roasting beans at the company's plant, and began to sell beans, ground jam, and other specialty goods.[47]

As demand increased, the company set up a national sales force to sell Kenco-branded coffee to other coffee shops. In 1972, Cadbury purchased Kenco, which it sold to Premier Foods in the mid-1970s. In 1987, General Foods purchased Kenco. And in 2012, Kenco became part of Mondelez International when Kraft, which had merged with General Foods in 1989, spun off its global snack and food brands. Mondelez also owns brands such as Oreo, Kraft Philadelphia, Toblerone, Cadbury, and Jacobs.[48]

More than a decade ago, Kenco purposefully set off on the path to become a WE brand, and today many users perceive it to be the brand that helps them improve the lives of people in coffee-growing regions. In the early to mid-2000s, Kenco took the first steps on its journey when it sought to engrain ethical production and sustainable distribution of coffee across all its operations—from sourcing and production to packaging design and brand communications. In 2005, at that time part of Kraft Foods, Kenco began a partnership with the Rainforest Alliance to source beans from certified farms. The Rainforest Alliance certification program ensures that coffee is farmed in an environmentally sustainable manner and that the rights of workers are protected. Today, Kenco products carry the Shop the Frog label, the Rainforest Alliance's stamp certifying products that are produced using sustainable methods and that provide ethical working conditions for farmers and their workers.

In the spring of 2005, Kenco launched its Sustainable Development product line, the brand's first to be 100 percent made from beans sourced from Rainforest Alliance Certified farms. Then in January of 2007, the brand helped move awareness of certified coffee more deeply into the public's consciousness through its partnership with McDonald's. McDonald's started selling Kenco Rainforest Alliance Certified coffee in 1,200 restaurants in the UK and Ireland.

By May of 2007, the Kenco Pure brand of instant coffees, like the Sustainable Development range, was 100 percent sourced from certified farms. And Kenco further committed to have 100 percent of its products sourced from Rainforest Alliance Certified Forests by 2010. Equivalent to approximately 13,000 tons of coffee beans (or 60 million cups of coffee) a week, this pledge would significantly progress sustainable farming. By 2008, people in the UK perceived Kenco to be the most ethical coffee brand in the country. The brand's advertising campaign highlighting its partnership with the Rainforest Alliance helped to grow Kenco's user base by 1.2 million people and maintained its coveted number two position in the market. By October of 2009, Kenco Pure and Sustainable Development had propelled the brand to be the number one instant ethical brand, with a 25.5 percent share of the ethical market.[49,50,51,52]

Packaging to Protect the Environment

In September of 2009, Kenco launched the second phase of its sustainability program with a product extension that reduced the impact of its packaging on the environment. The new Kenco Eco Refill pack had 97 percent less packaging weight than Kenco's glass jars at the time. To motivate users to switch to the new pack, Kraft invested £7.5 million into advertising and public relations.[53] With people walking around holding coffee in their hands as they went about their daily routines, the television ads offered a lighthearted, yet profound take on a world with no packaging. The popular British actress and activist Joanna Lumley provided the voiceover.[54] The brand complemented its advertising with a Waste Less challenge—a UK nationwide call to action encouraging people to reduce the amount of waste they throw away, led by Amanda

Holden, best known for being a judge on ITV's Britain's Got Talent, and eco-expert Oliver Heath.

Although some in the media claimed that the new packaging was more harmful than bottles, Kenco responded that the new packs reduced the overall mass of waste sent to landfill because, while a glass jar is re-cyclable, the lid, which is made of polypropolene, is not widely recycled in the UK. The Eco Refill pack weighs less than the jar lid alone. Kenco's new packaging encouraged people to reuse the old jar packaging rather than throw it away.[55] At the time of launch, Kenco also had established a partnership with TetraCycle® to close the loop and make the new packaging a circular product. Kenco offers Coffee Packaging Brigade lo-cations throughout the country: Users drop off their old packs, and TerraCycle turns them into new plastics to make eco-friendly products. Although Kenco has not yet made the bold move of eliminating its jars completely or pricing them so that they would be a one-time purchase to be refilled with coffee from the Eco-Refill pack, in March of 2011, the brand introduced a new slim-line glass jar that used 7 percent less glass than its old jar.

A Sustainable Future Through Entrepreneurship

In 2014, Mondelez International, Kenco's parent company, rolled out *Coffee Made Happy*. Committing a minimum of $200 million to the pro-gram, *Coffee Made Happy* aims to create, by 2020, 1 million coffee entre-preneurs in countries such as Brazil, Honduras, Indonesia, Peru, and Vietnam, as well as fostering a sustainable future for all small growers. Despite global consumption of coffee growing 2.5 percent every year since 2000, in addition to livelihood issues, coffee growers face difficult climate conditions and other challenges such as the increasing repurpos-ing of agricultural land suitable for coffee growing by other industries and urban developers.[56]

Coffee Made Happy recognizes the unique needs of each coffee region and measures its impact on three central variables: profitability, sustain-ability, and respectability. To ensure opportunities are created for young people locally and the country as a whole benefits, Mondelez and JDE work with community organizations like Ecom and its subsidiary ACOM, Pronatur, 4C, and Rainforest Alliance.

More specifically, as part of the *Coffee Made Happy* program, Kenco helps:

► Champion better agricultural practices, training farmers in soil nutrition, management of water and pests, and replanting and rejuvenation to improve productivity and sustain the environment.

► Equip farmers with the skills to be successful entrepreneurs, teaching farmers bookkeeping and accounting skills to manage their businesses more effectively and setting up farmer organizations for knowledge transfer.

► Make coffee farming attractive for future generations, showing economical and sustainable farming to be a good career option for women and young people.[57]

Kenco introduced a collect-to-give loyalty program in April of 2014, in conjunction with the *Coffee Made Happy* program. Users collected points from jars, which they could use to support charitable initiatives within coffee-growing communities, such as the donation of uniforms, stationery, and books to a Mondelez International–founded school in Honduras. Alternatively, fans had the option to choose to use their points toward programs closer to home in the UK, such as Street Style Surgery, which offered workshops to help young people across the country move into creative industries. There was also a reward available for loyalists themselves: They had the opportunity to also claim fitness trips or gardening kits. For the second phase of the program, Kenco planned a community aspect, which would enable people to join forces and pool their points in support of a single objective.[58]

Changing the Game Through Education, Training, and a Support Network

As part of *Coffee Made Happy*, Kenco pioneered a game-changing program. Developing a relationship with Fundes, a local NGO that works to rehabilitate youth in Honduras, Kenco launched *Coffee vs. Gangs*. Facing the realities of extreme poverty, young people in Honduras, one of the top murder capitals in the world, often are confronted with the difficult choice of fleeing the country or joining a gang. Offering young Hondurans a third choice, Kenco's *Coffee vs. Gangs* gives them the opportunity, training, and financial support to become coffee farmers.

In 2014, working with Fundes, Kenco recruited twenty young Hondurans at risk of joining gangs. Over one year, they were mentored in coffee agronomy and business skills and, importantly, given a necessary, dedicated support network. J. Walter Thompson, Kenco's agency—which you may recall also collaborated with Andrex on its Angolan toilet installation—and The Moment, an international content company, documented the program online. Using gang tattoos as an iconic communications vehicle, the campaign developed advertising for television and movie theaters that consequentially and compellingly told these young people's stories. The final series of videos, which celebrated the success of the program—the teenagers graduating and starting their own businesses—was released October 13, 2015. Videos of the individual program participants' stories were prominently featured on Kenco's Facebook page. In addition to coffevsgangs.com, "*The Telegraph* in Partnership with Kenco" has a dedicated news hub for the program, coffeevsgangs.telegraph.co.uk. At the end of May 2016, the beans planted during the 2015 program were used exclusively for the Kenco Coffee vs. Gangs Single Estate beans, which was available for sale through a number of food distributors in the UK.[59] With the pilot program successful, Kenco launched year two.

It's easy to envision a second phase of *Coffee vs. Gangs* in which Kenco collaborates with other coffee manufacturers and brands that also work with farming communities in the developing world to develop a Rural Farming Coalition. To have an even bigger impact, it needs scale. And Kenco can't do that alone. Competitors must join forces for this—like Unilever and Kimberly-Clark with the Toilet Board Coalition. While *Coffee vs. Gangs* impacts only a small number of people, it does so in a life-changing way.

HIGHLIGHTS

CHAPTER 8:
Contribution: Make Me Bigger Than I Am

► WE brands are not angry or radical activists. They're companies making choices congruent with their brand purpose—for-profit pragmatists integrating awareness of social issues, behavioral modification, sustainability, and progress into the marketing of their goods and services and their daily operations.

► Beginning as a creator and purveyor of natural bath and beauty products, Lush is the outcome of its founders' determined journey to live their personal purpose and embody the positive side of activism. The brand continually expands its reach and the ways in which it connects its fans to sustainable products, fair trade, and philanthropic causes.

► Also having more than one life, Seventh Generation has built sustainability into its purpose from the start and has evolved from a niche-oriented brand to a more mainstream leader in environmentally enlightened practices, delivering on the promise of its name.

► Kenco Coffee Company operates sustainably and demonstrates how a conventional brand can use education, training, and entrepreneurship to integrate a life-changing social program into its operations and transform itself from a ME to a WE brand.

PART III

CHOOSING CHANGE

PART III

CHOOSING CHANGE

CHAPTER 9

STEPPING FORWARD INTO BRAND CITIZENSHIP

Most people need to feel that they are here for a
purpose, and unless an organization can connect to this
need to leave something behind that makes this a better
world, or at least a different one,
it won't be successful over time.

—Peter Drucker

The playing field for companies of all types has changed. Technology and communications are continuously advancing. Dramatic sociopolitical events are occurring at an accelerating pace. And people's definitions of value are shifting. There is no going back. The old models for business—with businesses running the show and consumers and employees coming along for the ride—no longer speak to the needs, longings, and practical realities of our modern society.

Developed from the grassroots up, Brand Citizenship helps companies embrace change and lead from ahead rather than behind. The brand narratives highlighted in this book demonstrate that business is a social and cultural institution as much as it is a source of economic prosperity. Large multinational corporations, midsize companies, and start-up social enterprises alike have an opportunity to advance society, sustain the planet, and do good in the world, while simultaneously earning a profit for shareholders. Ultimately, Brand Citizenship's five steps precipitate a better, more sustainable future for an individual business by helping it to deliver significant benefits across the ME-to-WE continuum—to customers, employees, suppliers, business partners, other stakeholders, investors, and society.

There is not one type of Brand Citizenship company. As we've explored in Chapters 4 through 8, multiple approaches along the Me-to-We continuum resonate with customers, employees, investors, and other stakeholders. And while socially conscious brands, cool start-ups, and social enterprises have helped fuel the movement for Brand Citizenship, because of their size, the impact of their efforts will go only so far. More corporate giants like Unilever, Google, Apple, Walmart, IKEA, Kimberly Clark, and IBM must also take up the mantle. Even if they do so imperfectly—or as *CultureQ* research participants identified as "humanly"—at first.

With wider scopes of operations, more capital available, and bigger talent pools, big brands will affect impact on a much larger, global scale. When businesses of all sizes behave responsibly and operate more holistically, people, communities, society, and the whole planet will move forward together. Brand Citizenship necessarily acknowledges that any one brand is part of a vast ecosystem that includes customers, employees, suppliers, nonprofits, NGOs, communities, governments, society at large, the planet, and even competitors. Plum Organics, IKEA, Seventh Generation, and Kenco all advanced their industries as they raised the bar for their own operations.

MAKING THE DECISION TO CHANGE

The first step on the pathway of Brand Citizenship is a seemingly simplistic one: making the decision to change. Adopting the tenets of Brand Citizenship, however, requires courage to break from business as usual. It ultimately relies on distinctive departments, outside agency teams, and other partners working closely together to credibly deliver its benefits. Like the process of change itself, the five steps of Brand Citizenship are not prescriptive. Rather, they frame a journey that by necessity must adapt with the shifting cultural landscape. In a business climate seeking to eliminate risk through big data analytics, however, the notion of no absolute rights and wrongs can be discomforting. Accepting that trial and error is necessary to break the status quo and create meaningful social impact is a hallmark of charting new territory—and of Brand Citizenship.

Some companies embarking on the journey of Brand Citizenship will just be starting out. Others may be seeking a better way to focus existing efforts. And still others may be looking for a model to integrate initiatives. Shaking old habits and acculturating to new ways of doing things takes time. And, although most businesses today accept that continual innovation is necessary to remain relevant, many continue to be nervous about the financial risks implied in adapting dynamic frameworks. No matter where a brand is in the process, however, like many of the brands highlighted in this book, it may fail several times before being successful. Experiment, fine-tune processes, scale initiatives, measure impact, and begin again.

FOCUSING ON PURPOSE

Brand Citizenship begins with a clearly defined brand purpose. And placing purpose in the center of a business is a proactive choice. It rarely happens by accident. As I explained in Chapter 3, a powerful sense of purpose positions a brand on a distinguishable journey across the five steps of Brand Citizenship. Further, an effective purpose opens a brand up to endless possibilities across the ME-to-WE continuum by motivating action through greater meaning. Yet a brand purpose will create verifiable financial and social impact only when it is used to benchmark organizational systems and policies, product development, employee behaviors, relationships with stakeholders, sustainability, and corporate social responsibility, as well as brand development, marketing, and communications. More and more, the identification of purpose is being seen at a board level as a motivating tool for strategic business transformation, much in the same way a corporate brand was in the late 1990s and early 2000s.

Defining brand purpose—or why your business exists—is not an easy task. It must be true to who you are and what you do, not based on a competitor's position, advocacy group's demands, or politically correct definition. As discussed previously, a meaningful purpose is about much more than the products and services a company sells. Purpose sits at the intersection of the reason your business was created, the things that matter most to your customers and other stakeholders, and how you do business (Figure 9-1). Identifying it typically requires stepping back and reviewing your heritage; gaining a deep understanding of your customers', employees', and other key stakeholders' desires and expectations for your industry or category; and reflecting on the core competencies and values that drive business success today as well as those that will shape it in the future.

FIGURE 9-1. Framework for identifying brand purpose.

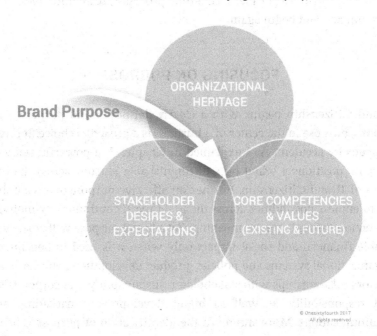

In investigating these three areas through management interviews, market research, and other audits, executives and managers may discover that a meaningful purpose was a part of their business all along yet had not been accentuated or was lost over the years. For others, especially those in traditional consumer goods, exploring how their brand impacts people's lives on a deeper level will help expand thinking beyond more traditional product features and benefits. For these businesses, identifying a social mission that is rooted in what the product does will help to illuminate a more significant purpose. As you'll recall, both *The Vaseline® Healing Project* and Andrex® *Toilets Change Lives* programs were developed in this manner.

When a purpose is true to what a brand delivers, it taps into universal truths that emotively stir employees at all levels across an organization, to do good and have an impact. For example:

SunTrust Bank: "To light the way to financial well-being."

Plum Organics: "To nourish little ones with the very best food from the very first bite."

Forest Stewardship Council: "To meet our current needs for forest products without compromising the health of the world's forests for future generations."

Seventh Generation: "To inspire a consumer revolution that nurtures health of the next seven generations."

As all the brands showcased throughout this book, not just the four above, corroborate, a meaningful purpose has the power to change the way people think, feel, and act. Importantly, though, as Chipotle learned, when a purpose is too high order, it may not successfully signpost product and service delivery, especially in a time of crisis.

To effectively guide your entire organization, the development of brand purpose should not be the purview of one department in isolation. In the same manner IKEA brought managers from across its business to develop its environmental plan, and IBM opened its values discussion to all employees, the most effective brand purposes are crafted with broad input. And while the final words chosen to communicate your purpose do matter, the passion and shared beliefs it encompasses mean more. When purpose reflects your organization's driving passion, like Apple's and Google's do, it will inspire employee behavior at a transactional level and cultivate the trust with stakeholders that is essential for gliding forward and back along the ME-to-WE continuum.

MOVING FROM PURPOSE TO
OPERATING PRINCIPLES

Socializing your brand purpose across your organization is crucial for it to be a driving force in day-to-day operations, not just in big, strategic decisions. Being clear on how you foster a culture that supports delivery of a brand's purpose through Brand Citizenship is as important as the purpose itself. Brand Citizenship necessitates collaborative and interconnected cultures rather than competitive and siloed ones. It motivates and enables managers to move beyond traditional divisional boundaries, create teams that cross borders, and build coalitions with stakeholders outside the organization, all in support of delivering meaning and impact alongside profit. Employees in turn embody the brand's purpose every day, through their attitudes, behaviors, and their every gesture.

While many organizations may first look to underpin brand purpose with a set of values, dissonance between stated company values and actual behavior has resulted in a deep cynicism toward corporate or brand values. Participants of *CultureQ* research into customers' and employees' relationships with brands have reported that they perceive values as empty words on a page. When describing the things they believe matter most to brands, they frequently name characteristics diametrically opposed to their published values. Further, in our client working sessions, employees often have expressed confusion about what values really mean for their day-to-day activities, noting they don't necessarily relate to operational processes and procedures. Rather than being a helpful way to engage employees in a brand's purpose and the five steps of Brand Citizenship, my experience in brand development has shown that values may actually be harmful.

By nature, values are subjective or relative, not universal. Indeed, when helping clients to internalize brand values, I've often described them as dials to be turned up or down dependent upon the situation. The word *values* is the plural of value, which you may recall from Chapter 2 originates from the thirteenth-century Latin word *valere*, meaning "to be strong and well." Over the ensuing 100 years or so, the word value evolved to mean intrinsic worth, and in 1918 it came to represent a "social principle" as appropriated from the language of painting.[2] Establishing rules for "ethical conduct" or behavior, operating principles that reinforce your brand purpose and promote behaviors to deliver it, every day and in every action taken, may be more practical—and can be more transformative—than values.

Easier for employees to relate to and recognize that their behaviors matter, operating principles more readily translate what you stand for into behaviors. They link the ambitions embedded in your purpose with your organizational focus, processes, and procedures. In the same way that peoples' morals and ethics form their behaviors over time, operating principles remain constant in the face of changing strategies. When effective, they act as a filter, helping to prioritize resources and activities. Although operating principles reflect the unique aspects of how a brand is delivered and help to distinguish one company culture from another, the best operating principles all:

▶ Capture the spirit of your brand purpose.

▶ Highlight the core competencies/capabilities that are essential to delivering your purpose.

▶ Are simple to understand yet introduce behaviors that will deliver your purpose.

▶ Reflect both the way your company does business and how your brand creates value.

▶ Communicate the experience you deliver to customers, employees, and other stakeholders.

While it's tempting to craft operating principles that are highly specific and prescribe exact behaviors, the most motivating are designed to engage, not constrain, employees, emphasizing what is important while leaving room to breathe. In other words, they effectively guide employees to determine the exact how-to's on their own. Like the five steps of Brand Citizenship themselves, operating principles in support of your brand purpose should be developed to incent employees to create win-win-win opportunities, not play zero sum games in which some people win and others lose or rights correct wrongs.

DETERMINING WHERE YOU ARE
AND WHERE YOU WANT TO BE

By clarifying why you exist at the highest level, your purpose dictates where on the ME-to-WE continuum your brand ultimately will sit. To effectively glide forward and back across the model of Brand Citizenship and fully realize your purpose, it's equally crucial to diagnose and benchmark where your brand is positioned on the five steps today relative to long-term ambitions over time. Magic is not needed to assess how your primary target audiences perceive your brand based on the attributes that define each of the five steps of the model. Market research developed specifically to determine the relative importance of attributes at each step and how you rate, both absolutely and as compared to competitors or out-of-category brands you identify as exemplars, provides the best insight for strategic planning and focus for innovation and implementation. While many tracking studies have a limited scope that includes only competitive brands in one industry or category, benchmarking your performance on the five steps of Brand Citizenship against leading out-of-category brands provides a valuable sideways perspective and parallel lessons that can lead to breakthrough thinking.

Over three years, through our *CultureQ* research project, we quantitatively tracked the characteristics—or attributes—people associated with Brand Leadership, Good Corporate Citizenship, and Favorite Brands. As an alternative to commissioning a Brand Citizenship research assessment, you can use existing tracking studies or other company data to evaluate your brand on a selection of the characteristics participants rated as most important, as illustrated in the worksheet in Figure 9-2. Armed with this data and financial knowledge about your company's overall focus on sustainable business performance versus short-term shareholder returns, you can gauge where your brand sits on a four-quadrant Brand Citizenship map to determine whether you are a Pioneer (a WE brand focused on sustainable performance, socially conscious, and often a social enterprise); an Active Contributor (a socially conscious ME brand centered on sustainable performance, maybe on a path to becoming a social enterprise); a Self-Server (a ME brand seeking short-term returns, perhaps already embarking on the pathway of Brand

FIGURE 9-2. Illustrative Brand Citizenship positioning worksheet.

BRAND CITIZENSHIP STEP	DEFINING ATTRIBUTES (in alphabetical order)	5–1 SCORE				
1. Trust Don't let me down	Affordable products and services	5	4	3	2	1
	Excellent customer service	5	4	3	2	1
	Produces reliable goods and services	5	4	3	2	1
	Value for quality	5	4	3	2	1
2. Enrichment Enhance daily life	Helps me accomplish my goals	5	4	3	2	1
	Is inspirational to me	5	4	3	2	1
	Simplifies daily routines	5	4	3	2	1
3. Responsibility Behave fairly	Betters local community	5	4	3	2	1
	Ethical supplier relationships	5	4	3	2	1
	Honest communications	5	4	3	2	1
	Sustainable environmental practices	5	4	3	2	1
	Treats employees fairly	5	4	3	2	1
4. Community Connect me	Connects me to communities I care about	5	4	3	2	1
	Connects me to the rest of the world	5	4	3	2	1
	Many generations use it	5	4	3	2	1
	Mirrors my personal values	5	4	3	2	1
5. Contribution Make me bigger than I am	Helps me to give back to society	5	4	3	2	1
	I feel proud when I use it	5	4	3	2	1
	Makes me a more responsible citizen	5	4	3	2	1

Citizenship); or a Pretender (a WE brand delivering short-term returns, a business whose communications and initiatives most likely are not aligned with its purpose). See Figure 9-3. Comparing this to where your purpose ultimately places your brand is a useful way to visualize position options as you move toward your ambition. Some brands also find it useful to develop a blueprint for change by plotting a pathway for transformation through initiatives, programs, and communications.

FIGURE 9-3. Four-quadrant Brand Citizenship map.

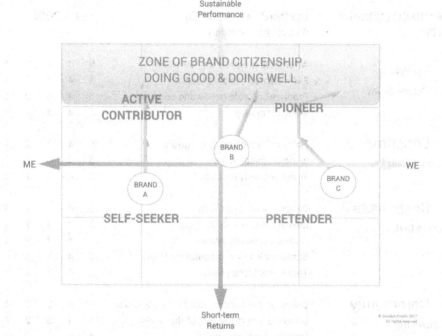

These two diagnostic tools bring an appreciation of where your brand can credibly move—and where it cannot—as well as highlight the level of organizational transformation required to fully deliver your brand purpose. The underlying insights frame the direction for prioritizing achievable goals, focusing resources, innovating new products and services, and identifying meaningful strategies to do good and do well. However, when developing implementation plans, it's paramount to be mindful that adapting Brand Citizenship is an iterative process. And as such, it's not necessary or realistic from a resource perspective to sequentially fill gaps identified from these assessments when moving from one step to another, with two exceptions, Step 1 and Step 3, which are each foundational elements in different ways.

► **Step 1:** Trust is a foundational element of the model. ME and WE brands must both deliver the basics and do what they say before they seek to embody the tenets of Enrichment, Responsibility, Community, or Contribution.

▶ **Step 3:** Responsibility, as we've previously considered, is the pivot point between ME and WE brands. Before a brand can believably claim WE sensibilities, it must be viewed first and foremost as treating employees well, followed by behaving ethically and operating in a sustainable manner.

While Brand Citizenship requires visible commitment from the CEO and entire executive team, responsibility for shaping and implementing programs across the five steps reaches across the organization. Although collaborative, cross-functional teams are necessary for innovation and greater impact, as Figure 9-4 highlights, different departments are typically responsible for leading the charge at different stages.

SETTING GOALS,
EMBRACING EXPERIMENTATION

As does any successful journey, Brand Citizenship requires milestones to benchmark and track performance. For example, most of the brands we explored in this book had clear, ambitious sustainability plans that included workplace, social, and environmental goals—and that expressed their brand purpose through the objectives set. As far as I know, none had comprehensively flushed out the strategies and tactics necessary to achieve these goals when they set them. Nonetheless, they publicly published their plans, committing to them wholeheartedly by raising the reputational risk of abandoning them.

Equally important, each of these businesses also challenged themselves to think differently, seeking inspiration from a wide range of resources inside and outside their organizations to deliver their goals and embed purpose more deeply into their day-to-day behavior. Each time they achieved a milestone, they set their aspirations higher using their purpose as the guiding compass for innovation and program development.

**FIGURE 9-4. Illustrative shift of leadership and accountability
for Brand Citizenship programs.**

BRAND CITIZENSHIP STEP	FUNCTIONAL LEADER/DEPARTMENT PRIMARILY ACCOUNTABLE FOR DELIVERY
1 Trust Don't let me down	Customer Service Product Development Marketing/Brand Finance
2 Enrichment Enhance daily life	Customer Service Customer Relationship Management Product Development Digital/Technology Marketing/Brand Communications
3 Responsibility Behave fairly	Human Resources Corporate Social Responsibility Sustainability Supply Chain Management Corporate Communications/Reputation Management Legal/Compliance Finance
4 Community Connect me	Human Resources Corporate Social Responsibility Digital/Technology Corporate Communications/Reputation Management Marketing/Brand
5 Contribution Make me bigger than I am	Corporate Social Responsibility Sustainability Supply Chain Management Product Development Corporate Communications/Reputation Management Marketing/Brand Comms

TRACKING YOUR JOURNEY

Measure impact and begin again. In the same way market share, profitability, and sustainability are tracked, ongoing metrics are essential to diagnose how a brand is performing on the five steps of Brand Citizenship over time. There are numerous ways to do this, from designing custom market research studies to producing balanced scorecards that combine existing brand equity and reputation management research with sustainability benchmarks and financial performance. Ultimately, any Brand Citizenship analytics should do more than illustrate performance on the five steps. They should supply insight that enables a business to continually adapt to a shifting landscape and develop programs that will increase trust, enrich lives, behave responsibly, cultivate community, and amplify a brand's greater contribution, all on the road to deliver its purpose. When Brand Citizenship metrics are tied to financial brand valuation and contribution assessments, they will form an even more intelligible picture of how a brand generates social and financial value—in other words, how it is doing good and doing well.

An understanding of the influence a brand has and the engagement it fosters with customers, employees, and other stakeholders will help strengthen the impact of Brand Citizenship. Brands that have influence contribute something meaningful, change how we do things, or even alter how we see the world, yet we may feel one step removed from them. Those that engage us and invite us to collaborate with them involve us on an emotional level, are more likely to mirror our values, and thereby cultivate more faithful relationships. Yet, as social media has increased people's interaction and involvement with brands—and brands have become content providers—the dynamics between influence and engagement have been shifting. Our three years of *CultureQ* research into Brand Leadership, Good Corporate Citizenship, and Favorite Brands yielded some insight into this dynamic. Figure 9-5 illustrates the relationship we uncovered.

FIGURE 9-5. Brand Citizenship model of influence and engagement.

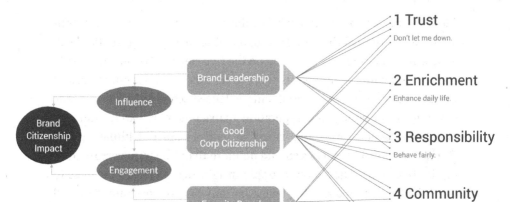

Based on our findings, elements of brand leadership and good corporate citizenship merge to command influence, and the characteristics of citizenship blend with those of favorite brands to stimulate engagement. Over the period we monitored these three benchmarks, we noted that the importance of influence as traditionally defined waned slightly as social media continued to increase the role of engagement. If this continues, customers, employees, and other stakeholders will demand to collaborate with brands even more in brand development, product improvements, and sustainability and corporate social responsibility initiatives. It also will mean that brands must wholeheartedly embrace Step 4, Community, and Step 5, Contribution, to sustainably create social and financial value.

SHAPING THE FUTURE TO CREATE FINANCIAL AND SOCIAL VALUE

Business leaders, management consultants, marketing executives, and people in general are always looking for the next big thing: reengineering, branding, innovation, digital transformation, green, purpose, and so on. Yet none of these have ever supplied magical formulas. That's because the idiosyncrasies of individual corporate cultures make a difference when solving problems, as do shifting marketplace dynamics, each of which are infinitely fascinating to study. No matter how far brands progress along the journey of Brand Citizenship, there will always be more changes to adapt to. Some will be welcome, and others will not. Some will be sudden, but most will be subtle and harder to recognize without continuously staying abreast of nascent cultural shifts as much as larger trends.

As companies reframe their priorities, social and political movements will continue to evolve, and culture will morph. Alongside this, people's relationships with brands will change, as will their expectations for good Brand Citizenship—whether they be customers, employees, business partners, investors, or other stakeholders. For brands to continue to lead from ahead rather than from behind and create a sustainable future, it's crucial that business leaders stay abreast of changes—no matter how subtle—as they are happening, not after they've occurred. It's also essential that they distinguish between what is important and what is not. Leaders need to be able to discern which trends are short-term blips and which represent long-term cultural transformations that need to be integrated into brand development and business operations.

Brand Citizenship evolved from the grassroots up. It wasn't something I set out to create. The model materialized over time, and the five steps started coming into view only after participants in *CultureQ* research told us they wanted brands to provide solutions to their personal ME problems, needs, and dreams *and* their generalized WE worries about the economy, the world, and the planet. Yet, as many of the stories I've shared throughout this book demonstrate, Brand Citizenship is in many ways a natural evolution of everything I have observed and learned during my tenure as a brand strategist and researcher.

Leadership is often characterized by a willingness to be brave—by the ability to unite people of different views and deploy capital to achieve important goals. Brands that understand how they impact people's lives through the products and services they offer and how this in turn creates financial *and* social value have always been able to tap into collective knowledge and transform markets. They shape the future because they

know the role they play today, where they want to be, and the assets they
have and need to acquire to get there. Brands that are clear about how
they advance society, that integrate sincere practices into their marketing
and operations, and that turn ethics into results exemplify good Brand
Citizenship. They do well by doing good, and they will always be touted
as leaders.

HIGHLIGHTS

CHAPTER 9:
Stepping Forward into Brand Citizenship

▶ Brand Citizenship is a journey, not an endgame. It requires courage to step forward and an understanding that experimentation and trial and error are parts of the process.

▶ Making the decision to change is the first step on the pathway of Brand Citizenship.

▶ Uncovering brand purpose and then using it as a guiding compass or benchmark is fundamental to doing good and doing well.

▶ Operating principles, which reflect the unique aspects of company culture and how a brand is delivered, are an effective way to socialize brand purpose and a reliable tool to help employees understand how purpose is relevant to their day-to-day jobs. Operating principles that leave employees room to breathe are the most motivating.

▶ Understanding where your organization is starting on the ME-to-WE continuum of Brand Citizenship is essential to developing a roadmap that will take you successfully to where you want to be.

▶ Developing metrics to measure performance and track your journey will hold you accountable to achieve your goals, as well as enable you to measure the perceptual, social, and financial impact of initiatives and programs.

▶ Brands that are clear about their purpose, integrate relevant policies and practices into operations, and emphasize creating social impact as much as bettering their reputation will shape a better future by doing good and doing well.

ENDNOTES

INTRODUCTION

1 Ross, Meghan. "5 Most Lucrative Retail Pharmacies in Rx Revenues." *Pharmacy Times*. August 24, 2015. http://www.pharmacytimes.com/news/5-most-lucrative-retail-pharmacies-in-rx-revenues

2 CVS Health 2014 Annual Report: Health Is Everything. http://www.graphis.com/entry/e47ed827-61ce-45f4-9578-32c373a713a8/

3 Nike. "The Flyease Journey." *Nike News*. July 13, 2015. http://news.nike.com/news/the-flyease-journey

4 Lee, MJ. "eBay to Ban Sale of Confederate Flag Merchandise." CNN Politics. June 24, 2015. http://www.cnn.com/2015/06/23/politics/confederate-flag-ebay/

5 H&M. "Presenting the Winners of the Global Change Award." http://about.hm.com/en/media/news/presenting-the-winners-of-the-global-change-award.html

6 *Harvard Business Review*. "The Business Case for Purpose." Harvard Business School Publishing. 2015.

7 Committee Encouraging Corporate Philanthropy. "Shaping the Future: Solving Social Problems Through Business Strategy." B Revolution Consulting. 2010.

CHAPTER 1

1 Giving USA. "Giving USA: 2015 Was America's Most-Generous Year." June 13, 2016. https://givingusa.org/giving-usa-2016/

2 Charity Navigator. "Giving Statistics." 2017. https://www.charitynavigator.org/index.cfm/bay/content.view/cpid/42

3 World Development Indicators database, World Bank, February 1, 2017.

4 Fortune. "Global 500." 2017. http://beta.fortune.com/global500/

5 Davis, Alyssa, and Mishel, Lawrence. "Top CEOs Make 300 Times More than Typical Workers." Economic Policy Institute. June 21, 2015. http://www.epi.org/publication/top-ceos-make-300-times-more-than-workers-pay-growth-surpasses-market-gains-and-the-rest-of-the-0-1-percent/

6   Committee Encouraging Corporate Philanthropy. "Creating a Better World Through Business." http://cecp.co/about/

7   Bachman, S. L. "A Stitch in Time?" *Los Angeles Times*. September 16, 2001. http://articles.latimes.com/2001/sep/16/magazine/tm-46210

8   Cushman Jr, John H. "International Business; Nike Pledges to End Child Labor and Apply U.S. Rules Abroad." *New York Times*. May 13, 1998. http://www.nytimes.com/1998/05/13/business/international-business-nike-pledges-to-end-child-labor-and-apply-us-rules-abroad.html

9   Sustainable Innovation Is a Powerful Engine for Growth, FY14/15 Nike Inc., Sustainable Business Report.

10 Carpenter, Dave. "McDonald's to Dump Supersize Portions." *Washington Post*. March 3, 2004. http://www.washingtonpost.com/wp-dyn/articles/A26082-2004Mar3.html

11 Burke, Jason. "Bangladesh Factory Collapse Leaves Trail of Shattered Lives." *The Guardian*. June 6, 2013. https://www.theguardian.com/world/2013/jun/06/bangladesh-factory-building-collapse-community

12 Heuermann, Hendrik. "H&M to Source More Garments from Bangladesh." *Apparel Resources*. March 14, 2016. http://news.appareiresources.com/trade-news/hm-to-source-more-garments-from-bangladesh/

13 Alderman, Liz. "Public Outrage over Factory Conditions Spurs Labor Deal." *New York Times*. May 19, 2013. http://www.nytimes.com/2013/05/20/business/global/hm-led-labor-breakthrough-by-european-retailers.html

14 Di Boscio, Chere. "Time for a Fashion Revolution." *Eluxe Magazine*. April 24, 2015. http://eluxemagazine.com/fashion/fashion-revolution/

15 Fashion Revolution. "2016 Impact." 2016. http://fashionrevolution.org/about/2016-impact/

16 Coscarelli, Joe. "AOL CEO on 401(k) Changes: Blame Obamacare and Two Pregnant Employees' 'Distressed Babies.'" *New York Magazine*. February 6, 2014. http://nymag.com/daily/intelligencer/2014/02/aol-tim-armstrong-distressed-babies-401k.html

17 Chipotle Mexican Grill. *The Scarecrow*. YouTube. September 11, 2013. 3:22. https://www.youtube.com/watch?v=lUtnas5ScSE

18 Chipotle. "Press Release." *Investor Relations*. February 3, 2015. http://ir.chipotle.com/phoenix.zhtml?c=194775&p=irol-newsArticle&ID=2013178_

19 McDonald's. "McDonald's Reports Fourth Quarter and Full Year 2014 Results." McDonald's Newsroom. January 23, 2015. http://news.mcdonalds.com/Corporate/news-stories/2015/McDonald-s-Reports-Fourth-Quarter-And-Full-Yea-(1)

20 Chipotle. "Press Release: Chipotle Mexican Grill, Inc. Announces First Quarter 2015 Results." *Chipotle Investor Relations*. April 21, 2015. http://ir.chipotle.com/phoenix.zhtml?c=194775&p=irol-newsArticle&ID=2038444

21 Mai-Duc, Christine. "Norovirus Caused Illness Outbreak at Ventura Chipotle Restaurant, Officials Say." *Los Angeles Times*. September 4, 2015. http://www.

latimes.com/local/lanow/la-me-ln-norovirus-chipotle-simi-valley-illness-20150904-story.html

22 Olson, Jeremy. "Minnesota Salmonella Outbreak Linked to Chipotle Restaurants." *Star Tribune*. September 11, 2015. http://www.startribune.com/twin-cities-salmonella-outbreak-linked-to-chipotle/326499341/

23 Baertlein, Lisa. "Chipotle E. coli Outbreak Reaches Six States, Shares Tumble." *Reuters*. November 20, 2015. http://www.reuters.com/article/us-chipotle-mexican-ecoli-idUSKCN0T92PV20151121

24 Fuhrmeister, Chris. "Has Chipotle's E. Coli Outbreak Spread to Massachusetts?" *Eater*. December 7, 2015. http://www.eater.com/2015 /12/7/9868796/chipotle-boston-college-athletes-sick-e-coli

25 Chipotle. "Press Release: Chipotle Mexican Grill, Inc. Announces Fourth Quarter and Full Year 2015 Results; CDC Investigation Over; Chipotle Welcomes Customers Back to Restaurants." *Investor Relations*. February 2, 2016. http://ir.chipotle.com/phoenix.zhtml?c=194775&p=irol-newsArticle&ID=2134993

26 Nasdaq. "Chipotle Mexican Grill, Inc. Common Stock Historical Stock Prices." http://www.nasdaq.com/symbol/cmg/historical

27 Centers for Disease Control and Prevention. "Multistate Outbreaks Of Shiga Toxin-Producing Escherichia coli O26 Infections Linked to Chipotle Mexican Grill Restaurants (final update)." February 1, 2016. https://www.cdc.gov/ecoli/2015/o26-11-15/

28 Chipotle. "Press Release: New Chipotle Food Safety Procedures Largely in Place; Company Will Share Learning's from 2015 Outbreaks at All-Team Meeting." *Investor Relations*. January 19, 2016. http://ir.chipotle.com/phoenix.zhtml?c=194775&p=irol-newsArticle&ID=2130375

29 Peterson, Hayley. "Here's Which Chipotle Ingredients Are Prepared Fresh in Restaurants." *Business Insider*. February 25, 2015. http://www.businessinsider.com/chipotle-address-food-preparation-2015-2

30 Chipotle Mexican Grill. *A Love Story*. YouTube. July 5, 2016. 4:07. https://www.youtube.com/watch?v=nKleQ1MXMCs

CHAPTER 2

1 Edelman. "2016 Edelman Trust Barometer." 2016. http://www.edelman.com/insights/intellectual-property/2016-edelman-trust-barometer/

2 Friedman, Milton. "A Friedman Doctrine—The Social Responsibility of Business Is to Increase Its Profits." *New York Times*. September 13, 1970. https://timesmachine.nytimes.com/timesmachine/1970/09/13/223535702.html?action=click&contentCollection=Archives&module=LedeAsset&region=ArchiveBody&pgtype=article&pageNumber=379

3 John Melloy, "Is the Buy & Hold Stock Strategy Officially Dead?" CNBC. June 25, 2012.

4   Justia USA Law. "Revlon, Inc. v. MacAndrews & Forbes Holdings." 1986. http://law.justia.com/cases/delaware/supreme-court/1986/506-a-2d-173-1.html

5   BlackRock. "Welcome to BlackRock." 2017. https://www.blackrock.com/ch/intermediaries/en/about-us/about-blackrock

6   Turner, Matt. "Here Is the Letter the World's Largest Investor, BlackRock CEO Larry Fink, Just Sent to CEOs Everywhere." *Business Insider*. February 2, 2016. http://www.businessinsider.com/blackrock-ceo-larry-fink-letter-to-sp-500-ceos-2016-2

7   DiChristopher, Tom. "Stop Thinking Short Term, CEOs: BlackRock's Fink." CNBC. February 3, 2016. http://www.cnbc.com/2016/02/03/stop-thinking-short-term-ceos-blackrocks-fink.html

8   Turner, Matt. "Here Is the Letter the World's Largest Investor, BlackRock CEO Larry Fink, Just Sent to CEOs Everywhere." *Business Insider*. February 2, 2016. http://www.businessinsider.com/blackrock-ceo-larry-fink-letter-to-sp-500-ceos-2016-2

9   Harper, Douglas. "The Online Etymology Dictionary." http://www.etymonline.com

10 William A. Vawter Foundation on Business Ethics. *The Ethical Problems Of Modern Finance. Lectures Delivered in 1929 on the William A. Vawter Foundation on Business Ethics, Northwestern University, School of Commerce* (New York: Ronald Press Company, 1930), pp. 23–48.

11 Stanford Business. "Theodore Kreps." https://www.gsb.stanford.edu/stanford-gsb-experience/leadership/history/theodore-kreps

12 Dodd, Merrick E. "For Whom Are Corporate Managers Trustees." *Harvard Law Review XLV*, no. 7 (May 8, 1932), 1152–4.

13 Stanford Business. "Theodore Kreps," https://www.gsb.stanford.edu/stanford-gsb-experience/leadership/history/theodore-kreps

14 Bowen, Howard R. *Social Responsibilities of a Businessman* (Iowa City: University of Iowa Press. 1953). Reprint in 2013.

15 Research and Policy Committee. "Social Responsibilities of Business Corporations." Committee for Economic Development. June 1971.

16 Bowie, Norman E. "Creating Public Value in a Multi-Sector, Shared-Power World." University of Minnesota. June 2012. PDF format.

17 Drucker, Peter F. *Management–Tasks, Responsibilities, Practices* (New York: Truman Talleey Books and E.P. Dutton. 1986), p. 47.

18 Unilever. *Unilever Sustainable Living Plan: Small Actions, Big Difference.* 2010. PDF format. https://webcache.googleusercontent.com/search?q=cache:DshA CONCEJcJ:https://www.unilever.com/Images/unileversustainable livingplan_tcm13-387356_tcm244-409855_en.pdf+&cd=1&hl=en&ct= clnk&gl=us

19 Haymarket Media. "Unilever's Quest for Magic." *Marketing*. November 2, 2011.

20 Cofino, Jo. "Will Unilever Become the World's Largest Publicly Traded B

Corp?" *The Guardian*. January 23, 2015. https://www.theguardian.com/
sustainable-business/2015/jan/23/benefit-corporations-bcorps-business-
social-responsibility

21 B Corporation. "About B Lab." https://www.bcorporation.net/what-are-b-
corps/about-b-lab

22 Cofino, Jo. "Will Unilever Become the World's Largest Publicly Traded B
Corp?" *The Guardian*. January 23, 2015. https://www.theguardian.com/
sustainable-business/2015/jan/23/benefit-corporations-bcorps-business-
social-responsibility

23 B Impact Assessment. "Measure What Matters: Your Company's Social and
Environmental Impact." 2017. http://bimpactassessment.net/

24 Coen Gilbert, Jay. Interview by author. Co-founder of B Lab. May 27, 2015.

25 Vaseline. "The Vaseline® Story." http://www.vaseline.co.uk/article/vaseline
story.html

26 Interview Kathleen Dunlop, Global Brand Director, Vaseline, January 6, 2017.

27 Interview Kathleen Dunlop, Global Brand Director, Vaseline, January 6, 2017.

28 Vaseline. "The Vaseline Healing Project." Unilever. http://healingproject.
vaseline.us/

29 Kathleen Dunlop. Interview by author. Global Brand Director, Vaseline.
January 6, 2017.

30 Vaseline. "The Vaseline Healing Project & Viola Davis Help Heal Skin
Worldwide." YouTube. 0:30. https://www.youtube.com/watch?v=ArQNgzd
W2rw

31 Vaseline. "Build a Relief Kit to Help Someone in Need." 2017. http://www.
vaseline.us/kitbuilder

CHAPTER 3

1 Rick Tetzeli, "Tim Cook on Apple's Future: Everything Can Change Except
Values." *Fast Company*. March 18, 2015. https://www.fastcompany.
com/3042435/steves-legacy-tim-looks-ahead

2 Blagdon, Jeff. "Apple Hires Former EPA Chief Lisa Jackson to Coordinate
Environmental Policy." *The Verge*. May 28, 2013. http://www.theverge.
com/2013/5/28/4374474/apple-tim-cook-d11-interview-taxes

3 Tsukayama, Hayley. "Apple's Lisa Jackson to Lead All of Apple's Social Policy
Initiatives." *Washington Post*. June 23, 2015. http://www.politico.com/
story/2013/05/lisa-jackson-epa-apple-091971

4 Barbosa, Greg. "Apple SVP Lisa Jackson Details Apple's Environmental Effort
Including Recycling Program During Event." 9TO5MAC. March, 21 2016.
https://9to5mac.com/2016/03/21/apple-svp-lisa-jackson-details-apples-
environmental-effort-including-recycling-program-during-event/

5 Musil, Steven. "Apple to Donate Portion of Holiday Sales to AIDS Fight."

CNET. November 23, 2014. https://www.cnet.com/news/apple-to-donate-portion-of-holiday-sales-to-aids-fight/

6   Mooney, Chris. "Apple Just Found a Powerful New Way to Make People Care About the Planet." *Washington Post*. April 14, 2016. https://www.washingtonpost.com/news/energy-environment/wp/2016/04/14/whats-so-different-and-powerful-about-apples-newest-green-initiative/?utm_term=.afea995eb91b

7   Drozdiak, Natalia, and Schechner, Sam. "Apple Ordered by EU to Repay $14.5 Billion in Irish Tax Breaks." *Wall Street Journal*. Updated August 30, 2016. https://www.wsj.com/articles/apple-received-14-5-billion-in-illegal-tax-benefits-from-ireland-1472551598

8   Mill, Chris. "Understanding Apple's Tax Mess: Why Apple Owes $14.5 Billion, and Why Ireland Doesn't Want It." BGR. August 30, 2016. http://bgr.com/2016/08/30/apple-tax-evasion-ireland-eu-explained-penalty-fine/

9   David Byrne Press Officer. "Minister Noonan Disagrees Profoundly with the Commission on Apple." An Roinn Airgeadais Department of Finance. August 30, 2016. http://www.finance.gov.ie/news-centre/press-releases/minister-noonan-disagrees-profoundly-commission-apple

10 Engler, John. "Business Roundtable Letter to EU Heads of State or Government Regarding State Aid Investigations." *Business Roundtable*. September 16, 2016. http://businessroundtable.org/resources/business-roundtable-letter-eu-heads-state-or-government-regarding-state-aid-investigations

11 BBC News. "Apple Fights Back with Appeal Against EU Irish Tax Ruling." December 19, 2016. http://www.bbc.com/news/business-38362434

12 Harper, Douglas. "The Online Etymology Dictionary." http://www.etymonline.com

13 Google.org. "A Better World Faster." https://www.google.org/

14 George Tharakan, Anya. "Bye Bye Google, Hello Alphabet." *Reuters*. October 2, 2015. http://www.reuters.com/article/us-google-restructuring-alphabet-idUSKCN0RW21H20151002

15 Page, Larry. "G Is for Google." Alphabet. https://abc.xyz/

16 Paton, James. "Alphabet's Verily, Sanofi to Invest $500 Million in Diabetes." Bloomberg News. September 12, 2016. https://www.bloomberg.com/news/articles/2016-09-12/alphabet-sanofi-to-invest-500-million-in-diabetes-venture

17 Alphabet Investor Relations. "Press Release: Alphabet Announces Second Quarter 2016 Results." Alphabet. July 28, 2016. https://abc.xyz/investor/news/earnings/2016/Q2_alphabet_earnings/

CHAPTER 4

1   Roberts, Kevin. *Lovemarks: The Future Beyond Brands* (New York: powerHouse Books, 2005).

2   "Top Scoring Meaningful Brands Enjoy a Share of Wallet 46% Higher Than

Low Performer." *Havas Media*. April 28, 2015. http://www.havasmedia.com/press/press-releases/2015/top-scoring-meaningful-brands-enjoy-a-share-of-wallet-46-per-cent-higher-than-low-performers

3   "Results of Reader's Digest Most Trusted Brands in America Announced." *PR Newswire*. September 15, 2015. http://www.prnewswire.com/news-releases/results-of-readers-digest-most-trusted-brands-in-america announced-300142306.html

4   "Reader's Digest Announces 2016's Trusted Brands." *Business Wire*. September 20, 2016. http://www.businesswire.com/news/home/2016092 0005039/en/Reader%E2%80%99s-Digest-Announces-2016%E2%80%99s-Trusted-Brands

5   Denend, Lyn, and Plambeck, Erica. "Wal-Marts sustainability strategy." *Stanford Business*. 2007. https://www.gsb.stanford.edu/faculty-research/case-studies/wal-marts-sustainability-strategy

6   Barbaro, Michael. "Wal-Mart to Expand Health Plan for Workers." *New York Times*. October 24, 2005. http://www.nytimes.com/2005/10/24/business/walmart-to-expand-health-plan-for-workers.html?_r=0

7   Barabaro, Michael, and Greenhouse, Steven. "Wal-Mart Memo Suggests Ways to cut Employee Benefit Costs." *New York Times*. October 26, 2005. http://www.nytimes.com/2005/10/26/business/walmart-memo-suggests-ways-to-cut-employee-benefit-costs.html

8   Brave New Films. "Walmart: The High Cost of Low Price" Full Documentary Film. YouTube. November 26, 2014. https://www.youtube.com/watch?v=RXmnBbUjsPs

9   Brave New Films. "Walmart: The High Cost of Low Price." Full Documentary Film. YouTube. November 26, 2014. https://www.youtube.com/watch?v=RXmnBbUjsPs

10 Bloomberg News. "Wal-Mart Promotes Executive Who Warned of Sick Workers." *The Boston Globe*. April 6, 2006. http://archive.boston.com/business/globe/articles/2006/04/06/wal_mart_promotes_executive_who_warned_of_sick_workers/

11 "Wal-Mart Rolling Out New Company Slogan." *Reuters*. September 12, 2007. http://www.reuters.com/article/us-walmart-advertising-idUSWEN0918 20070912

12 Wal-Mart. "Our history." http://corporate.walmart.com/our-story/our-history

13 "Wal-Mart Awards $2 Billion to U.S. Hourly Employees." *Reuters*. March 19, 2009. http://www.reuters.com/article/us-walmart-bonus-idUSTRE52I4PS2 0090319

14 Wal-Mart. "Walmart Launches Major Initiative to Make Food Healthier and Healthier Food More Affordable." *Wal-Mart Health and Wellness*. January 20, 2011. http://corporate.walmart.com/_news_/news-archive/2011/01/20/wal mart-launches-major-initiative-to-make-food-healthier-healthier-food-more-affordable

15 Wal-Mart. "Walmart and GE Transforming Retail Lighting with Energy-Efficient LEDs Globally." *Wal-Mart Sustainability*. April 9, 2014. http://

corporate.walmart.com/_news_/news-archive/2014/04/09/walmart-and-ge-transforming-retail-lighting-with-energy-efficient-leds-globally

16 Jena McGregor. "Wal-Mart CEO Speaks Out Against 'Religious Freedom' bill in Arkansas." *The Washington Post*. April 1, 2015. https://www.washingtonpost.com/news/on-leadership/wp/2015/04/01/wal-mart-ceo-speaks-out-against-religious-freedom-bill-in-arkansas/

17 Lee, M. J. "Walmart, Amazon, Sears, eBay to Stop Selling Confederate Flag Merchandise." *CNN Politics*. June 24, 2015. http://www.cnn.com/2015/06/22/politics/confederate-flag-walmart-south-carolina/

18 Smith, Aaron and Alesci, Cristina. "Walmart to Stop Selling AR-15s and Similar Guns." *CNN Money*. August 26, 2015. http://money.cnn.com/2015/08/26 /news/companies/walmart-ar-15-guns/

19 Walmart. "Global Responsibility Report: Opportunity, Sustainability, Community." 2015. PDF format.

20 Walmart. "Sustainability Report: Using Our Strengths to Help Others." 2016. PDF format.

21 Walmart. "Walmart Offers New Vision for the Company's Role in Society." November 4, 2016. http://news.walmart.com/2016/11/04/walmart-offers-new-vision-for-the-companys-role-in-society

22 "James Marsden Chosen as Chipotle's Food Safety Leader." *Food Safety Magazine*. March 24, 2016. http://www.foodsafetymagazine.com/news/james-marsden-chosen-as-chipotlee28099s-food-safety-leader/

23 Kate Taylor. "Chipotle Spent Millions Launching an Incredible Rewards Program for Customers—but Nobody Cared." *Business Insider*. September 22, 2016. http://www.businessinsider.com/chiptopia-failed-to-win-over-customers-2016-9

24 Ells, Steve. "Our Food Safety Advancements: A Letter from Chipotle Founder Steve Ells." Chipotle. https://chipotle.com/openletter

25 Chipotle Mexican Grill. "Our Food Safety Advancements: Click to Watch the Video and Explore the Steps We've Taken Below." https://chipotle.com/foodsafety

26 Chipotle Mexican Grill. Ingredients Reign. YouTube. September 4, 2016. 1:00. https://www.youtube.com/watch?v=fW_9toMB4Mo

27 Ells, Steve. "Barclays 2016 Eat, Sleep, Play—It's Not All Discretionary Conference." Chipotle Mexican Grill. December 6, 2016. https://cc.talkpoint.com/barc002/120516a_as/?entity=9_QYCBN1K

28 Arnold, Chris. "Chipotle Founder Steve Ells Returns to Sole CEO Role; Outlines Plans for Company's Future." *Chipotle Mexican Grill: Investor Relations*. December 12, 2016. http://ir.chipotle.com/phoenix.zhtml?c= 194775 &p=irol-newsArticle&ID=2228998

29 The Chipotle Cultivate Foundation. "About the Foundation." https://www.cultivatefoundation.org/about

30 Trader Joe's. "Our Story." 2017. http://www.traderjoes.com/our-story

31 Trader Joe's. "Our Story." 2017. http://www.traderjoes.com/our-story

32 Google. "Trader Joe's Number of Stores." February 16, 2017. https://www.google.com/search?q=trader+joe%27s+number+of+stores&ie=utf-8&oe=utf-8 March 7, 2017

33 Kowitt, Beth. "Inside the Secret World of Trader Joe's—Full Version." *Fortune.* August 23, 2010. http://archive.fortune.com/2010/08/20/news/companies/inside_trader_joes_full_version.fortune/index.htm

34 Trader Joe's. "A Word About Being Part of the Neighborhood." http://traderjoes.com/fearless-flyer/article/2910

35 Stryker, Sam. "18 Incredible Things You Didn't Know About Trader Joes." *Buzzfeed.* June 6, 2014. https://www.buzzfeed.com/samstryker/trader-joes-is-the-bomb-dot-com?utm_term=.isdBBjKQZ#.wuyEEPe6J

36 "Very High Levels of Arsenic Found in Top-Selling Wines." CBS News. March 19, 2015. http://www.cbsnews.com/news/lawsuit-claims-high-levels-arsenic-found-some-california-made-wines/

37 Scheiber, Noam. "At Trader Joe's, Good Cheer May Hide Complaints." *New York Times.* November 3, 2016. https://www.nytimes.com/2016/11/04/business/at-trader-joes-good-cheer-may-hide-complaints.html

38 Rossy, Ph.D., Gerry, and Mallinger, Mark, Ph.D. "The Trader Joe's Experience: The Impact of Corporate Culture on Business Strategy." *Pepperdine University Graziado Business Review 10,* no. 2. https://gbr.pepperdine.edu/2010/08/the-trader-joes-experience/

39 "The *New York Times* to Offer Open Access on Web and Apps for the Election." *New York Times.* November 3, 2016. https://www.nytimes.com/ 2016/ 11/04/homepage/new-york-times-open-access-election-2016.html

40 "Standards and Ethics." *New York Times.* 2017. http://www.nytco.com/who-we-are/culture/standards-and-ethics/

41 Berry, Jeff. "Colloquy Report: The 2015 Colloquy Loyalty Census, Big Numbers, Big Hurdles." *Colloquy Report.* February 2015. PDF format.

42 "Industry Report: Insights from Consumers and Marketing Decision Makers, The State of the Customer Journey." *Kitewheel.* 2014. PDF format.

43 Gesenhues, Amy. "A CMO's View: How SunTrust Is Maximizing Its Super Bowl 50 Campaign." *Marketing Land.* June 3, 2016. http://marketingland.com/cmos-view-suntrust-bank-susan-somersille-johnson-179533

44 SunTrust Banks Inc. "SunTrust Starts a National Conversation to Help Americans 'onUp' Toward Financial Confidence." PR Newswire. February 7, 2016. http://investors.suntrust.com/news/news-details/2016/SunTrust-Starts-a-National-Conversation-to-help-Americans-onUp-toward-Financial-Confidence/default.aspx

45 Gesenhues, Amy. "A CMO's View: How SunTrust Is Maximizing Its Super Bowl 50 Campaign." *Marketing Land.* June 3, 2016. http://marketingland.com/cmos-view-suntrust-bank-susan-somersille-johnson-179533

46 "Super Bowl Commercials 2016 30 Hold Your Breath SunTrust onUp Movement." SuperBowl Ads Online. YouTube. February 9, 2016. 0:30. https://www.youtube.com/watch?v=xp6kv0cV0hw

47 Operation HOPE. "The Global Leader for Financial Dignity." https://www.
    operationhope.org/

48 Operation HOPE. "SunTrust to Donate a Dollar to Operation HOPE for
    Every New onUp Participant." PR Newswire. February 8, 2016. http://www.
    prnewswire.com/news-releases/suntrust-to-donate-a-dollar-to-operation-
    hope-for-every-new-onup-participant-300216493.html

49 Gesenheus, Amy. "A CMO's View: How SunTrust Is Maximizing Its Super
    Bowl 50 Campaign." *Marketing Land*. June 3, 2016. http://marketingland.
    com/cmos-view-suntrust-bank-susan-somersille-johnson-179533

50 onUp. "Money Bloggers Get Real and Tell All." SunTrust. https://
    onupmovement.suntrust.com/stories/

51 SunTrust. "Philanthropy." https://www.suntrust.com/about-us/community-
    commitment/philanthropy

52 Amazon. "About." Facebook. https://www.facebook.com/Amazon/about

53 "Video from Jeff Bezos about Amazon and Zappos." YouTube. July 22, 2009.
    8:09. https://www.youtube.com/watch?v=-hxX_Q5CnaA

54 Parr, Ben. "Here's Why Amazon Bought Zappos." *Mashable*. July 22, 2009.
    http://mashable.com/2009/07/22/amazon-bought-zappos/#Mrg7.6CI9Sqj

55 Amazon Jobs. "Leadership Principles." https://www.amazon.jobs/principles

56 Zappos. "Zappos Family Core Values." http://www.zappos.com/core-values

57 "Amazon Workers Face 'Increased Risk of Mental Illness'." BBC News.
    November 25, 2013. http://www.bbc.com/news/business-25034598

58 Kantor, Jodi, and Streitfeld, David. "Inside Amazon: Wrestling Big Ideas in a
    Bruising Workplace." *New York Times*. August 15, 2015. https://www.
    nytimes.com/2015/08/16/technology/inside-amazon-wrestling-big-ideas-in-
    a-bruising-workplace.html

59 Ciubotariu, Nick. "An Amazonian's Response to 'Inside Amazon: Wrestling
    Big Ideas in a Bruising Workplace.'" LinkedIn. August 16, 2015. https://
    www.linkedin.com/pulse/amazonians-response-inside-amazon-wrestling-
    big-ideas-nick-ciubotariu

60 Bezos, Jeff. "Amazon Chief's Message to Employees." *New York Times*. August
    17, 2015. https://www.nytimes.com/2015/08/18/business/amazon-chiefs-
    message-to-employees.html

61 Sullivan, Margaret. "Was Portrayal of Amazon's Brutal Workplace on Target?"
    New York Times. August 18, 2015. https://publiceditor.blogs.nytimes.
    com/2015/08/18/was-portrayal-of-amazons-brutal-workplace-on-target/

62 Kantor, Jodi and Streitfeld, David. "Inside Amazon: Wrestling Big Ideas in a
    Bruising Workplace." *New York Times*. August 15, 2015. https://www.
    nytimes.com/2015/08/16/technology/inside-amazon-wrestling-big-ideas-in-
    a-bruising-workplace.html

63 Byrnes, Nanette. "How Amazon Loses on Prime and Still Wins." *MIT
    Technology Review*. July 12, 2016. https://www.technologyreview.com/s/601
    889/how-amazon-loses-on-prime-and-still-wins/

64 Shi, Audrey. "Amazon Prime Members Now Outnumber Non-Prime

Customers." *Fortune.* July 11, 2016. http://fortune.com/2016/07/11/amazon-prime-customers/

65 Cause Marketing. "Amazon Prime Diversity Ad: 'A Priest and Imam Meet for a Cup Of Tea'." YouTube. December 5, 2016. 1:36. https://www.youtube.com/watch?v=cllWl1u1fj0

66 Rodionova, Zlata. "Amazon Christmas Advert 2016: Imam and Priest Push Festive Message of Friendship." *Independent.* November 2, 2016. http://www.independent.co.uk/news/business/news/amazon-christmas-advert-2016-video-priest-imam-xmas-a7420856.html

67 Walmart. "Walmart Completes Acquisition of Jet.com, Inc." *Walmart News.* September 19, 2016. http://news.walmart.com/2016/09/19/walmart-completes- acquisition-of-jetcom-inc

68 Walmart. "Walmart Completes Acquisition of Jet.com, Inc." Walmart News. September 19, 2016. http://news.walmart.com/2016/09/19/walmart-completes-acquisition-of-jetcom-inc

CHAPTER 5

1 Reese, Megan L., "Monica Nassif, Caldrea & Mrs. Meyer's Clean Day: 5 Steps to Creating a Powerful Attraction Marketing Plan for 2010." *Ladies Who Launch.* January 19, 2010. http://www.ladieswholaunch.com/magazine/monica-nassif-mrs-meyers-clean-day/

2 Mrs. Meyer's. "Our Inspiration." 2017. http://www.mrsmeyers.com/our-story/our-inspiration/

3 Mrs. Meyer's. "Ingredient Glossary." 2017. http://www.mrsmeyers.com/our-story/ingredients-glossary/

4 Mrs. Meyer's. "Leaping Bunny Program." 2017. http://www.mrsmeyers.com/leaping-bunny/

5 Carbone, Ken. "Unify, Simplify, Amplify: How the Mrs. Meyer's Brand Conquers a Tough Market." *Fast Company & Inc.* June 7, 2011. https://www.fastcodesign.com/1664014/unify-simplify-amplify-how-the-mrs-meyers-brand-conquers-a-tough-market

6 Lee, Thomas. "Mr. Muscle Marrying Mrs. Meyer." *Star Tribune.* April 28, 2008.http://www.startribune.com/mr-muscle-marrying-mrs-meyer/18351 899//

7 Anderson, Corey. "S.C. Johnson Integrating Caldrea/Mrs. Meyer's in Racine, Ceasing Minneapolis Operations." *Minnpost.* February 11, 2014. https://www.minnpost.com/business/2014/02/sc-johnson-integrating-caldreamrs-meyers-racine-ceasing-minneapolis-operations

8 Hanson Dodge. "Mass Marketing a Niche Brand." 2017. http://www.hansondodge.com/work/mrs-meyers-clean-day/mass-marketing-a-niche-brand/

9 Mrs. Meyer's Clean Day. "The Hunt for the First Ever Mrs. Meyer's Home

Maker." Facebook. September 2, 2015. https://www.facebook.com/mrs meyerscleanday/videos/973616642681354/

10 Mrs. Meyer's. "Making the World a Greener Place One Garden at a Time." 2017. http://www.mrsmeyers.com/our-story/celebrating-service/

11 Mrs. Meyer's. "Mrs. Meyer's Clean Day Make Something Day." Facebook. December 13, 2016. https://www.facebook.com/search/top/?q=mrs.%20meyer %27s%20clean%20day%20make%20something%20day

12 A Bullseye View. "16 Better-for-You Brands. 1 First-of-Its Kind Collection." Target. April 8, 2014. https://corporate.target.com/article/2014/04/target-introduces-made-to-matter-collection

13 D'Innocenzio, Anne. "Target Doubling Initiative on Organics, Naturals." *Chicago Sun Times.* February 20, 2015. http://chicago.suntimes.com/news/target-doubling-initiative-on-organics-naturals/

14 Burt's Bees. "Our Philosophy." 2017. https://www.bee2bee.com/story-philosophy.html

15 Burt's Bees. "Operational Footprint." 2017. https://www.burtsbees.com.au/w/about-us/sustainability/operational-footprint.html

16 Burt's Bees. "Our History." 2017. https://www.burtsbees.co.uk/c/root-our-history-burt-s-bees.html

17 Feloni, Richard. "Burt's Bees Cofounder Burt Shavitz Died at Age 80—Here's His Crazy Success Story." *Business Insider UK.* July 6, 2015. http://uk.businessinsider.com/success-story-of-burts-bees-late-cofounder-burt-shavitz-2015-7?r=US&IR=T

18 McFeeters, Stephanie. "Maine Artist Recalls Making Iconic Burt's Bees Logo." *Boston Globe.* July 6, 2015. https://www.bostonglobe.com/lifestyle/2015/07/06/maine-artist-recalls-making-iconic-burt-bees-logo/zeVDVmePq8OE7 g35WmLajI/story.html

19 Story, Louise. "Can Burt's Bees Turn Clorox Green?" *New York Times.* January 6, 2008. http://www.nytimes.com/2008/01/06/business/06bees.html

20 Funding Universe. "Burt's Bees, Inc. History." http://www.fundinguniverse.com/company-histories/burt-s-bees-inc-history/

21 Ritter, Beth. "Why Live the Greater Good?." SVP HR, Burt's Bees. 2010.

22 AEA Investors. "AEA Differentiator: Ability to Transform a Family-Owned Business." 2017. http://www.aeainvestors.com/private-equity/middle-market/case-studies/burts-bees//

23 The Clorox Company. "Clorox to Acquire Burt's Bees; Expands into Fast-Growing Natural Personal Care." October 31, 2007. https://investors.thecloroxcompany.com/investors/news-and-events/press-releases/press-release-details/2007/Clorox-to-Acquire-Burts-Bees-Expands-Into-Fast-Growing-Natural-Personal-Care/default.aspx

24 Story, Louise. "Can Burt's Bees Turn Clorox Green?" *New York Times.* January 6, 2008. http://www.nytimes.com/2008/01/06/business/06bees.html

25 Story, Louise. "Can Burt's Bees Turn Clorox Green?" *New York Times.* January 6, 2008. http://www.nytimes.com/2008/01/06/business/06bees.html

26 Calbi, Christina and Cammaker, Meredith. "Julianne Moore Casts Her Vote for Natural at Burt's Bees Voting Day in New York City." Burt's Bees. September 2008. https://www.burtsbees.co.uk/wcsstore/Bee2C/upload.../VoteForNatural%20Sept2008.pdf

27 Talking Makeup. "Actress Julianne Moore Casts Her Vote at Burt's Bees Election Day." September 10, 2008. http://talkingmakeup.com/beauty/actress-julianne-moore-casts-her-vote-at-burts-bees-election-day/

28 Burt's Bees. "Burt's Bees Publishes 2009 Social and Environmental Report." CSR Wire. February 3, 2010. http://www.csrwire.com/press_releases/28810-Burt-s-Bees-Publishes-2009-Social-And-Environmental-Report

29 Shorty Awards. "Raise Your Burt's: Part Social Contest Part Love Fest." February 19, 2013. http://shortyawards.com/5th/raise-your-burts-part-social-contest-part-love-fest

30 Sharp, David. "Turkey Coop Home of Burt's Bees Co-Founder to Be Saved." *Washington's Top News.* September 4, 2016. http://wtop.com/media-galleries/2016/09/turkey-coop-home-of-burts-bees-co-founder-to-be-saved/slide/1/

31 Burt's Bees. "Burt's Bees Joins Healthy Child, Healthy World." CSR Wire. October 16, 2012. http://www.csrwire.com/press_releases/34755-Burt-s-Bees-reg-Joins-Healthy-Child-Healthy-World

32 David Sharp, "AP—The Big Story." Associated Press. September 4, 2016.

33 Lee Chang, Gigi. Interview by author. January 25, 2017.

34 "Gigi Lee Chang." *Ladies Who Launch.* January 13, 2009. http://www.ladieswholaunch.com/magazine/1209/

35 Cooper, Steve. "The Hot List." *Entrepreneur.* December 1, 2006. https://www.entrepreneur.com/article/170426

36 Lee Chang, Gigi. Interview by author. January 25, 2017.

37 Carroll, Sina. "The Nest Collective Announces Acquisition of Plum Organics." PR Web. February 19, 2009. http://www.prweb.com/releases/Nest_Collective/Organic_Baby_Food/prweb2097444.htm

38 Schwartz, Ariel. "How the Nest Collective Is Making Children's Food Fun." *Fast Company.* November 12, 2010. https://www.fastcompany.com/1701982/how-nest-collective-making-healthy-childrens-food-fun

39 Plum Organics. "What Is Nutritional Intelligence?" 2017. http://www.plumorganics.com/resource_center/what-is-nutritional-intelligence/

40 Mand, Ben. Interview by author. January 20, 2017.

41 Mand, Ben. Interview by author. January 20, 2017.

42 Campbell Team. "Plum 'Super Smoothie' Fuels Little Ones." Campbell Soup Company. April 15, 2014. https://www.campbellsoupcompany.com/newsroom/news/2014/04/15/plum-super-smoothie-fuels-little-ones/

43 Campbell Team. "Plum 'Super Smoothie' Fuels Little Ones." Campbell Soup Company. April 15, 2014. https://www.campbellsoupcompany.com/newsroom/news/2014/04/15/plum-super-smoothie-fuels-little-ones/

44 Plum Organics. "Nourishing Little Ones: Mission Report 2016." 2016. PDF format.

45 Singh, Aman. "Campbell Becomes America's First Public Company to Acquire a Public Benefit Corporation: In Conversation with Plum Organics' Cofounder." CSR Wire. September 9, 2013. http://www.csrwire.com/blog/ posts/1005-campbell-becomes-america-s-first-public-company-to-acquire-a-public-benefit-corporation-in-conversation-with-plum-organics-cofounder

46 Mand, Ben. Interview by author. January 24, 2017.

47 Schwartz, Ariel. "Inside Plum Organics, the First Benefit Corporation Owned by a Public Company." *Fast Coexist.* January 22, 2014. https://www. fastcoexist.com/3024991/world-changing-ideas/inside-plum-organics-the-first-benefit-corporation-owned-by-a-public-co

48 B Lab. "Benefit Corporations and Certified B Corps." Benefit Corporation. 2017. http://benefitcorp.net/businesses/benefit-corporations-and-certified-b-corps

49 Mand, Ben. Interview by author. January 24, 2017.

50 The Soulful Project, PBC. "What Is the Soulful Project." 2015. https:// thesoulfullproject.com/

51 Yi, Karen. "Baby Food Recall: Plum Organics Recalls Pouch Food for Possible Botulism Contamination." *Daily News.* October 20, 2009. http://www. nydailynews.com/news/national/baby-food-recall-plum-organics-recalls-pouch-food-botulism-contamination-article-1.385470

52 News Desk. "Plum Organics Recalls Kids' Food Products for Possible Spoilage." *Food Safety News.* November 9, 2013. http://www.foodsafetynews. com/2013/11/plum-organics-recalls-kids-food-for-possible-spoilage/#. WIqFXxCNNVU

53 Mand, Ben. Interview by author. January 24, 2017.

54 Anne Westpheling. Interview by author. January 30, 2017.

55 Plum Organics. "Plum Organics Enters Earliest Feeding Category with Organic Infant Formula." *PR Newswire.* March 8, 2016. http://www.pr newswire.com/news-releases/plum-organics-enters-earliest-feeding-category-with-organic-infant-formula-300232480.html

56 Mommyhood101. "Best Organic Baby Formula Options for 2017." 2017. http://mommyhood101.com/best-organic-baby-formula-2017

57 Mand, Ben. Interview by author. January 24, 2017.

58 Mand, Ben. Interview by author. January 24, 2017.

59 Plum Organics. "Nourishing Little Ones: Mission Report 2015." 2015. PDF format.

60 Plum Organics. "Nourishing Little Ones: Mission Report 2015." 2015. PDF format.

61 Westpheling, Anne. Interview by author. January 30, 2017.

62 IKEA. "IKEA History—How It All Began." 2016. http://www.ikea.com/ms/ en_AU/about_ikea/the_ikea_way/history/

63 Farlex. "IKEA." The Free Dictionary. http://acronyms.thefreedictionary.com/ IKEA

64 Goggle search. "Number of IKEA Employees." 2016. https://www.google. com/search?q=ikea+number+employees+&ie=utf-8&oe=utf-8

65 IKEA. "Welcome Inside Our Company." August 31, 2016. http://www.ikea. com/ms/en_US/this-is-ikea/company-information/index.html

66 IKEA. "IKEA Launches Pilot Virtual Reality (VR) Kitchen Experience for HTC Vive on Steam." April 5, 2016. http://www.ikea.com/us/en/about_ikea/ newsitem/040516_Virtual-Reality

67 IKEA. "IKEA Shares Global Insights on How the World Wakes Up in New Life at Home Report." June 3, 2014. http://www.ikea.com/us/en/about_ikea/ newsitem/FY14-IKEA_Life-At-Home-Report

68 IKEA. "We're on the Road Helping America Improve Life at Home with Simple Design Solutions." 2017. https://www.hometourseries.com/

69 IKEA. "Life at Home." http://lifeathome.ikea.com/morning

70 Jackson, Amy. "IKEA Hits the Road to Help Homeowners Tackle Home Design Challenges with 'IKEA Home Tour.'" IKEA. April 2, 2014. http:// www.ikea.com/us/en/about_ikea/newsitem/pr_IKEA-home-tour-hits-road

71 IKEA. "The Testament of a Furniture Dealer." 2013. PDF format. http:// webcache.googleusercontent.com/search?q=cache:3ta3n5URJAEJ:www.ikea. com/ms/en_US/pdf/reports-downloads/the-testament-of-a-furniture-dealer. pdf+&cd=1&hl=en&ct=clnk&gl=us

72 Torekull, Bertil, and Kamprad, Ingvar. *Leading by Design: The IKEA Story* (New York: Harper Collins, 1999).

73 IKEA. The Testament of a Furniture Dealer." 2013. PDF format. http:// webcache.googleusercontent.com/search?q=cache:3ta3n5URJAEJ:www.ikea. com/ms/en_US/pdf/reports-downloads/the-testament-of-a-furniture-dealer. pdf+&cd=1&hl=en&ct=clnk&gl=us

74 IKEA. The Testament of a Furniture Dealer." 2013. PDF format. http:// webcache.googleusercontent.com/search?q=cache:3ta3n5URJAEJ:www.ikea. com/ms/en_US/pdf/reports-downloads/the-testament-of-a-furniture-dealer. pdf+&cd=1&hl=en&ct=clnk&gl=us

75 Nattrass, Brian. *The Natural Step for Business: Wealth, Ecology & the Evolutionary Corporation* (New Society Publishers, 50, January 1999), p. 50.

76 Owens, Heidi Ph.D. "IKEA Case Study." The Natural Step Network. October 28, 2008. http://thenaturalstep.nl/ikea/

77 Nattrass, Brian. *The Natural Step for Business: Wealth, Ecology & the Evolutionary Corporation* (New York: New Society Publishers, 50, January 1999), pp. 51– 52.

78 Nattrass, Brian. *The Natural Step for Business: Wealth, Ecology & the Evolutionary Corporation* (New York: New Society Publishers, 50. January 1999), p. 51.

79 Nattrass, Brian. *The Natural Step for Business: Wealth, Ecology & the Evolutionary Corporation* (New York: New Society Publishers, 50. January 1999), p. 53.

80 Nattrass, Brian. *The Natural Step for Business: Wealth, Ecology & the Evolutionary Corporation* (New York: New Society Publishers, 50. January 1999, pp. 52–53.

81 Doppelt, Bob. *Leading Change Toward Sustainability* (Abingdon, UK: Greenleaf Publishing, 2003), p. 111.

82 Greenpeace. "The Forest Stewardship Council." 2016. http://www.greenpeace.org/international/en/campaigns/forests/solutions/alternatives-to-forest-destruc/

83 Woolford, Justin. "World's Largest Print Run Now Carries FSC Label." Forest Business Network. August 12, 2015. https://www.forestbusinessnetwork.com/50873/worlds-largest-print-run-now-carries-fsc-label/

84 Doppelt, Bob. *Leading Change Toward Sustainability* (Abingdon, UK: Greenleaf Publishing, 2003), p. 111.

85 IKEA. "Social Initiative Backgrounder." February 2009. PDF format. https://www.unicef.org/media/files/IKEA_social_initiative_backgrounder_01.doc

86 IKEA Foundation. "History." https://www.ikeafoundation.org/about-us/history/

87 Save the Children. "IKEA Foundation." 2017. http://www.savethechildren.org/site/c.8rKLIXMGIpI4E/b.8275809/k.BB87/IKEA.htm

88 IKEA. "IWAY Standard." http://www.ikea.com/ms/en_JP/about_ikea/our_responsibility/iway/index.html

89 IKEA. "The IKEA Way on Purchasing Home Furnishing Products (IWAY)." January 10, 2007. PDF format.

90 IKEA. "The IKEA Way on Preventing Child Labor." January 10, 2007, pp. 2–3. PDF format.

91 IKEA. "IKEA Live Lagom." 2017. http://www.ikea.com/gb/en/ikea/ikea-live-lagom/

92 IKEA. "People & Planet Positive: IKEA Group Sustainability Strategy for 2020." First published October, 2012, updated June, 2014. PDF format www.ikea.com/ms/en_US/.../sustainability-strategy-people-and-planet-positive.pdf

93 Perella, Maxine. "A Sustainable Life at Home: How IKEA Plans to Become Circular." Sustainable Brands. September 22, 2016. http://www.sustainablebrands.com/news_and_views/brand_innovation/maxine_perella/sustainable_life_home_ how_ikea_plans_become_circular_

94 McKernan, Bethan. "IKEA Builds Syrian Home Replica in Store to Show Horrors Of War." *Independent*. November 2017. http://www.independent.co.uk/news/world/middle-east/ikea-builds-syrian-home-replica-in-store-to-show-horrors-of-war-a7409896.html

95 The Local SE. "IKEA Opens Massive Museum in Sweden." July 1, 2016. https://www.thelocal.se/20160701/ikea-opens-mammoth-museum-in-sweden

CHAPTER 6

1 Office of the Press Secretary. "Fact Sheet: White House Launches American Business Act on Climate Pledge." The White House. July 27, 2015. https://www.whitehouse.gov/the-press-office/2015/07/27/fact-sheet-white-house-launches-american-business-act-climate-pledge

2 Breitbart News. "#DumpKelloggs: Breakfast Brand Blacklists Breitbart, Declares Hate for 45,000,000 Readers." November 30, 2016. http://www.breitbart.com/big-government/2016/11/30/dumpkelloggs-kelloggs-declares-hate-45-million-americans-blacklisting-breitbart/

3 Kellogg's Company. "Stock Chart." 2017. http://investor.kelloggs.com/stock-information#stock-chart

4 Employee Benefit Research Institute. "Facts from EBRI." November 2013. https://www.ebri.org/publications/facts/index.cfm?fa=0398afact)

5 Employee Benefit Research Institute. "History of Health Insurance." March 2002. https://www.ebri.org/publications/facts/index.cfm?fa=0302fact

6 Ford. "Our History." 2015. https://corporate.ford.com/history.html

7 Cox, Peter. *Spedan's Partnership: The Story of John Lewis and Waitrose* (N.p.: Labatie Books, 2011).

8 John Lewis Partnership. "Our Responsibilities." https://www.johnlewispartnership.co.uk/csr.html

9 John Lewis Partnership. "Employee Ownership, a Shared Passion." January 6, 2011. https://www.johnlewispartnership.co.uk/resources/library/video/employee-ownership-a-shared-passion.html

10 John Lewis Partnership. "Working for Us." https://www.johnlewispartnership.co.uk/work.html

11 John Lewis Partnership. "Annual Report and Accounts 2016." 2016. http://www.johnlewispartnership.co.uk/content/dam/cws/pdfs/financials/annual-reports/jlp-annual-report-and-accounts-2016.pdf

12 John Lewis. "John Lewis Christmas Advert 2016- #bustertheboxer." YouTube. November 9, 2016. 2:10. https://www.youtube.com/watch?v=sr6lr_VRsEo

13 Jenkins, Heather. "Waitrose Awards." *Compassion in Food Business.* 2017. https://www.compassioninfoodbusiness.com/award-winners/retailer/john-lewis-partnership/waitrose/

14 Smithers, Rebecca. "Waitrose Commits to Sustainable Farming." *The Guardian.* April 26, 2007. https://www.theguardian.com/environment/2007/apr/26/food.supermarkets

15 Waitrose. "Waitrose Wins Double Title at Compassion in World Farming Awards for Its Work on Welfare." July 7, 2011. http://waitrose.pressarea.com/pressrelease/details/78/CORPORATE percent20NEWS_13/3015

16 Waitrose. "The Waitrose Foundation: Treating People Fairly in Global Partnership." 2017. http://www.waitrose.com/home/inspiration/about_waitrose/the_waitrose_way/foundation.html

17 Waitrose. "Waitrose Farm Assessment." 2017. http://www.sustainable agriculturewaitrose.org/research/waitrose-farm-assessment/

18 Waitrose. "2015 The Waitrose Way Awards." 2015. http://www.waitrose. com/home/inspiration/about_waitrose/the_waitrose_way/waitrose-way-awards.html

19 John Lewis Partnership. "Achieving More Through Collaboration." 2013. http://static.globalreporting.org/report-pdfs/2013/8519e7f8ccd7a626bc6df0c f78df717b.pdf

20 Business in the Community. "Waitrose—The Waitrose Way." June 2014. http://www.bitc.org.uk/our-resources/case-studies/waitrose-waitrose-way

21 Waitrose. "Waitrose Hot Ideas." 2017. http://www.waitrose.com/home/ inspiration/about_waitrose/our_company/WaitroseHotIdeas.html

22 Chapman, Matthew. "Waitrose to Launch Hiku Home Scanner as Part of New Incubator Programme." Retail Week. October 15, 2014. https://www. retail-week.com/technology/innovation/waitrose-to-launch-hiku-home-scanner-as-part-of-new-incubator-programme/5065178.article

23 Hiku. "The Shopping Button." http://hiku.us/

24 Butler, Sarah. "John Lewis to Cut Staff Bonus After Pound's Brexit Slide." *The Guardian.* January 12, 2017. https://www.theguardian.com/ business/2017/jan/12/john-lewis-cut-staff-bonus-market-waitrose-christmas

25 Kimberly-Clark. "Leading the World in Essentials for a Better Life. That's What Kimberly Clark Is All About." http://www.Kimberly-Clark.com/our company/overview.aspx

26 Lewis, Jenny. Interview by author. January 24, 2017.

27 Federovitch, John. Interview by author. February 9, 2017.

28 Lewis, Jenny. Interview by author. January 24, 2017.

29 Lewis, Jenny. Interview by author. January 24, 2017.

30 Brown, Rob. "Britain's Biggest Brands 2016." *The Grocer.* March 18, 2016. http://webcache.googleusercontent.com/search?q=cache: nNJ8ivfMxjkJ: www. thegrocer.co.uk/buying-and-supplying/britains-biggest-brands-2016/+ &cd=7&hl=en&ct=clnk&gl=us

31 Andrex. "Andrex Extended Film 2014 'How Andrex Do You Feel?'" YouTube. September 24, 2014. https://www.youtube.com/watch?v=qxcUwBvTeAU

32 Mumsnet. "How Andrex Do You Feel?" https://www.mumsnet.com/ microsites/andrex-index

33 Berry, Tom. Interview by author. February 9, 2017.

34 Unicef. "Andrex Working with UNICEF" https://www.unicef.org.uk/ corporate-partners/andrex/

35 Berry, Tom. Interview by author. February 9, 2017.

36 Deighton, Katie. "Event TV: Andrex and UNICEF Stage Angolan Toilet Experience." *Event Magazine.* November 20, 2015. http://www.eventmagazine. co.uk/event-tv-andrex-unicef-stage-angolan-toilet-experience/brands/ article/1373640

37 Berry, Tom. Interview by author. February 9, 2017.

38 Kimberly-Clark. "Sustainability for a Better Life." 2015. http://www.Kimberly-Clark.com/sustainability/Content/PDF/Report_FA.pdf

39 Lewis, Jenny. Interview by author. January 24, 2017.

40 Federovitch, John. Interview by author. February 9, 2017.

41 Kimberly-Clark. "National & International Awards and Recognition." 2012. http://www.careersatkc.com/awards-recognition.aspx

42 Ethical Fashion Forum. "The Issues." http://www.ethicalfashionforum.com/the-issues/ethical-fashion

43 Remy, Nathalie, Speelman, Eveline, and Swartz, Steven. "Style That's Sustainable: A New Fast-Fashion Formula." McKinsey & Company, October 2016.

44 Savers. "State of Reuse Report." 2016. https://www.savers.com/reusereport

45 BBC News. "Why East Africa Wants to Ban Second Hand Clothes." March 2, 2016. http://www.bbc.com/news/world-africa-35706427

46 H&M. "The History of H&M Group." https://about.hm.com/en/about-us/history.html

47 H&M. "Markets & Expansion." https://about.hm.com/en/about-us/markets-and-expansion.html

48 H&M. "About H&M Conscious." http://sustainability.hm.com/en/sustainability/about/hm-conscious/about-hm-conscious.html

49 Secondary Materials and Recycled Textiles. "Recycling Fact Sheet." 2013.

50 H&M. "Recycle Your Clothes." https://about.hm.com/en/sustainability/get-involved/recycle-your-clothes.html

51 I:CO. "H&M First Fashion Company to Launch Global Clothes Collecting Initiative." December 20, 2012. http://www.ico-spirit.com/en/news/hm-first-fashion-company-to-launch-global-clothes-collecting-initiative,13.html

52 H&M. "H&M Foundation." http://sustainability.hm.com/en/sustainability/about/hm-conscious/hm-conscious-foundation.html

53 Green Strategy. "Review of Copenhagen Fashion Summit." May 10, 2014. http://www.greenstrategy.se/review-copenhagen-fashion-summit-2014-2/

54 Clevercare. "How to Reduce Climate Impact, Effort and Money Caring for Fashion the Clever Way." Ginetex. http://www.clevercare.info/en

55 H&M. "Vision & Policy." http://sustainability.hm.com/en/sustainability/about/governance/vision-and-policy.html

56 H&M. "Conscious Actions Sustainability Report." 2015. PDF format.

57 McCarthy, Lauren. "Olivia Wilde Hosts Dinner for H&M Conscious Exclusive Collection." Womens Wear Daily. April 15, 2015. http://wwd.com/eye/parties/olivia-wilde-hosts-dinner-for-hm-conscious-exclusive-collection-10112107/

58 "H&M and Olivia Wilde Present the Conscious Exclusive 2016 Collection." Business Wire. April 5, 2016. http://www.businesswire.com/news/home/20160405005931/en/HM-Olivia-Wilde-Present-Conscious-Exclusive-2016

59 Abrams, Rachel. "Retailers like H&M and Walmart Fall Short of Pledges to Overseas Workers." New York Times. May 31, 2016. https://www.nytimes.

com/2016/05/31/business/international/top-retailers-fall-short-of-commitments-to-overseas-workers.html?_r=1

60 H&M. "A Clear Stand Against Child Labour." http://sustainability.hm.com/en/sustainability/commitments/choose-and-reward-responsible-partners/code-of-conduct/clear-stand-against-child-labour.html

61 H&M. "A Clear Stand Against Child Labour." http://sustainability.hm.com/en/sustainability/commitments/choose-and-reward-responsible-partners/code-of-conduct/clear-stand-against-child-labour.html

CHAPTER 7

1 Maslow, A. H. "A Theory of Human Motivation." 1943. *Psychological Review 50*, no. 4, 370–396.

2 Kahn, Brad. Interview by author. November 29, 2016.

3 FSC US. FSC: One Simple Action." YouTube. October 7, 2016 https://www.youtube.com/watch?v=dfIC6Edsu5A

4 Kahn, Brad. Interview by author. November 29, 2016.

5 Burn-Callander, Rebecca. "Giffgaff, the Bonkers Mobile Network, Proves That the Crowd Can Run Your Business for You." *Telegraph.* May 26, 2015. http://www.telegraph.co.uk/finance/newsbysector/media technology and telecoms/telecoms/11630738/Giffgaff-the-bonkers-mobile-network-proves-that-the-crowd-can-run-your-business-for-you.html

6 Burn-Callander, Rebecca. "Giffgaff, the Bonkers Mobile Network, Proves That the Crowd Can Run Your Business for You." *Telegraph.* May 26, 2015. http://www.telegraph.co.uk/finance/newsbysector/mediatechnologyand telecoms/telecoms/11630738/Giffgaff-the-bonkers-mobile-network-proves-that-the-crowd-can-run-your-business-for-you.html

7 Mobile. "2012 Winners." 2012. http://www.mobiletoday.co.uk/awards/2012/winners/list

8 Elliott, Nate. "Winners of the 2010 Forrester Groundswell Awards (Consumer International)." Forrester. November 19, 2010. http://74.201.44.71/nate_elliott/10-11-19-winners_of_the_2010_forrester_groundswell_awards_consumer_international

9 Giffgaff. "Giffgaff Community." 2016. https://community.Giffgaff.com/

10 Mobile. "2012 Winners." 2012. http://www.mobiletoday.co.uk/awards/2012/winners/list

11 Elliott, Nate. "Winners of the 2010 Forrester Groundswell Awards (Consumer International)." Forrester. November 19, 2010. http://74.201.44.71/nate_elliott/10-11-19-winners_of_the_2010_forrester_groundswell_awards_consumer_international

12 Farey-Jones, Daniel. "Industry Leaders Vote John Lewis as Brand of the Year." Campaign. November 19, 2010. http://www.campaignlive.co.uk/article/1042012/industry-leaders-vote-john-lewis-brand-year?src_site=brandrepublic

13 Mobile. "2012 Winners." 2012. http://www.mobiletoday.co.uk/awards/2012/winners/list

14 Leggett, Jonathan. "Giffgaff Named Best Network in Night for Underdogs at uSwitch Awards." uSwitch Mobiles. February 11, 2016. https://www.uswitch.com/mobiles/news/2016/02/Giffgaff-named-best-network-uswitch-awards/

15 Ghosh, Shona. "Giffgaff Moves into Personal Finance to Disrupt Banks." Campaign. May 14, 2015. http://www.campaignlive.co.uk/article/1347118/giffgaff-moves-personal-finance-disrupt-banks

16 Haggerty, Angela. "Kiss FM Teams Up with Giffgaff to Pay a Listeners Rent for a Year in Social Media Contest." *The Drum*. August 28, 2014. http://www.thedrum.com/news/2014/08/28/kiss-fm-teams-Giffgaff-pay-listeners-rent-year-social-media-competition

17 Admin. "Your Place, Your Space Winner—Kiss FM (UK)." Photoshop Adobe. November 15, 2016. http://www.photoshopadobe.com/your-place-your-space-winner-kiss-fm-uk

18 Nunwood. "UK Customer Experience Excellence Analysis." September 22, 2016. http://www.nunwood.com/?portfolio=08-Giffgaff-uk-customer-experience-excellence-analysis-2016

19 IBM. "Chronological History of IBM." https://www-03.ibm.com/ibm/history/history/decade_1880.html

20 IBM. "Annual Report." 2015.

21 IBM. "IBM Research." http://www.research.ibm.com/labs/index.shtml

22 IBM. "History: 2002." http://www-03.ibm.com/ibm/history/history/year_2002.html

23 IBM. "IBM's Chairmen." https://www-03.ibm.com/ibm/history/exhibits/chairmen/chairmen_1.html

24 Hemp, Paul, and Stewart, Thomas A. "Leading Change When Business Is Good." *Harvard Business Review*. December 2004.

25 Interview by author with former IBM employee. Brand Research and Strategy group. February 2, 2017.

26 IBM. "A Business and Its Beliefs." http://www-03.ibm.com/ibm/history/ibm100/us/en/icons/bizbeliefs/

27 IBM. "The IBM Beliefs Plaque." http://ibmcollectable.com/gallery/BobLadden1/basic_beliefs?full=1

28 Former IBM employee. Interview by author. Brand Research and Strategy Group. February 2, 2017.

29 Hemp, Paul, and Stewart, Thomas A. "Leading Change When Business Is Good." *Harvard Business Review*. December 2004.

30 IBM. "Employee Values." PDF format. www.ibmemployee.com/PDFs/Values percent20Jam.pdf

31 Former IBM employee. Interview by author. Brand Research and Strategy Group. February 2, 2017.

32 Hemp, Paul, and Stewart, Thomas A. "Leading Change When Business Is Good." *Harvard Business Review*. December 2004.

33 IBM. "A Global Innovation Jam." https://www-https://www-03.ibm.com/employment/ca/en/newhire/regular_work.html

34 Hemp, Paul, and Stewart, Thomas A. "Leading Change When Business Is Good." *Harvard Business Review*. December 2004.

35 IBM. "Client Experience Jam." 2008. https://www.collaborationjam.com/IBMJam/

36 IBM. "A Global Innovation Jam." http://www-03.ibm.com/ibm/history/ibm100/us/en/icons/innovationjam

37 Former IBM employee. Interview by author. Brand Research and Strategy Group. February 2, 2017.

38 Tiebout Hanson, Janet. Interview by author. February 20, 2017.

39 Tiebout Hanson, Janet. Interview by author. February 20, 2017.

40 Tiebout Hanson, Janet. Interview by author. February 20, 2017.

41 Tiebout Hanson, Janet. Interview by author. February 20, 2017.

42 Krawcheck, Sallie. "Why a Woman's Network? Why Now?" LinkedIn. May 15, 2013 https://www.linkedin.com/pulse/20130515130547-174077701-why-a-woman-s-network-why-now

43 Alden, William. "Sallie Krawcheck Opens an Index Fund Focused On Women." *New York Times*. June 4, 2014. https://dealbook.nytimes.com/2014/06/04/sallie-krawcheck-opens-an-index-fund-focused-on-women/?_r=0

44 Thompson, Sherry. "Women's Fund Fall Luncheon Speaker Brings Leadership Message to Omaha." *Today's Omaha Woman*. 2014. http://www.todays omaha woman.com/news/summer-2014/sallie-krawcheck/

45 Wallace, Kristy. Interview by author. December 19, 2016.

46 Ellevate Network. "Ellevate Network's Values & Guiding Principles." https://www.ellevatenetwork.com/articles/7677-ellevate-network-s-values-guiding-principles

47 Wallace, Kristy. Interview by author. December 19, 2016.

48 Natura Brazil. "Cosmetics Leader in Brazil." https://www.naturabrasil.fr/en/about-us/cosmetics-leader-in-brazil

49 Hashiba, Luciana. "Innovation in Well-Being—The Creation of Sustainable Value at Natura." *Management Exchange*. May 18, 2012. http://www.managementexchange.com/story/innovation-in-well-being

50 Antunes, Anderson. "Brazil's Natura, the Largest Cosmetics Maker in Latin America, Becomes a B Corp." Forbes. December 16, 2014. http://www.forbes.com/sites/andersonantunes/2014/12/16/brazils-natura-the-largest-cosmetics-maker-in-latin-america-becomes-a-b-corp/#2fc49eee9779

51 World News. "Natura Exercises Options to Acquire 100% of Aesop." *Direct Selling News*. January 3, 2017. http://directsellingnews.com/index.php/view/natura_exercises_options_to_acquire_100_of_aesop

52 Natura. "History." http://www.natura.com.br/a-natura/sobre-a-natura/historia (Translated with Google translator.)

53 Seale, Barbara. "Natura: Blending Being Well with Well-Being." *Direct Selling News*. January 1, 2012. http://directsellingnews.com/index.php/view/blending_beingwell_with_well_being#.WLWztBCNNVU

54 Sivakumaran, Suba. "Natura Cosmeticos Empowers Women in Mexico." United Nations Development Programme. March 8, 2013. http://www.undp.org/content/undp/en/home/presscenter/pressreleases/2013/03/08/natura-cosmeticos-empowers-women-in-mexico.html

55 Sivakumaran, Suba. "Natura Cosmeticos Empowers Women in Mexico." Business Call to Action. March 8, 2013. http://businesscalltoaction.org/news/natura-cosmeticos-empowers-women-mexico

56 Certified B Corporations. "Natura B Impact Report." https://www.bcorporation.net/community/natura

57 Movi Mento Natura. "Explore the Initiatives." Natura. 2016. http://www.movimentonatura.com.br/cs/movimentonatura/home

58 Porter, Michael. "Why Social Progress Matters." Project Syndicate. April 9, 2015. https://www.project-syndicate.org/commentary/economic-development-social-progress-index-by-michael-porter-2015-04

59 *Natura Annual Report 2015*. http://www.natura.com.br/en/annual-report/2015/our-processes/valuing-the-amazon

60 Antunes, Anderson. "Brazil's Nature, the Largest Cosmetics Maker in Latin America, Becomes a B Corp." *Forbes*. December 16, 2014. http://www.forbes.com/sites/andersonantunes/2014/12/16/brazils-natura-the-largest-cosmetics-maker-in-latin-america-becomes-a-b-corp/#2fc49eee9779

61 Schwartz, Ariel. "A Public Company Finally Becomes a B Corp." *Fast Coexist*. December 23, 2014. https://www.fastcoexist.com/3040158 /a-public-company-has-finally-become-a-b-corp12.23.14

62 United Nations Environment Program. "Natura Brazil 2015 Champion of the Earth." 2015. http://web.unep.org/champions/laureates/2015/natura-brasil

CHAPTER 8

1 Long, Pia. "The Guerrilla Perfumers: An Interview with Mark and Simon Constantine (Lush & B Perfumery)." *Basenotes*. December 19, 2008. http://www.basenotes.net/features/402-The-guerrilla-perfumers-An-interview-with-Mark-and-Simon-Constantine-(Lush-amp-B-Perfumery)

2 Kwilkison. "The History of Lush Cosmetics." 2013. https://storify.com/kwilkison/the-history-of-Lush-cosmetics

3 Lush. "Our History." 2017. https://www.lushusa.com/about-history.html

4 Long, Pia. "The Guerrilla Perfumers: An Interview with Mark and Simon Constantine (Lush & B Perfumery." *Basenotes*. December 19, 2008. http://www.basenotes.net/features/402-The-guerrilla-perfumers-An-interview-with-Mark-and-Simon-Constantine-(Lush-amp-B-Perfumery)

5   Lush. "Our History." 2017. https://www.lushusa.com/about-history.html
6   Long, Pia. "The Guerrilla Perfumers: An Interview with Mark and Simon Constantine (Lush & B Perfumery." *Basenotes*. December 19, 2008. http://www.basenotes.net/features/402-The-guerrilla-perfumers-An-interview-with-Mark-and-Simon-Constantine-(Lush-amp-B-Perfumery)
7   Teather, David. "Lush Couple with a Shed Load of Ideas." *The Guardian*. April 12, 2007. https://www.theguardian.com/business/2007/apr/13/retail2
8   Long, Pia. "The Guerrilla Perfumers: An Interview with Mark and Simon Constantine Lush & B Perfumery." *Basenotes*. December 19, 2008. http://www.basenotes.net/features/402-The-guerrilla-perfumers-An-interview-with-Mark-and-Simon-Constantine-(Lush-amp-B-Perfumery)
9   Lush. "Blackboards and Handwritten Signage." 2017. https://www.lushusa.com/Article_Blackboard-And-Handwritten-Signage.html?fid=history
10 Oxford Dictionaries. "Lush." https://en.oxforddictionaries.com/definition/Lush
11 Macdonald, George. "Secret Success: Lush—From the Body Shop Supplier to Retail Rival." *Retail Week*. February 15, 2017. https://www.retail-week.com/analysis/secret-success-how-Lush-came-to-rival-the-body-shop/7018593.article
12 Bowles, Elizabeth. Lush press information provided to author.
13 Pilkington, Diana. "Shop Staff Strip Off in Protest at Packaging." *Your Local Guardian*. July 12, 2007. http://www.yourlocalguardian.co.uk/news/1541894.shop_staff_strip_off_in_protest_at_packaging/
14 Lush. "Lush Prize." 2017. http://lushprize.org/2016-prize/
15 Hall, James. "Britain's Favourite and Least Favourite Shops Revealed in Which? Poll." *The Telegraph*. May 22, 2012. http://www.telegraph.co.uk/finance/newsbysector/retailandconsumer/9283363/Britains-favourite-and-least-favourite-shops-revealed-in-Which-poll.html
16 Press Association. "Lush 'Favourite High Street Shop.'" May 21, 2014. http://money.aol.co.uk/2014/05/21/Lush-favourite-high-street-shop/
17 The Excellence Centre Team. "How the Customer Experience Strategy of Lush Made It the UK's Number One Customer Experience Brand." Nunwood. September 14, 2015. http://www.nunwood.com/customer-experience-strategy-Lush-made-uks-number-one-customer-experience-brand/
18 Lush. "What to Expect at the Lush Summit 2017." 2017. https://uk.Lush.com/article/what-expect-Lush-summit-2017
19 Jeffery Hollender. "Who We Are." http://www.jeffreyhollender.com/?page_id=803
20 Jeffery Hollender. "Jeffery Hollender." From Scratch Radio. 2017. http://www.fromscratchradio.com/show/jeffrey-hollender
21 Jeffery Hollender. "Jeffery Hollender." From Scratch Radio. 2017. http://www.fromscratchradio.com/show/jeffrey-hollender
22 Jeffery Hollender. "Jeffery Hollender." From Scratch Radio. 2017. http://www.fromscratchradio.com/show/jeffrey-hollender

23 Welker, Glenn. "Constitution of the Iroquois Nations." August 5, 2016. http://www.indigenouspeople.net/iroqcon.htm

24 Deganawida and the Chiefs. "Wampum #28, a New Chief Must Make Pledge via Four Strings of Wampum." http://www.ganienkeh.net/thelaw.html

25 Seventh Generation Backgrounder. "About Seventh Generation." PDF format. https://www.seventhgeneration.com/sites/default/files/assets/pdf/Seventh Generation_Backgrounder.pdf

26 Jeffery Hollender. "Jeffery Hollender." From Scratch Radio. 2017. http://www.fromscratchradio.com/show/jeffrey-hollender

27 Jeffery Hollender. "Jeffery Hollender" From Scratch Radio. 2017. http://www.fromscratchradio.com/show/jeffrey-hollender

28 Seventh Generation Backgrounder. "About Seventh Generation." PDF format. https://www.seventhgeneration.com/sites/default/files/assets/pdf/Seventh Generation_Backgrounder.pdf

29 Clark Steiman, Hannah. "A New Kind of Company: A 'B' Corporation." *Inc.* July 1, 2007. http://www.inc.com/magazine/20070701/priority-a-new-kind-of-company.html

30 B Lab. "Seventh Generation: Committed to Impact." Certified B Corporations. February 28, 2013. https://www.bcorporation.net/blog/seventh-generation-committed-to-impact

31 Masterson, Kathleen. "Safer Cleaning Products? Seventh Generation Among Companies Using New EP Label." WNPR. September 20, 2016. http://wnpr.org/post/safer-cleaning-products-seventh-generation-among-companies-using-new-epa-label

32 Rizzuto, Pat. "Seventh Generation to Lobby for Chemical Ingredient Disclosure." Bureau of National Affairs. January 12, 2017. https://www.bna.com/seventh-generation-lobby-n73014449734/

33 Seventh Generation. "Seventh Generation Names John Replogle to Serve as CEO and President." Marketwire. February 9, 2011. http://www.marketwired.com/press-release/seventh-generation-names-john-replogle-to-serve-as-ceo-and-president-nyse-ipg-1393156.htm

34 US Department of Agriculture. "Fact Sheet: Overview of USDA's BioPreferred program." https://www.usda.gov/wps/portal/usda/usda home? content id= 2016/02/0047.xml

35 Seventh Generation. "Seventh Generation's 2020 Vision for Sustainability." The Seventh Generation Corporate Consciousness Report. 2011. PDF format.

36 Seventh Generation. "Future Tense: Corporate Consciousness Report for 2012." 2012. PDF format.

37 Schwartz, Ariel. "Seventh Generation Is Buying a Mini Empire of Sustainable Companies." *Fast Coexist.* October 14, 2014. https://www.fastcoexist.com/3036957/seventh-generation-is-buying-a-mini-empire-of-sustainable-companies

38 French Dunbar, Meghan. "How Seventh Generation Made Sustainable Cleaning Products Mainstream." Conscious Company Media. July 4, 2015.

https://consciouscompanymedia.com/social-entrepreneurship/scaling-with-values/how-seventh-generation-made-sustainable-cleaning-products-mainstream/

39 Ng, Serena. "Seventh Generation Picks Up Bobble Brand." *Wall Street Journal*. May 30, 2013. https://www.wsj.com/articles/SB100014241278873246822045785155512439788042

40 Schwartz, Ariel. "Seventh Generation Is Buying a Mini Empire of Sustainable Companies." *Fast Coexist*. October 14, 2014. https://www.fastcoexist.com/3036957/seventh-generation-is-buying-a-mini-empire-of-sustainable-companies

41 Tugend, Alina. "Seventh Generation Taps Maya Rudolph for Its Biggest Campaign Yet." *New York Times*. April 17, 2016. https://www.nytimes.com/2016/04/18/business/media/seventh-generation-taps-maya-rudolph-for-its-biggest-campaign-yet.html?_r=0

42 Seventh Generation. "Seventh Generation + Maya Rudolph | Vajingle." YouTube. June 13, 2016. 1:40. https://www.youtube.com/watch?v=OoL29u5XmpI

43 Seventh Generation. "Seventh Generation + Maya Rudolph | Maya Knows Clean." YouTube. September 12, 2016. 1:18. https://www.youtube.com/watch?v=rnIi9hRTHAQ&t=1s

44 Seventh Generation. "Seventh Generation + Maya Rudolph | BayBay." YouTube. November 21, 2016. 0:26. https://www.youtube.com/watch?v=VTKo5mPj7YE

45 B Corp. "Seventh Generation's New Way of Transforming Commerce." B Corporation. https://www.bcorporation.net/blog/seventh-generationpercentE2 percent80 percent99s-new-way-of-transforming-commerce-0

46 Chaudhuri, Saabira, and Terlep, Sharon. "Unilever Buys 'Green' Products Maker Seventh Generation." *Wall Street Journal*. September 19, 2016. https://www.wsj.com/articles/unilever-to-buy-u-s-home-and-personal-care-company-seventh-generation-1474303177

47 The Kenco Coffee Company. "About Us." 2017. https://www.thekencocoffeecompany.co.uk/about-us/

48 John. "History of Kenco." *Kencovending Blog*. October 17, 2011. http://www.kencovending.co.uk/blog/index.php/coffee-machine/history-of-kenco.html

49 The Marketing Society. "Kenco's Brand Revitalization: Coffee vs. Gangs." 2015. PDF format.

50 Green Futures Magazine. "An End to Premium Prices for Ethical Coffee?" *Forum for the Future*. June 18, 2012. https://www.forumforthefuture.org/greenfutures/articles/end-premium-prices-ethical-coffee

51 Talking Retail. "Kenco Expands Partnership with Rainforest Alliance." May 7, 2008. http://www.talkingretail.com/products-news/grocery/kenco-expands-partnership-with-rainforest-alliance/

52 IGD. "Kraft Foods—Ethical Sourcing of Coffee." October 23, 2009. http://www.igd.com/Kraft_Foods_Ethical_Sourcing_of_Coffee

53 Golding, Amy. "Kenco Kicks Off £7.5m Green Packaging Campaign." Campaign. September 30, 2009. http://www.campaignlive.co.uk/article/942333/kenco-kicks-off-75m-green-packaging-campaign

54 Kevin Masters. "Kenco Eco Refill Ad." YouTube. February 3, 2013. 0:30. https://www.youtube.com/watch?v=2_kgd5Z9rgw

55 Mrs. Green. "Mrs. Green Talks to Kenco About Their Packaging." *My Zero Waste.* November 26, 2009. http://myzerowaste.com/2009/11/mrs-green-talks-to-kenco-about-their-packaging/

56 "Coffee Made Happy: Empowering Coffee Farmers." *The Telegraph.* October 24, 2014. http://www.telegraph.co.uk/sponsored/lifestyle/honduras-gangs/11173039/coffee-made-happy.html

57 "Coffee Made Happy: Empowering Coffee Farmers." *The Telegraph.* October 24, 2014. http://www.telegraph.co.uk/sponsored/lifestyle/honduras-gangs/11173039/coffee-made-happy.html

58 Joseph, Seb. "Kenco to Reward Coffee Drinkers for Doing Good." *Marketing Week.* April 7, 2014. https://www.marketingweek.com/2014/04/07/kenco-to-reward-coffee-drinkers-for-doing-good-deeds/

59 Briggs, Fiona. "Kenco's 'Coffee Versus Gangs' Project Returns for 2016 as First Cycle's Coffee Is Harvested for Sale." *Retail Times.* May 31, 2016. http://www.retailtimes.co.uk/kencos-coffee-versus-gangs-project-returns-2016-first-cycles-coffee-harvested-sale/

CHAPTER 9

1 Kantrow, Alan M., "Why Read Peter Ducker?" *Harvard Business Review.* November 2009. Reprint.

2 Harper, Douglas. "The Online Etymology Dictionary." http://www.etymonline.com

INDEX

Printed in the USA
CPSIA information can be obtained
at www.ICGtesting.com
JSHW032346070824
67729JS00008B/48

9 781400 245673